The Lincoln Highway

The

LINCOLN HIGHWAY

"THE SPIRIT OF LINCOLNWAY"

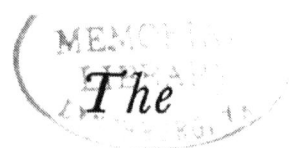

The
LINCOLN HIGHWAY

THE STORY OF A CRUSADE
THAT MADE
TRANSPORTATION HISTORY

WITH ILLUSTRATIONS

DODD, MEAD & COMPANY
NEW YORK   1935

TO

The score of the Nation's Leading Business Men, who served so earnestly and faithfully as Directors:

To the several scores of early "Contributors" who envisioned and assisted in founding this enterprise:

To the several hundred "Consuls" who for many years gave so generously of their time, of their efforts and of their private funds:

To the many thousands of "Sustaining Members" who for years paid annual dues, thereby assisting in financing what to many once seemed like a fantastic dream:

THIS BOOK IS GRATEFULLY DEDICATED

PREFACE

THE Lincoln Highway ushéred in an era of land transportation in which American civilization has been changed more profoundly, within only a few years, than in the century preceding.

When man made use of natural or unimproved means of transportation only, his progress socially and culturally was slow; when he developed mechanical means of moving from place to place, it was accelerated. The modern highway and its complement, the automobile, together represent the broadest means of land transportation yet attained.

It is impossible to separate these two factors; the automobile is worthless without the improved road and the road is of limited value without the automobile. Together, they have lengthened the span of average life appreciably. They have reduced the amount of time we must spend in travel. They have emancipated man from provincialism. They have given him quick and easy means of direct contact with distant communities. They have opened up to him, for business or enjoyment, thousands of square miles of country, educated him to the healthfulness of outdoor travel and recreation, enabled him to live amid more healthful surroundings àt no sacrifice of convenience.

They have knit the many detached groups of the American people into a compact and homogenous nation. They have unified interests, brought rural communities into contact with governmental and educational centers, helped the farmer get more for his products and given the manufacturer a wider market. They have both reduced and increased congestion in cities.

Between them, they are responsible for a vast new group of industries, giving employment to hundreds of thousands, with tremendous stimulation of related industries and promoted development of new methods of manufacture which have brought yesterday's luxuries into reach of today's millions.

Now, if highways are jointly responsible for all this —and the fact is incontestible—then the Lincoln Highway Association, which initiated the movement that brought these highways to realization, is likewise responsible. The value of the example set by this public-spirited organization, the stimulus it gave to the creation of automobile routes everywhere and the enlightened educational work it performed cannot be overestimated.

The Lincoln Highway Association's labor is done. This is its official history. It is an effort to account, not for money received and spent, for that was done years ago, but for those remarkable results of which the Lincoln Highway was the germinating cause.

It is written while the dreamer who first envisioned this great highway still lives, while the practical men to whom he entrusted his vision are still active. It is fashioned from their statements, their records, both personal and official, and from their very painstaking reminiscences, though it is characteristic of them that each has sought to keep himself in the background. It has been only by painstaking effort on the part of the compilers that it has been possible to assure credit where it is due.

It is hoped that this record of a great altruistic movement and its consequences necessarily condensed will be of value as history and that the recital of methods employed may be of benefit to the road-builders to come, as the Lincoln Highway was of benefit to the country in its generation.

CONTENTS

xii CONTENTS

LIST OF ILLUSTRATIONS

CHAPTER I

CARL FISHER had an idea. Not that new ideas—hard, solid, practical ideas—were anything new to Carl G. Fisher. He had been associated with the motor industry almost from its beginning. He had seen the first automobile lighted by a mixture of lard oil and kerosene, similar to the old brakeman's lantern. Then some bright genius had devised a method of dissolving calcium carbide by the slow addition of water, enabling each car to use a gas light much more penetrating and making much safer night driving from its own generating unit.

Carl Fisher perfected the means of compressing this carbide gas in tanks and supplying vehicles with a constant, dependable gas flow, good for several hundred hours without the dangers and nondependability of the individual unit. The great Prest-O-Lite Company which has been supplying lights for automobiles for more than twenty five years grew from this beginning.

Another Carl Fisher idea was the great Indianapolis speedway, which supplied a proving ground for makers of motor cars and has been one of the principal factors in developing the present high speed, dependable travel unit ever since.

But the big idea referred to here is one out of which has grown thousands of miles of modern highways, whole new systems of highway administration, vast changes in American social and economic life. Revolu-

1

tionary in character, it was nevertheless so simple that a few words sufficed to describe it. It was in his own phrasing:

"A road across the United States; Let's build it before we're too old to enjoy it."

Today, when hard-surfaced highways are a commonplace and a man may pick and choose among routes to almost any destination, the exceeding boldness of such a proposal is obscured; but in 1912, when Mr. Fisher presented it to the astonished leaders of an infant automobile industry, there were plenty to term him visionary and his idea impossible of accomplishment.

That he was able to obtain pledges of more than $4,000,000 for this project, and attract to its support some of the most hard-headed and practical men in American business life, speaks volumes for his own magnetic salesmanship as well as for the vision of the industrial leaders who joined forces to make his dream a reality.

At that time there were almost no roads, as roads are known today, in the United States. There was no system of connecting roads covering even so large an area as a state, probably none which even covered a county. And yet one of the earliest activities of the colonists who settled this country was the laying out of overland routes and their improvement into more or less passable condition as roads. In fact, such operations go back farther than they can be traced with historical certainty.

Lack of good roads was not due to any failure to appreciate the value of land transportation; on the contrary, it was directly attributable to the American genius for seeking the swiftest, easiest and most convenient means of transporting persons and goods. The idea that highways were needed existed but it had simply been obscured for nearly eighty years by the canal-building movement of the eighteen thirties and forties and the railroad-building era which followed, and which monopolized the public's attention.

The steel rails which laced the country served well as main channels for the collection of raw materials and distribution of finished products. They connected the important cities and towns. But they did not, and could not, serve for primary assembly of such things as agricultural and forest products, or for ultimate distribution of any sort. They could get from town to town, but not from store to store, or farm to warehouse. For that, improved, all weather, roads were necessary.

And so there had grown two million miles of unrelated, unconnected roads, broken into thousands of star-like independent groups, each railroad station or market town the center of a star. As these carried little traffic, they were left practically unimproved. At their best, they were graded and gravelled or macadamized; at their worst they were little, if any, better than the backwoods byways of Colonial times.

There were some toll roads, and particularly in states which had been little affected by the canal-building frenzy there were considerable mileages of macadamized turnpikes, but compared with the total mileage of so-called roads in the country, these faded into insignificance.

Nobody knew or cared where any road went except that which led to his home: and rarely did a farmer close to town know the farther terminus of the route that passed his front gate.

There was little engineering, little maintenance, and what organization for building and maintenance existed was mostly dominated by politics; only one or two states had effective systems of highway administration. Indeed, as late as 1912, the Office of Public Roads—now known as the Bureau of Public Roads—was compelled to estimate what had been spent on roads for the year because state records were lacking.

Of the 48 states, only 28 spent anything whatever on roads. One of these failed to report expenditures; the others jointly spent $11,427,000. The estimated total spent for road work by all governing units for the year was $177,537,000, more than $166,000,000 of which was thus expended, and mostly wasted, by local governmental bodies.

In the decade beginning that year the United States was to spend two billions of dollars for roads—and still lack a national system of highway transportation!

Road signs giving direction to travellers were a rarity. Carl G. Fisher, founder of the movement which later became the Lincoln Highway Association, recounts an incident illustrative of this point which, he says, was one of the galvanizing circumstances of this project.

"Three of us drove out nine miles from Indianapolis," said Mr. Fisher, "and being delayed, were overtaken by darkness on the return trip.

"To complicate matters, it began to rain pretty hard, and you know automobiles didn't have any tops on them in those days, so we all three got pretty wet.

"We guessed our way along as well as we could, until we came to a place where the road forked three ways.

CARL G. FISHER, WHO CONCEIVED AND PROMOTED THE IDEA OF
A TRANSCONTINENTAL HIGHWAY

It was black as the inside of your pocket. We couldn't see any light from the city, and none of us could remember which of the three roads we had followed in driving out; if, indeed, we had come that way at all.

"So we stopped and held a consultation. Presently, by the light of our headlamps, reflected up in the rain, one of us thought he saw a sign on a pole. It was too high up to read and we had no means of throwing a light on it, so there was nothing to be done but climb the pole in the wet and darkness and see if we could make out some road direction on the sign.

"We matched to see who should climb. I lost. I was halfway up the pole when I remembered that my matches were inside my overcoat and I couldn't reach them. So down I had to come, dig out the matches, put them in my hat, and climb up again.

"Eventually, by hard climbing, I got up to the sign. I scratched a match and before the wind blew it out I read the sign.

"It said: 'Chew Battle-Ax Plug.' "

There was not, in 1900, or even 1905, a single mile of rural paved road, as pavement now is known, in the United States.

It was into this condition that the automobile was born, and within a very few years the owners of motor cars had wearied of driving over the streets of their home towns, or the driveways of their parks and were clamoring for durable road construction.

Wayne County, Michigan, of which Detroit is the seat, was one of the first communities to respond to this clamor. Here, in 1908, just north of what was then the Detroit city limit, on Woodward Avenue, was laid the first mile

of rural concrete highway paving ever put down in the
United States. Edward N. Hines, who designed and built
it, is still a commissioner in charge of highways in Wayne
County.

, But the country was not made up of Wayne Counties.
True, the good roads gospel was beginning to make con-
verts in New York, in Pennsylvania, and in some counties
in California. True, there were some highway and trail
promotion organizations. Equally true, however—the
country as a whole was by no means enamored of road
improvement; city men opposed taxation for the purpose of building roads anywhere "for city dudes to run
their gas buggies over"; farmers hadn't yet realized that
it costs them 30 cents a ton to haul hay a mile over a poor
road and only 15 cents over a good one; nobody took
the motor truck seriously; nobody regarded operation of
a motor car as anything but idle sport.

Yet, there was no lack of enterprising souls to drive
them. Some even dared a transcontinental motor trip.

J. M. Murdock of Johnstown, Pennsylvania, was outstanding among these long-distance tourists. His first trip
was made from Los Angeles to New York City in 1898.
It required 32 days and he had the courage to take his
family with him!

Between then and 1913 he made five additional transcontinental trips.

The motor manufacturers were not long in grasping
the publicity possibilities of such ventures and presently
began to sponsor long trips, partly to test factory developments in actual service, partly for the resultant advertising. One of the earliest of these was made by Tom Fetch,
who was sent out in 1902 by Col. Sidney D. Waldon,

General Manager of the Packard Motor Car Company.
Says Colonel Waldon:

"I realized that we had to attract public attention with
a spectacle, but it had to be a useful spectacle.

"So I sent a man named Tom Fetch and a mechanic
named Allen, a great, big, six-footer, and a man named
Swetland, late of the McGraw-Hill organization, and a
photographer named Krarup, out to San Francisco and
arranged for them to make a San Francisco-New York
trip in 'Old Pacific,' a car which later became famous.

"I didn't understand the difficulties and consequently
selected the wrong route—from San Francisco to Emigrant Gap, Reno, Lovelock, Winnemucca, around the
north end of Great Salt Lake, and from Salt Lake City
told them to go right through the center of Colorado.
Like a dumb fool, I was thinking from the standpoint of
publicity, with pictures of the mountains and canyons,
but what I sent them into was something terrific. However, Fetch finally got through with many fine pictures
and came on to New York. The trip took 51 days. This
performance created a very favorable public impression."

Thereafter, Packard cars made transcontinental trips
annually for many years.

Henry C. Ostermann, who was later to be one of the
Lincoln Highway Association's important staff workers,
made a trip across in 1908 when, he later said, sixty
to ninety days was good time for the average non-
professional driver to make from the Atlantic to the
Pacific.

William R. Peck, in 1909, driving a Midland car, with
Frank Mayo as mechanic, drove from Moline, Illinois,

to Los Angeles, blazing the "Midland Trail."

Henry B. Joy, President of the Packard Motor Car Company, took many of these test trips himself, often through some terrible conditions. Once, plodding through a test trip, he asked the Packard distributor in Omaha for directions to the road west.

"There isn't any," was the answer.

"Then how do I go?" asked Mr. Joy.

"Follow me and I'll show you."

They drove westward until they came to a wire fence.

"Just take down the fence and drive on and when you come to the next fence, take that down and go on again."

"A little farther," said Mr. Joy, "and there were no fences, no fields, nothing but two ruts across the prairie."

But some distance farther there were plenty of ruts, deep, grass-grown ones, marked by rotted bits of broken wagons, rusted tires and occasional relics of a grimmer sort, mementoes of the thousands who had struggled westward on the Overland Route in 1849 and '50, breaking trail for the railroad, pioneering the highway of today.

CHAPTER II

A DEFINITE PLAN PRESENTED

At the opening of 1912, the community of interest between the automotive vehicle and the improved highway was becoming apparent. The fact was being recognized that roads through which the non-stalling power of horse-flesh could drag a lightly-laden wagon were no roads at all for the use of motor cars that already weighed a ton and more.

As the motor car manufacturers found themselves able to produce more automobiles than the market would absorb, and as motorists were demanding more and better roads, the leaders of the industry gave serious thought to road improvement as a means of stimulating sales.

Mr. Fisher, being the manufacturer of Prest-O-Lite lighting systems used on many automobiles, knew what the motor car manufacturers were thinking, and as an enthusiastic motorist in his own right he knew what the automobile owners wanted.

From this knowledge he conceived the idea of a road that would go as far as any road could go in America, from the Atlantic to the Pacific, a road that should be a hard-surfaced, improved highway capable of bearing traffic in all weathers, and that should be accurately signed through its length. Not knowing of a more feasible material than rock, he called it "The Coast-to-Coast Rock Highway."

9

The only question was, who should finance such a road?

That question was not one to be answered in a hurry, but Mr. Fisher talked it over with his partner, James A. Allison, and it seemed to them that the automotive industry was the best available source of the necessary money. He outlined the project to some of the motor car manufacturers then located in Indianapolis and received encouragement.

Details were worked out in these discussions and on September 6, 1912, Mr. Fisher formally laid his proposal before the leaders of the automobile world and asked for support. The sum needed, he estimated, would be $10,-000,000, and this he proposed should be raised through contributions from automobile manufacturers, jobbers, dealers, producers of automobile accessories, and persons from whom these concerns bought supplies.

For equity's sake, he suggested that these contributions be based on a percentage of gross revenue, either $\frac{1}{3}$ of 1% a year for each of three years, or $\frac{1}{5}$ of 1% a year for five years, as might be determined later.

The contributions, he said, should be handled by a trust company under bond. No contribution should become due unless the set goal of $10,000,000 were reached and no money should be spent for actual construction. It was his idea that the entire fund should be used to buy road-building material which would be donated to road authorities for use on the projected road, according to specifications which he anticipated government engineers would prepare free. He also counted on supervision by government engineers.

What route the road should follow he did not attempt

to prescribe, leaving that important question to a national committee to be selected later. He proposed that all contributions be signed and the fund closed on January 1, 1913, and that the road itself be completed ready for travel by May 1, 1915, so that "a corps of 25,000 automobiles can be taken over this road to the opening of the Exposition in San Francisco either in May or June, 1915."

Realizing that private citizens outside the motor industry would be interested in the road, and might be willing to assist in its development, Mr. Fisher suggested that an association of such be formed to sponsor it and that membership be offered the public in two classes, one involving an annual payment of $5 and the other yearly dues of $100 or even more.

On such a basis, he declared, a road actually costing $25,000,000 or more could be made available to the public. Finally, to make sure that all the funds donated should go into actual improvement, he and Mr. Allison proposed to pay all preliminary expenses themselves.

The letters brought quick and encouraging results and on September 1, Mr. Fisher called a group of leaders in the automotive world to a dinner at Indianapolis' famed old Deutsches Haus, where he presented his plan and in half an hour obtained subscriptions exceeding $300,000. Promises of favorable consideration, practically all of which netted definite subscriptions later, were also obtained from a number of those present who lacked power to commit their companies to the project.

While the meeting was still a topic of ardent discussion in the industry, tangible results from Mr. Fisher's letter-writing campaign began to come in.

"A letter from Carl Fisher to me outlined the idea of a transcontinental road and asked for pledges to make up a total of $10,000,000," said Frank A. Seiberling, now President of the Lincoln Highway Association, then President of the Goodyear Tire and Rubber Co. "He asked 1 percent of the gross sales of all automobile and accessory companies' earnings. I pledged $300,000 without even consulting my directors."

Next day Mr. Fisher was telegraphing to prospective contributors all over the country that Goodyear had come in for $300,000 and asked whether they would not please hurry up their pledges.

The Goodyear contribution stirred the interest of the whole automobile world. A. G. Batchelder, secretary of the American Automobile Association, promptly invited Mr. Fisher down to New York to describe his project to the annual meeting of the American Road Congress.

"Someday," wrote Secretary Batchelder to Mr. Fisher, "there will be erected to you one of the finest pieces of statuary obtainable, signifying that you were the man who deserved credit for giving America its first transcontinental road."

"Dear Batch," the Indianapolis man replied, "I am not much on statuary—and right now I think it is a good time to pull out personally and take away from our possible subscribers the idea that this road plan is mine. If any particular noise is made for any particular person or small clique of persons, this plan is going to suffer."

While Mr. Fisher desired no prominence for himself, he was perfectly willing to do three men's work for the plan's success, dashing up to Detroit for meetings with the heads of automobile companies, dashing back to

Indianapolis to dictate stacks of letters that kept his stenographers working nights; arguing, persuading, urging, and in between times finding spare moments to think out new schemes for advancing his project.

As he worked, his plans expanded; he wrote of twelve million, fifteen million, twenty million dollars possible to be obtained from the automobile and allied industries; of a road that would represent thirty million, fifty million, even a hundred million dollars in actual investment. Why not? In thirty days a million dollars had been subscribed! But now he wrote only to those whom he knew intimately, or to those who already knew of his connection with the enterprise; for the general promotion he transferred operations to a separate office where his secretary was soon sending out letters signed, "Coast-to-Coast Highway, Temporary Committee, Will J. Dobyns," and getting back subscriptions at the rate of $10,000 a day.

There was no doubt the idea was taking hold. Alvan Macauley, general manager of Packard, wrote that his company liked the size of Mr. Fisher's ideas and that while their contribution would amount to $150,000, nevertheless such a subscription would be forthcoming if Mr. Fisher could convince Col. Sidney D. Waldon that it should be made.

Probably Mr. Macauley didn't know it, but Colonel Waldon was already heart and soul in the movement, working hard to convince manufacturers of other motor cars that they, too, should join the procession. Roy D. Chapin, of the Hudson Motor Car Company, was working with him.

George W. Bennett, vice-president of Willys-Overland, suggested that Mr. Fisher take the matter before the motor car manufacturers' association and sell them the idea *en masse*.

Batchelder forwarded commendatory resolutions passed by the American Road Congress and Mr. Fisher wrote back that "there's already been enough resolutions passed to pave the road across the country," but that he really believed so much interest had been created that something good was bound to come of it in the very near future. It took courage to write that last phrase for he had just had word from Colonel Waldon that the Ford Company probably would not contribute to the movement. Losing the Ford contribution would be bad enough, he said, but a worse thing would be the effect of the Ford Company's refusal on other manufacturers.

Henry Ford was the dominant figure in the automotive industry. He made three-quarters of all the cars produced and while Mr. Fisher had once feared that without Ford's assistance the entire plan would fail, he was now so encouraged by what had been accomplished that he believed the road could be built anyway. Nevertheless, he redoubled his efforts to win Mr. Ford's support.

He approached the motor manufacturer through his business associate, James Couzens, Senator Albert J. Beveridge, Thomas A. Edison and others, including President William Howard Taft. However modest Mr. Fisher might be personally, he had no hesitation in appealing to the mighty in behalf of his plan.

One of the most interesting records in the Lincoln Highway Association's files is a gracious note from Charles Warren Fairbanks, vice-president of the United States, saying that he had written to Mr. Ford, and that if Mr. Fisher did not think the enclosed letter was strong enough, he would gladly supplement it.

In a further effort to enlist Mr. Ford's support, Mr. Fisher wrote to Elbert Hubbard, publisher of "The Fra" and "The Philistine":

"Of agitating good roads there is no end, and perhaps this is as it should be, but I think you'll agree that it is high time to agitate less and build more.

"The enclosed booklet describes a plan whereby the automobile industry of America can build a magnificent 'Appian Way' from New York to San Francisco, having it completed by May 1, 1915 and present it to the people of the United States.

"The fund necessary is ten million dollars. The project is twelve days old today and one million has been pledged—over $300,000 of it in Indianapolis alone. With Henry Ford enlisted in this movement the entire fund can be pledged in thirty days. A letter from you to Henry Ford will, I know, carry considerable influence."

Then on September 24th, 1912, followed a paragraph which expressed in brief, but completely, the principles which were to guide the Lincoln Highway Association's work for a full score of years. Here it is:

"As you know, Mr. Hubbard, the highways of America are built chiefly of politics, whereas the proper material is crushed rock, or concrete. We believe one magnificent highway of this kind, in actual existence, will stimulate as nothing else could the building of enduring highways everywhere that will not only be a credit to the American people but that will also mean much to American agriculture and American commerce. Will you pitch in and help?"

The idea of educating America to the value of good roads by building one magnificent transcontinental highway as an object lesson appealed to The Sage of East Aurora. He pitched in.

No wonder Mr. Fisher was disgusted when such efforts failed to bring Mr. Ford's approval of the plan into which he had thrown himself heart and soul. Yet there was encouragement at hand. Batchelder wrote him that, with Ford or without Ford, he had started a roadbuilding era, and the eventual result would be the same though Ford's help would hasten it. Presently he was on a train for Detroit determined to win Mr. Ford's co-operation if humanly possible.

In connection with this visit there is an apocryphal incident related that serves, as nothing else can, to illustrate Mr. Fisher's tremendous personal magnetism and his deep and sincere belief in his project.

The state fair was in progress at Detroit, and when Mr. Fisher reached the Ford factory, he was told that Mr. Ford was at the Fair. He found the manufacturer in the livestock exhibit, studiously observing the pigs, and while both leaned their arms on the top rail of the pigpens, dark, magnetic Fisher convinced lank, conservative Ford that the plan was righteous and worthy of support.

"Come to my office tomorrow and bring your papers and I will sign up," the story quotes Ford.

That night Mr. Fisher gave a dinner in celebration. But when he went to the office next day, Mr. Ford's secretary informed him that Mr. Ford had changed his mind.

Whether this story is true or not, there never was a contribution from the Ford Motor Company, although

years later, Edsel Ford became a heavy personal contributor.

However, so much interest had been aroused, and the
support of so many influential figures had been obtained,
that the project was going ahead almost of itself. The
whole west was on fire with enthusiasm for it.

The Denver Chamber of Commerce had sent some
automobiles, under leadership of the veteran road-scout,
A. L. Westgard, to lay out a trail between Denver and
Salt Lake City. At every stop the personnel of this tour
formed Midland Trail Association units to seek routing
of the proposed road their way. Cities as far south as
Santa Fe and Phoenix were clamoring to be placed on
its route. Chambers of Commerce, civic bodies and public
officials wanted all sorts of information. Westgard wrote
in that a dozen letters a day were coming to him on the
subject. Evidently the plan looked like a winner to the
shrewd old road man and he hinted that perhaps he
might be persuaded to go to work for it. And Los Angeles
saw the road's value as a producer of tourist business and
was sending telegrams about it. Competition between
various sections for the route of the highway was stirring
action as nothing ever had done.

Success was sure eventually; moreover Colonel Waldon, Mr. Chapin, Mr. Seiberling, Mr. Fisher and the
others who had placed themselves solidly behind the
movement were not men to withdraw any proposition
until it had been completed satisfactorily.

Then on December 3, Colonel Waldon wired from
Detroit:

"Packard Company voted enthusiastically to join
movement and start the ball rolling in Detroit."

The effect was electric. This contribution of $150,000 was proof that not everyone would wait for Mr. Ford. Mr. Fisher began thinking of creating a small office staff to organize publicity efforts and take some of the work off Secretary Dobyns' sagging but uncomplaining shoulders.

Delegations were coming in to talk things over and promise support; Utah and Wyoming men said if the road went through their states all necessary improvement would be done without expense to outside interests, and Mr. Leslie T. McCleary, executive secretary of the Lincoln Memorial Road Association, wrote in to propose a "Fisher Foundation for Highway Improvement."

Henry B. Joy, president of Packard, came forward whole-heartedly with support for the project. While the Packard directors had viewed it skeptically at first, he said, they had come to regard it as of paramount value as an object lesson.

"If a transcontinental highway can be fathered by means of the Ocean-to-Ocean highway organization, the good roads improvement which will result within the next ten years can hardly be conceived of in advance," he wrote. "Such highway improvement would benefit almost every person in the United States.

"We have investigated the proposition with great care and the directors unanimously endorsed the project."

And just to start Mr. Fisher's new year off right, on January 17, 1913, the Willys-Overland Company subscribed to the movement, giving it another estimated $150,000 toward its ten million dollar goal.

Clubs and individuals began pledging real support to

HENRY B. JOY, FIRST PRESIDENT OF THE LINCOLN HIGHWAY ASSOCIA-
TION. MR. JOY'S BUSINESS ABILITY PLACED THE MOVEMENT ON A SOUND
BASIS, AND HIS PROMOTIONAL QUALIFICATIONS ENLISTED A NATION-
WIDE INTEREST AND SUPPORT

the movement. The Hoosier Motor Club, Carl Fisher's own home organization, subscribed $2,000; Terre Haute business men subscribed $5,750.

Now the movement was booming. Secretary Dobyns, instead of diplomatically stalling off chamber of commerce officials who wanted to know how much money had been raised, was writing back asking what had been done in their communities toward raising their share of the fund. Newspapers were asking for regular releases and magazines were asking for articles even before Paul R. Martin, the latest addition to the staff, could write them. Private individuals and the motoring public became enthusiastic; even orders for automobiles were being conditioned on completion of the Ocean-to-Ocean highway. And Mr. Fisher was saying sagely that the people wouldn't be satisfied with one coast to coast road but would demand that three or four others be built.

This spirit reached Washington and Representative William P. Borland, of Missouri, introduced in Congress a bill to reassume jurisdiction over the old National Road Congress had abandoned eighty years before and complete it to the Pacific Ocean.

Early in February Roy D. Chapin's Hudson Motor Car Company subscribed, thus providing another $100,000, and Salt Lake City automobile interests gave assurance their state would raise a million and a half for the road, if Colorado would do likewise. The challenge was accepted and a bill was introduced in the Colorado legislature for a $1,000,000 bond issue to bring available funds up to the mark desired.

And now Mr. Fisher got some help he had not sought. Without any preliminaries whatever, a letter came in from A. Y. Gowen, president of the Lehigh Portland Cement Company, saying the cement industry was interested in the proposed highway, that Mr. Gowen had been talking to leaders of the industry, that he believed a donation of at least a million and a half barrels of cement—perhaps double that quantity—could be obtained for the construction of the road, and that the cement men had appointed a committee to study the matter, of which committee he was one.

Here was news!

Not only was the donation thrice-welcome, but Mr. Gowen himself was a tower of strength. March 12, 1913, the day he wrote his letter, was an eventful date for what was to become the Lincoln Highway Association.

CHAPTER III

THERE were now two important objectives to be attained. One was the project that had brought Mr. Gowen into the movement—arranging for the cement industry to coöperate in building the road—the other was the creation of a representative group to take sponsorship of the organization on behalf of the motor industry.

Both represented long, hard labor. Meanwhile, things had been happening in other directions which were to have a profound effect upon the plan. Chief of these were that the Hoosier Motor Club had begun plans for the famous Indiana Motor Car Manufacturers' tour, which is so important it must be treated later by itself; and that A. R. Pardington had become vitally interested in the Fisher project.

Mr. Pardington had been affiliated with the general movement for good roads since the cinder-path days of the League of American Wheelmen. He had worked hard for the New York state road movement. He had taken an active part in creating the Long Island Motor Parkway. As referee of the Vanderbilt races he had met Mr. Fisher, who loved automobile racing, and the two had formed a fast friendship.

Small wonder, then, that in the previous October, hardly a month after public announcement of the Coast-to-Coast highway, he wrote to the Indianapolis man:

"I always like to hear of you starting something big, because you never start anything you can't finish. If you find a place where I can help out, call on me."

The correspondence so begun went forward steadily. Soon Mr. Pardington was virtually a New York representative of the highway organization, writing letters, sending out booklets and telling the newspapers about the plan.

Not least of his volunteer services was to hearten Mr. Fisher when the Detroit group lagged in making up its several minds to subscribe.

However, the Detroiters did not always lag. On April 14, 1913, there was held in Mr. Joy's office in Detroit, a meeting which carved the pattern to which the Fisher project was to be molded and set the reshaped plan well on the way to active realization.

Mr. Fisher called this meeting by telegraph Those present, beside himself, Mr. Joy and Mr. Gowen, were Paul R. Deming and Russell A. Alger, Detroit men in whose judgment and ability Mr. Joy had great confidence, Mr. Pardington and A. L. Westgard.

The two last named were there to give the others the benefit of their knowledge of road conditions and road sentiment.

The session began at 10:30 in the morning and ended at 5:30 that evening.

The decisions reached were that, if investigation showed facts to be as those present understood them, Messrs. Gowen, Deming, Fisher, Alger and Joy would form an organization to sponsor the plan, which organization Mr. Joy agreed to head; that the organization should have a corporate form, which they outlined in general terms; that Mr. Pardington should repair immediately to Indianapolis, go over Mr. Fisher's records and prepare a statement showing what financial backing had been obtained for the road, which statement he was to embody in a prospectus; that the organization's headquarters should be in Detroit; that its name should embody the word "Lincoln"; and that Mr. Pardington should be its chief administrative official.

Mr. Pardington and Mr. Fisher hurried back to Indianapolis to compile the statement and prepare certificates to be awarded members of the highway association which was being formed.

Indirectly, this caused Mr. Pardington considerable difficulty, because he found it almost impossible to get Mr. Fisher and Mr. Joy to agree finally upon the name it was to bear. The meeting had decided on "Lincoln" but not on the exact manner of its use.

The steps leading up to the adoption of the title finally selected are not all clear. Mr. Joy had brought the name of the great president into the Association's records in December, 1912, when he wrote to Colonel Waldon and Mr. Fisher criticizing congressional plans to use the national Lincoln Memorial fund of some $1,600,000 for a building. Mr. Joy felt that roads, rather than marble architecture of no matter what nobility, would form the finest memorial to such a man as Lincoln, whose life had been devoted to public service.

Then in January, 1913, while they were using "Coast-to-Coast Highway" as a title, Congressman Borland had given Mr. Fisher the idea that the popularity of his plan could be enhanced by introducing some patriotic appeal into its title or routing.

The two ideas acted and reacted in Mr. Fisher's mind, so that when the time came for permanent organization and a definite title must be chosen, the suggestion of his good friend Elbert Hubbard, "The American Road," was over-ruled and he came out flatfootedly for "Lincoln Memorial Highway."

That name was the property of the "Lincoln Memorial Road Association," organized by McCleary, which had projected a Lincoln Memorial Road from Gettysburg to Washington. However, Congress, in the closing hours just before the advent of Woodrow Wilson, had dashed the McCleary plans by voting as Mr. Joy had feared, against roads and for architecture. Consequently the Mc-Cleary association was virtually moribund and Mr. Fisher thought it would gladly relinquish the name to the new highway organization rather than see so good a title go unused. He wrote McCleary:

"It might be a good thing for us to change the name from Ocean-to-Ocean Highway to Lincoln Memorial Road. Kindly advise me if you have the name incorporated and if it would suit your plans to turn it over to us in order that we might continue it."

As he had expected, the McCleary group gladly relinquished the name, but, what he had not anticipated, McCleary strongly advised the use of "Jefferson Memorial Highway" instead.

His grounds were largely political and Mr. Fisher, who hadn't much faith in politicians as roadbuilders, was not persuaded. They stuck to the name "Lincoln" and it appears that way in the prospectus which Mr. Pardington prepared.

While Mr. Joy and Mr. Pardington were correspond-
ing about the form and details of this prospectus and
about an audit of the subscriptions already made, which
was to be part of it, Mr. Gowen wrote the Packard chief
enthusiastically that it appeared the cement industry
would be willing to contribute cement on the same basis
that motor car manufacturers contributed; that is, ⅓ of
one percent of the annual gross each year for three years,
and that this would mean 2,350,000 barrels of cement,
equivalent to about $3,000,000.

Such support added much to the prospects of success,
and opportunely, too, for Mr. Joy was none too sanguine
of the plan's future.

"The enterprise has strewn in front of it insurmount-
able difficulties," he wrote, "yet, on account of so much
work having already been put into the matter I feel that
everything possible should be done to push it on. Fisher
is ready for the audit so it's up to you. Get it in shape
to convince Paul Deming and it will convince me."

So Mr. Pardington hurried back to Indianapolis,
picked up a representative of the auditing firm Mr. Joy
preferred and by working nights, got the audit in shape
to be presented to a meeting which the Packard chief had
called for May 8, in his office.

This audit, made by Marwick, Mitchell, Peat & Co.,
demonstrated the tremendous appeal the plan had exerted. It showed actual definite subscriptions totalling
$2,316,040. There were additional indefinite subscrip-
tions which Mr. Fisher estimated would yield $366,700,
and fifty-six subscriptions in which the amount was given
simply as ⅓ of 1 percent of the subscribers' gross business annually for three years, the amount of which the

auditors declined to appraise. Mr. Pardington estimated
them however, at approximately $4,000,000.

The showing was highly satisfactory, especially as many
of those whose subscriptions were for indefinite amounts
were the largest concerns in the automotive world. The
organizing group settled down at once to put the Lincoln
Highway Association into active being. Those who participated in this meeting were the same as those who had
attended the former one, except that Roy D. Chapin had
been added and A. L. Westgard was not present. The
gathering was thus well representative of the automobile
industry.

Mr. Joy acted as chairman, agreed to sign the prospectus
as chairman of the organization committee and also consented to serve as President of the association when its
organization had been completed. Messrs. Deming, Alger
and Gowen agreed to serve on the executive committee
which would govern the new body, and Mr. Fisher announced that F. A. Seiberling was also willing to serve
on it. Mr. Joy requested that Emory W. Clark, a leading
Detroit banker—the only treasurer the Lincoln Highway
Association has ever had—be asked also to serve on this
group. Mr. Pardington, it was agreed, should be secretary and also vice-president, so he could act for Mr. Joy
in the leader's absence. The prospectus was discussed in
detail.

Next day the committee picked the prospectus to
pieces once more, redrew portions of it with the assistance
of Henry E. Bodman, Mr. Joy's attorney, and tentatively
approved it.

Mr. Gowen and Mr. Fisher went to Chicago and, with
the aid of Charles A. Bookwalter, former mayor of In-

dianapolis, presented the case of the Lincoln Highway to the Portland Cement Association. Technical difficulties prevented them from obtaining an outright donation of cement but they made good progress, aroused much interest, and laid the ground for later contributions which played an important part in Lincoln Highway work.

What the cement men wanted was assurance that their product would be used exactly as specified by their engineers, so that good results would be obtained, as they had in Wayne County, Michigan. They feared that otherwise, the cement might be used wrongly and the whole idea of constructing roads out of concrete thereby given a tremendous setback.

Meanwhile, the business of the new organization went forward rapidly in other quarters.

Secretary Pardington closed up his business in New York; Mr. Bodman put the final revisions into the prospectus; and on May 22, the day Mr. Pardington took up his headquarters in Detroit, the organization group met again, approved the articles of incorporation Mr. Bodman had drawn and instructed that they be filed with the Secretary of State.

Now Mr. Joy started off to investigate in person certain routes in the west, to be gone three weeks. Mr. Fisher was very busy preparing for the Hoosier Tour and Secretary Pardington plunged into a perfect fever of activity, establishing headquarters and getting the Association into operation.

Almost his first act was to employ F. T. Grenell, city editor of the Detroit Free Press, to serve part time as a publicity man. Another function claiming his attention was the sale of the certificates he had spent so much time perfecting. This was important, because all the money the Association had to work with was a $1,000 check sent in by Mr. Fisher a month before and one of similar size which Mr. Gowen forwarded a little later.

There was also to be arranged a transfer of activity from the Indianapolis headquarters over which Will Dobyns had presided for so long.

Mr. Pardington and Mr. Dobyns solved this by a letter giving notice that the Lincoln Highway Association had superseded the Coast-to-Coast Rock Highway and asking that all further correspondence be addressed to the Detroit headquarters. At the same time, Mr. Pardington took steps to enlist in the work of the Lincoln Highway all those who had aided in developing Mr. Fisher's plan, so that there would be continuity of effort throughout.

There was always the closest and most cordial cooperation between these two, and brilliant as Mr. Pardington's work showed him to be, credit must be given Mr. Dobyns for invaluable aid in starting off the Lincoln Highway Association's activities without a misstep of any kind. His assistance was especially important in enabling the Lincoln Highway Association to benefit from the Hoosier Tour, now due to start west in a few days.

A PORTION OF THE FIRST ARMY TRANSCONTINENTAL MOTOR CONVOY REFERRED TO IN CHAPTER NINE

AROUND a table in the Claypool Hotel, four Indianapolis men sat chatting after luncheon one autumn day in 1912. They were W. S. Gilbreath, secretary of the Hoosier Motor Club; W. D. Edenburn, advertising manager of the Apperson Automobile factory; W. McK. White, Marion automobile executive, and John Guy Monihan, a noted driver. Edenburn had just brought word of Carl Fisher's plan for an ocean to ocean road.

All four had participated in the "Four State Tours" which the motor club and the Indiana Automobile Manufacturers' Association jointly had arranged annually for several years. Someone, either Captain Gilbreath or Monihan, suggested that the next year's tour be held on the road Mr. Fisher proposed, and that Mr. Fisher himself be persuaded to help finance it.

There was some argument over whether such a trip was feasible but Mr. Edenburn, who with Mr. Monihan had taken a caravan of 17 Premier cars across the country earlier that same year, believed it was, and so did Mr. White. Captain Gilbreath supplied them with such maps as were available and after they had made a study of the conditions, they convinced Mr. Fisher that the project could be carried through.

Mr. Fisher appreciated the value of such a trip in stimulating interest for roads but he was loath to associate his project for a transcontinental highway definitely with the trip because he foresaw that the public would assume the route taken by the Indianapolis men was the route selected for the Lincoln Highway. This was exactly what happened in several instances, though Mr. Fisher had stated expressly and often that the Lincoln ·Highway's route would be laid out only after very complete investigation and careful study.

Instead of proceeding as an adjunct to the Lincoln Highway Organization, therefore, the promoters of this trip sought and obtained the sponsorship of the Indiana Automobile Manufacturers' Association and the Hoosier Motor Club of Indianapolis. Under these conditions, Mr. Fisher cooperated heartily.

Captain Gilbreath promptly began to give publicity to the newspapers, while Messrs. White and Edenburn settled down to a long grind of preparation to insure the trip's success.

As word of the plan got out and was hammered home by Captain Gilbreath's propaganda, high interest was aroused in the west. Indeed, it is probable that it was the plans for this trip that sent the Denver people trailblazing across Colorado and started a furore of excitement in that and other western states for construction of the road Mr. Fisher proposed. Certainly the plans for the tour fanned the flames of excitement all through the west. Whether or not the tour followed the route to be selected for the Lincoln Highway, it would certainly lay out a road which could be followed by automobiles, and would stimulate motor tourist traffic to follow in its path. And so the western states and cities and even villages made strenuous efforts to have the Indiana men pass their way.

In one day, telegrams were received from more than 100 communities asking to be placed on the tour's itinerary!

Some communities went to the expense of sending delegations to Indianapolis to seek inclusion in the itinerary. One such was Price, Utah. The mayor headed the delegation in person. There was no road through Price Canyon from the east, however, and Captain Gilbreath regretfully told the mayor that the tour could not, therefore, pass through his town.

"We'll build one, then," said the mayor.

And sure enough, they did. More, when later on it appeared the contractor would not be able to finish the road in time for the tour to use it, the energetic mayor declared a legal holiday and called out all the town's able-bodied men to assist. With picks, shovels, crowbars and dynamite, they labored until 10 o'clock on the road that night and while it was no boulevard, the tour came over it, as Captain Gilbreath said, "without a broken axle, a broken part of any kind, or even a puncture. It was rough but we got through."

Nevada appropriated $25,000 to improve the road from the Utah border to the California line. Colorado practically rebuilt 60 miles of the route across Berthoud Pass. More than thirty new concrete bridges were constructed at various points along the tour's line of travel. Many of them, it is true, had been planned for construction in any event, but their building was advanced to facilitate the passage of the tour. Mr. Fisher in his report to the Lincoln Highway Association on the results of the trip, estimated that not less than $500,000 was spent on improving the road.

If the west was thus flaring up, the automobile people were equally busy back in Indianapolis preparing for the trip. Every motor car manufacturer in Indiana entered at least one car. Two trucks were entered. Mr. White and Mr. Edenburn laid down a prescribed list of equipment for each vehicle and even specified where it should be packed, so that everyone would always know where to find the needed implement when a car got into trouble.

Mr. Edenburn knew by experience what was likely to be needed and as the tour was going through some places where few, if any, automobiles had ever gone before, he saw that all necessities were taken along. Here is his list:

One pick or one mattock
One pair of tackle blocks
600 feet of ¾ inch rope
One barn lantern, hung on the rear tire carrier, to be lighted if the car's regular lights failed, so the following driver could see it and keep in line.
One steel stake 3 feet long, 1½ inches wide at top, tapered to point, for use as anchor to pull car out of sand or mud.
12 mudhooks
1 full set of chains
1 sledge
Chocolate bars in cans, beans, canned goods, stowed under rear seat
West of Salt Lake City each car also carried:
4 African water bags, kept filled at all times
1 4 x 6 foot tent, envelope type, made especially for the tour. This tent was intended to be tied to the top and the wheels of the car. It could be raised from inside

and was provided with ground-cloth and mosquito-bar ventilating windows.

Camp equipment sufficient to shelter and feed the entire tour was carried on one of the trucks; the provisions in the cars were for emergency use only.

This lengthy catalog of items which are as foreign to modern motoring as a packsaddle would be, was no idle collection. Practically every car in the group used every item at some stage of the journey. There were unbridged creeks and muddy places to be crossed with the aid of mudhooks and chains, gullies from which the cars could be extricated only with the aid of the ropes and tackle-blocks; arid spots where the steel pin had to be driven deep in the ground to afford a purchase for the tackle.

Lighting systems not being then so reliable as now, and the vicissitudes of travel hard on tail-lamps, the barn lanterns were used more than once. As for the tentage, it saw little employment, but the emergency supplies were raided frequently. Good management could assure the tour of reaching a settlement or recognized stopping place every night, but the mud of eastern Colorado, the rocky washes and narrow, boulder-cluttered canyons of the Rocky Mountains, kept the Indianans on the road long hours after regular meal-times.

Thanks to Mr. Edenburn's foresight, every car had whatever was needed to meet each circumstance as it arose. However, there were not lacking amateurs to suggest improvements and additions to the selected equipment and novel means of traversing difficult spots. He tells with delight how Elmer Apperson insisted that he take with him two rolls of canvas, 7½ feet wide and 100 yards in length, and how he refused.

"The idea was," said he, "that if we ran into sand we could unroll one of these strips, drive onto it, then unroll the other ahead and drive onto that, then roll up the first one, carry it ahead and repeat the process until the sand had been passed. I didn't take the canvas.   ·

"But when we got to Salt Lake City, I was notified that there were two packages awaiting me at the express office. There was this canvas. Each package weighed 750 pounds. As far as I know that canvas is still there."

This tour was not just a case of picking up anyone who wanted to go; the personnel was selected very carefully. Neither Mr. White nor Mr. Edenburn, respectively chairman and vice-chairman, anticipated that the trip would be a pleasure jaunt; both had high ideas of what could be accomplished for touring generally and for advancing the interests of the participating manufacturers, and they made sure that such guests as were taken along were personages able to further the objects of the tour. There was practically no deadwood anywhere in the personnel, which numbered more than 70.

More, every man was a selected specimen from a physical standpoint. As the itinerary called for traversing points 11,000 feet above sea level, where exertion would be difficult for unacclimated persons, and as exertion of the most strenuous sort would surely be necessary to get the cars through, each man was required to pass a strict physical examination before acceptance.

The tour had its own treasurer, R. P. Henderson, and its own secretary, Joseph M. Ward, who was also secretary of the Indiana Automobile Manufacturers' Association. It carried its own medical corps in the persons of two Indianapolis doctors, C. R. Strickland and J. C. Sexton. It had its own photographer, Edward McArdle, and its own official representatives from the telegraph companies, P. W. Williams from the Postal and Charles Kent from the Western Union. Among those who went on the trip were Mr. Fisher, Charles A. Bookwalter of Indianapolis, who was the tour's official speechmaker; Elwood Haynes, pioneer automobile manufacturer; C. A. Brenston, tour observer for the Royal Automobile Club of England; Ray Harroun, famous automobile driver; W. O. L. Westgaard, touring representative of the American Automobile Association; A. L. Westgard, representative of the American Highway Association; Chris Cox, mapmaker for the Blue Book Corporation; Fred Wellman, press representative for the Lincoln Highway Association and the Indiana Automobile Manufacturers' Association; J. B. Dudley of the Hearst newspaper syndicate; A. S. Blakely, of the Indianapolis *Star;* E. I. Lewis of the Indianapolis *News;* Reed Parker of the Chicago *Tribune* and J. W. Morgan, field representative of the American Automobile Association.

The automobiles, all of which finished the trip, were the Marmon, two Marions, Pilot "60," two Haynes, two Americans, McFarland, two Appersons, two Hendersons, Empire, Pathfinder "40," two Premiers and one Brown truck and one Premier truck, which carried a supply of tires provided by the G. & J. Tire Company. The Brown truck carried camp equipment, repair parts and supplies.

The tourists started from Indianapolis at 2 p.m. July 1, 1913, and had proceeded only to Brazil, Indiana, barely 50 miles, before they began to perceive evidence of the enormous amount of road improvement work that had been done in anticipation of their advent. From this point to the Pacific Coast, Mr. Fisher said, "practically every mile of the road had been scraped, dragged, graded or otherwise improved" for the use of the tour.

Some of these improvements were of a very minor nature, sometimes no more than the removal of large rocks on which crank-cases were likely to come to grief, sometimes merely the cutting down of "high centers" and the partial filling-in of ruts; western road improvement work in that day was nothing like what is understood by the term at present.

At Brazil, too, began a round of dinners, luncheons, impromptu roadside entertainments, road meetings and banquets that presently had every member of the tour worn out and begging for rest. Demands that the tour stop for speechmaking and refreshments were so numerous it was difficult to make even the moderate schedule of 150 miles a day.

Every night there was a banquet, a supper or some other celebration, with more speechmaking, and as the local newspaper representatives and the news men with the party vied in sending out stories about each meeting, the tour evoked tremendous publicity and interest.

As the trip proceeded westward, the celebrations became less numerous but more strenuous. At some places, the hospitality of the warm-hearted westerners was almost overpowering. For instance, at one point in Colorado, gasoline had been hauled by team 70 miles for the benefit of the tourists, and was offered them free! At another place it had been hauled 65 miles, and was also free.

Near Bishop, California, citizens prepared a complete camp for the tourists in the heart of the mountains, where the president of one of Bishop's banks acted as cook and leading citizens as waiters. There the easterners were, most of them, introduced to mountain trout for the first time.

When the tourists neared Oakland, California, more than 1,200 automobiles came out to escort them into the city.

Frequently they were importuned to change the route of the tour, or to turn aside and examine new roads.

Mr. Fisher sent back reports to headquarters as often as the pressure of hospitality permitted. The first came from Springfield, the tour's second stop. There Governor Dunne had told him Illinois had set aside $1,200,000, and the several counties of the state had set aside an equal sum, for highway improvement and a state highway commission was being created. Governor Dunne said his only fear was that his term of office would expire before a hard surfaced road could be completed across the state.

Governor Hodges of Kansas met the visitors at Topeka and travelled with them three days, making speeches in behalf of improved highways. At the Colorado state line a delegation from the Denver Chamber of Commerce met the Indianans and escorted them into Denver, where they remained over a day. Governor E. M. Ammons joined the tour at Colorado Springs and accompanied it as far as Grand Junction, three days' travel. At Grand Junction the visitors were given a reception which Mr. Fisher described as "the largest yet received." Fully

4,000 persons, he said, were gathered to greet them, the town was decorated and a rousing meeting was arranged for that night.

Governor Ammons, he reported, was very much in earnest and intended to make the road across Colorado "16 feet wide, 4 feet berm or shoulder of rock and 2 foot 6 inch rock wall around all bad turns, with 6 percent grades."

"If we can allow him $1,000 per mile in material we will get a $5,000,000 road across Colorado," Mr. Fisher added.

The Grand Junction celebration apparently was strenuous; the tour was almost an hour late in getting under way next day. And the going was tough. They were until 11:15 p.m. getting to Green River, Utah, a matter of 121 miles. The next day they rolled through Price Canyon, over the road the mayor had so energetically pressed to a passable condition, and stopped for the night at Price. Governor Spry of Utah met them and accompanied them into Salt Lake City.

At a banquet there, he made what Mr. Fisher pronounced one of the strongest speeches in favor of the Lincoln Highway that was given on the tour. Unfortunately, more than half the Indianans were too weary to attend.

West from Salt Lake City the tour faced the desert and everyone figuratively tightened his belt for the struggle. Up to this point they had faced hardships which to a tourist of this day would be almost unbearable. For instance, their whole tour across Colorado was about as strenuous as anyone could desire. Here are the times and distances from Mr. Fisher's personal log:

"Left Denver 9:30 a.m., arrived Hot Sulphur Springs 11:30 p.m., 105.2 miles."

That was the day they crossed Berthoud Pass, up grades so steep some of the cars had to turn around on the narrow road and back up the worst stretches because the gasoline tanks were lower than the carburetors.

"Left Hot Sulphur Springs 8 a.m., arrived Glenwood Springs 6 p.m., 108.4 miles.
"Left Glenwood Springs 7:45 a.m., arrived Grand Junction 3:30 p.m., 133.1 miles."

Once the tour had been divided by a sudden rush of water down an arroyo when half the cars had crossed and the others were preparing to cross. All that was nothing, said the experienced ones, but trouble lay just ahead.

It came at one of their nearby stops, a plague of enormous and voracious bedbugs; bedbugs so energetic and so hungry that Mr. Fisher abandoned his couch and spent the remainder of the night dozing precariously atop a chicken-coop; bedbugs so large that next morning one member of the tour, awakening to find a mandolin hanging on the wall above him, smashed it with a chair and vowed that, seeing it move, he had mistaken it for one of the night's too numerous companions; bedbugs of such character and parts that Mr. Fisher, for years, never mentioned the place without a note of identification: "where I do believe they have the biggest bedbugs in the whole world."

Though they left Salt Lake City in a broiling sun, a mountain storm that came up as they travelled soon drenched the hills and salt flats, set arroyos running bank-full, washed many a gully across the road, and started streams running down the ruts of former traffic. Presently it was a case of "out shovels and all hands dig" to get down into, across and up out of the arroyos.

The tackle came out and lines were run from cars behind to cars that had already worked their way across. It was a battle but they stuck to it gamely and by nine that night were drawing into Callao, or Kearney's Ranch, where a delegation of eight cars from Ely, Nevada, headed by Gael S. Hoag, was awaiting them.

It was their last hard fight. From then on they had no more than ordinary difficulties to encounter. The heralded difficulties of the desert were as nothing to those encountered farther east.

Governor Oddie of Nevada met them at Ely and travelled with them practically all the way across the state. The Governor promised Mr. Fisher he would call a special session of the legislature, if need be, to act on any proposals the Lincoln Highway Association might put before it.

The tour was late reaching Lake Tahoe, on the Nevada-California border, so the Indianans missed Governor, later U. S. Senator, Hiram Johnson of California, who had intended to meet them, but Mr. Fisher saw him later in Sacramento and reported: "It will not be necessary for us to build a foot of road in California as they have sufficient funds and a sufficient amount can be diverted from their main highways to this cross-continental road."

At Bishop the party divided and some went on to San Francisco while others continued down the Owens Valley toward Los Angeles. At Owensmouth, just north of Los Angeles, they reunited on August 3, the 34th day of their travels, and were greeted by a crowd which stood patiently in the broiling sun to listen to the speeches, to cheer the visitors and to shout a welcome.

Not all who were present that day were so happy. The tour members were worn and weary. Captain Gilbreath, sunburned and picturesque in high boots, red silk hand-kerchief bound around his head, khaki trousers and open-throated khaki shirt, was trying to find some shade where he could rest a few minutes before addressing the crowd. A photographer asked him to pose.

"I guess he picked me because I was sunburned and carried flags and wore no hat," said the Captain. "When we started, I had a couple of transcontinental highway pennants on the car; one from the Indianapolis Chamber of Commerce and one from the Hoosier Motor Club. As we went along I gathered others. Finally I got so many that the staff of the Hoosier Motor Club pennant, to which I had fastened them, would not hold any more. So at Price, Utah, I bought a rake, took the rake off and tacked the pennants on the handle. It made quite a show.

"This photographer had been trying to photograph me but he couldn't get a picture to satisfy him. It was 112 in the shade and I was getting tired. Just then somebody shouted that they wanted me to come and make a speech. The photographer asked for one more shot. I jumped up and stuck my hands up in the air, with the flags in one hand and the other one right up. 'How's this?' I said. He snapped it—and it was the best picture of the whole lot."

So was born a picture known ever afterward as The Spirit of the Lincoln Highway, which the Association used freely in propaganda work and which perhaps expresses better than anything else the flaring spirit of youth, adventure and daring embodied in the dream created by Mr. Fisher and the realization carried out by Messrs. Joy, Gunn, Seiberling and others.

Some time later, at the instance of President Joy, a statue in bronze, about one-sixth lifesize, was made in the same vein, using the picture and Gilbreath himself as models.

The completion of this tour with its large personnel and wide variety of cars of different powers and different requirements, without a casualty of any sort, without delays exceeding a day at any time, was a major feat in organization. More, it showed the public as nothing else could, that transcontinental touring was possible. Unquestionably the result was a tremendous spurt in long distance driving for sport or pleasure.

What this 34 day tour did for the Lincoln Highway was less spectacular but more valuable.

ROY D. CHAPIN, PRESIDENT HUD-
SON MOTOR CAR COMPANY. MEM-
BER OF EXECUTIVE COMMITTEE OF
THE LINCOLN HIGHWAY ASSOCIA-
TION

ALVAN MACAULEY, PRESIDENT
PACKARD MOTOR CAR COMPANY.
MEMBER OF LINCOLN HIGHWAY AS-
SOCIATION EXECUTIVE COMMITTEE

COL. SIDNEY D. WALDON, RE-
TIRED. PROMINENT DETROIT CIVIC
LEADER; EXECUTIVE COMMITTEE-

ALBERT Y. GOWEN, EX-PRESIDENT
OF LEHIGH PORTLAND CEMENT AS-
SOCIATION. A MEMBER OF ONE OF

CHAPTER V

JUST half an hour before Mr. Fisher departed from Indianapolis July 1, 1913, on the tour which was to accomplish so much for the Lincoln Highway, the other leaders whom he had drawn into the movement gathered in Detroit to close the work of the old Coast-to-Coast Rock Highway group and to bring its successor, the Lincoln Highway Association, into the world.

It seems too bad that Mr. Fisher could not have attended this meeting. His modest and unselfish spirit would undoubtedly have taken great pride in attending and probably the only thing that could have kept him away was just such an activity as that on which he was engaged—a fresh effort, in a new channel, for the success of the project.

The organizers met for the first time in the Lincoln Highway's own offices—"National Headquarters, 2115 Dime Savings Bank Building, Detroit, Mich.," the minutes note with pardonable pride. Those attending were Messrs. Joy, Chapin, Clark, Pardington and Bodman.

Under the skilled guidance of Mr. Bodman, they went swiftly through the legal formalities of completing their incorporation and establishing The Lincoln Highway Association as a legal entity, then elected Messrs. Alger, Beveridge, Chapin, Clark, Deming, Fisher, Gowen, Joy, Pardington and Seiberling as active members and directors of the new organization.

Officers were elected as follows:

President, Henry B. Joy

Vice-Presidents, Carl G. Fisher and Arthur R. Pardington

Treasurer, Emory W. Clark

Secretary, Arthur R. Pardington

Executive Committee: Henry B. Joy, Chairman; Paul R. Deming, Carl G. Fisher, Russell A. Alger, Roy D. Chapin, A. Y. Gowen, A. R. Pardington, secretary.

Then Mr. Bodman, who had only signed the articles of incorporation as a matter of convenience, resigned and the Directors adjourned, leaving to the executive committee, which was to be the active working unit of the Association, the task of clearing away matters which had arisen during the organization period

The legal routine by which this Association was created served afterward as a pattern for many other highway organizations. It was incorporated as a non-profit body under the laws of Michigan, statutes similar to which are to be found in most states.

The articles of incorporation fixed the name as "The Lincoln Highway Association" and declared the purpose, from which the Association never once wavered:

"To procure the establishment of a continuous improved highway from the Atlantic to the Pacific, open to lawful traffic of all description without toll charges: such highway to be known, in memory of Abraham Lincoln, as 'The Lincoln Highway.' "

In the articles of incorporation provision was made for active members, directors, and an executive committee to be composed of five directors with the President and Secretary as ex-officio members.

The Directors were given power to name the executive committee, to elect the president and other officers and to fill vacancies in their own number, but only the active members could elect the Directors. In turn, the Directors elected the active members. Provision was also made for other classifications of membership to be created by the Directors, but in practice the Directors themselves were the only active members and the only other classifications were "Sustaining Members" and "Founders." Sustaining Members were on a $5 annual membership basis; Founders were those who contributed $1,000 or more annually for at least three years.

The Association was thus a self-perpetuating body with control vested in the Directors.

The work was generally done by the executive committee. It had power to act and its personnel was chosen always with a view to the convenience and speed with which its members could assemble.

Its first meeting was on that day of repeated meetings, July 1, 1913. Its first act was to refuse to affiliate with the National Highways Association, a group seeking federal government construction and maintenance of interstate highways throughout the nation. The Lincoln Highway men declined because their aim was to procure the construction of one road only, and to enlarge their activities would dissipate their energies.

The executive committee also set in motion the long train of propaganda which the Association was to sponsor through so many years by authorizing the reprinting of a report on Mr. Fisher's road project. This report had been made by the Good Roads Committee of the National Association of Automobile Manufacturers. The com-

mittee ordered it sent to all manufacturers of automobiles, accessories and supplies with a view to enlisting
their aid in the Lincoln Highway movement.

Thus, when Mr. Fisher returned from his transcontinental trip with a glowing report and a project for
brand-new action, he found an interested and alert group
to listen and a well-knit organization to carry out his
proposal.

The plan was to go before the annual Conference of
Governors soon to be held at Colorado Springs, tell them
the story, and see how much money they could induce
the western leaders to spend in immediate improvement
of the road. This idea was suggested by Governor Hodges
of Kansas. Mr. Fisher thought it good and had talked
to other western governors about it. They too, found it
good. So did the Lincoln Highway leaders when he came
to Detroit and amplified in person the written report he
had already made on the tour.

"All the governors from each state along our road
will be glad to be at Colorado Springs," said Mr. Fisher,
"and if we can make our plans complete by that time
we can close up the west solid to the coast and have at
least three or four million spent next year on the Lincoln
Highway.

"If the directors could meet at Colorado Springs
August 22, it would clinch all matters now partially
closed. These governors want to get busy at once."

This step involved considerable amendment of Mr.
Fisher's own original plan to raise $10,000,000 for con-
struction of a road and then select the route it should
follow. For this, it substituted the immediate selection
of a route and the enlistment of such support as could

be obtained for improvement of that specific line. The $10,000,000 idea was not discarded, but it was thrust into the background. It never fully emerged.

As for the difficulty of selecting a route quickly, that offered but a small obstacle, since they were agreed that only the shortest, best and most direct route was worthy to be the great memorial they planned and they had not only personal knowledge and experience, but a great mass of collected data on which to base their decision.

The new move proposed by Mr. Fisher had important advantages. To offer this route first to the governors, as the leaders of the states through which it would pass, for approval and endorsement would start the new road off with a backing of influence obtainable in no other way. Moreover, consultation with the governors prior to public announcement would afford opportunity for correcting any errors that might have been made.

Not that they suspected the presence of errors; on the contrary, they believed they could select a route so logical, so obviously right, that its very reasonableness must win it universal support.

In fact, they knew that any route along which they could be successful in procuring the creation of a road must have just this reasonableness; they knew that there must never be a possibility of any critic saying: "Here you were swayed; at this point you deviated from your announced principle."

Mr. Fisher's proposal was so sound and offered so much of benefit that President Joy's only hesitancy in accepting it instantly was his doubt that the governors had specifically invited representatives of the Association to present their plan to the conference. Mr. Fisher, however, convinced him they would be welcome.

Secretary Pardington opened correspondence with the governors eligible to attend the conference, urging them to attend and support the Lincoln Highway plan, or to send representatives who would do so in their behalf. He began preparing the presentation of the project. And he kept up the campaign of letter-writing necessary to pacify western communities who were literally bombarding him with demands to be placed on the route of the Lincoln Highway or at least to be told where that route would lie. The form letter he devised to answer their inquiries was a masterpiece of diplomacy.

In one or two phrases, at least, it was highly significant in that it voiced a policy which became permanent, and from which the Association declined to deviate even at the request of the President of the United States.

"The route of the Lincoln Highway must, when finally adopted," Mr. Pardington wrote, "be governed by the following factors: the directness of the route between New York and San Francisco; second, points of scenic and historic interest and centers of population, between these points which can be most advantageously and economically incorporated; third, the character and the amount of support afforded this Association by the local communities which will receive the direct and immediate benefit of the establishment of this great memorial to Abraham Lincoln."

Only one of these factors counted with President Joy—directness. As his influence became more and more the controlling factor in the Association's work, centers of population and scenic beauties were pushed farther and farther into the background. By the time of the governors' meeting they had become indistinguishable.

Mr. Joy knew about roads; for years he had been travelling them, alone and with engineers. He knew what motor traffic required. And he particularly knew about roads in the west, where it was already evident the Association must center its first and greatest efforts. In fact, while Mr. Fisher was preparing for his trip, Mr. Joy was making one along a different and more northerly route, checking up at first hand on reports of road conditions, local enthusiasm and promises of construction. He had a very thorough knowledge of desert conditions, having spent years mining in southwestern Utah and having often travelled the western deserts.

Moreover, he had had intimate contact with men like Colonel Sidney D. Waldon and Frank H. Trego, engineers who had made many trips into the, from a motoring standpoint, uncharted spaces of the west.

Mr. Chapin, too, knew about roads. He was chairman of the Good Roads Committee of the National Association of Automobile Manufacturers, of which Colonel Waldon was a member.

Before the Association was formally organized, Mr. Chapin wrote to Colonel Waldon for his opinion concerning the route. The reply not only laid down the general line which eventually was followed but gave very sound reasons why that line, and no other, should be adopted.

"The selection of a route to bear the name Lincoln Memorial Highway requires more careful consideration than appears on the surface," said Colonel Waldon. "It is easy to say that the route should be through the southwestern states to provide touring conditions all the year round. The trouble is that when conditions are right for touring in the level country of Arizona, the mountains to the east and west of it are snowbound.

"If a route is considered still farther south, then the worst possible conditions are encountered in the wind-shifted sand around Yuma, together with the fact that the route becomes a winter route only, inasmuch as the heat is so intense during the summer. When the northern tier of states thaws out, the great volume of touring west begins. In April conditions were actually better for touring east of Detroit than they were for touring across Arizona.

"If, apparently, we must wait until the mountain passes of Arizona and California dry out, we will have waited longer than is necessary for the level plains of Nebraska and Wyoming to get into excellent touring condition. By this time, all the east will also be in shape for cross-country work. In fact, it will be ready before the Sierras permit the passage of automobiles. We can, therefore, practically eliminate any route that doesn't furnish the most direct line from New York to San Francisco.

"The route through the center of Colorado, of course, offers wonderful scenic beauties. This, however, introduces difficulties not experienced on the route through Wyoming.

"This fact has been recognized by practically every transcontinental motorist since 1903.

"The northern route, the original Emigrant Trail, is not nearly so well known as what I may call the central route and, besides, it does not lead to a destination that would be as popular as San Francisco would be.

"All things considered, I believe the Lincoln Memorial Highway should run from New York to San Francisco; that it should touch Chicago. From Chicago there are no two questions in my mind about the Omaha-Cheyenne-Salt Lake-Reno route being the shortest and offering the least possible trouble to the tourist. All parts of the line will be in condition for travel at about the same time and there is obviously no use in selecting a route where, as in our Arizona experience last April, we made three quarters of the way and then were blocked when almost in sight of the coast."

And here it is interesting to note that Colonel Waldon, whose judgment was so signally confirmed in the Association's final choice, confesses himself in 1933 to have been somewhat pessimistic about the whole project in 1913! Said he in the later year:

"I realized the importance of having possible routes across the country, north and south, and the importance of having highways that connected up; but it looked to me like a wild dream to spend $30,000,000 on a concrete highway connecting the Atlantic and Pacific. Nevertheless, the route interested me.

"As soon as Joy took hold, we felt we must decide where to put the link across the desert and Joy studied several alternates. From Salt Lake we had a choice of going north or south of the Lake. The terrain dictated selection of the southern alignment. We realized that the road must lie in the place where we put it for a number of years. We knew the Pony Express had taken the southern route but that didn't decide us; it only confirmed our own judgment that that was best.

"Our idea was to get a continuous route traversable through the largest portion of the year at the least cost. On that basis we selected the route."

Other leaders of the Association, too, had knowledge of roads. But they did not rely entirely on the facts they had. They gathered information wherever they could. They laid out tentative routes and compared the mileages, the numbers of cities on each route and the percentages of the country's population which each would serve.

They studied the maps. And in the end, it was Nature which compelled them to decide for a central routing with San Francisco as the western terminus; there never had been any question but that the nation's metropolis should be the eastern end of the line.

Let us also look at the map. North and south through this country run two major mountain chains, the Appalachians in the east and the Rockies in the west. Commerce had found many routes through the lower Appalachians; the Lincoln Highway could get through that range almost anywhere. But away west, at the far boundary of the plains country, the Rockies towered almost impenetrably.

There were but three practicable places to get through this vast mountain barrier—at Raton Pass, leading from southern Colorado into New Mexico, the pass taken by the Santa Fe Railroad; the great South Pass where the Union Pacific crossed the mountains, the pass through which streamed the gold-hunters of 1849; and the third, far to the north, the one taken by the Old Emigrant Trail.

It was necessary to use one of these three gateways; there was no other way.

To have taken the northernmost pass would logically have led the Lincoln Highway to some northern seacoast city, perhaps Seattle, perhaps Portland. There were many objections to such a routing; history showed that

PRESIDENT JONES SHOWN AS HE ATTEMPTED

the emigrants themselves had practically deserted this route for one through the South Pass as soon as the latter had become generally known.

Between the two remaining gateways there was less to choose. But the climatological factors outlined in Colonel Waldon's letter were potent arguments for the route through South Pass as it would be available *throughout its entire length,* for a greater portion of each year than that through Raton Pass. The studies also indicated it would eventually carry a heavier proportion of the national traffic than the one following the Santa Fe Trail.

Use of the South Pass dictated San Francisco as the logical western terminus. At the same time it afforded access to a greater portion of the Pacific Coast region than any other routing.

Basing their decision on these facts of climate and topography, President Joy and his associates felt they could go before the governors, the states and the world, with complete confidence that they were right. Their judgment in this matter, based on facts as they then existed, has never been successfully impugned.

At Mr. Joy's direction a map was prepared showing the route beginning at Jersey City—there being only a ferry connection with New York—and running to Philadelphia, thence by way of Gettysburg to Pittsburgh, across Ohio to Fort Wayne, Indiana; then around Chicago to join the old Overland Trail at Geneva, Illinois, and so westward to the bridge across the Mississippi at Clinton, Iowa; thence to Omaha and through Cheyenne to the Great South Pass and on to Salt Lake City, whence they followed the Old Pony Express route south of Great

Salt Lake to Ely, Reno, Carson City, Sacramento and San Francisco.`

There was good, sound, solid reasoning behind every step of this routing. Between Jersey City and Philadelphia they followed a route on which was probably performed the first highway improvement work ever done in America. This road, if such a meager thing can be called a road, was laid out by the Dutch as part of a route to link New Amsterdam with the settlements on the Delaware River, sometime prior to 1675.

Certainly a part of this route—between Elizabeth and New Amsterdam—was a regularly travelled way as early as 1664. It ran then from "Elizabethtown Point to Indian's Ferry"; that is, from what is now Elizabeth to what is now New Brunswick; and thence to Trenton, or as it then was known, "Falls-of-the-Delaware."

The sturdy burghers were wont to travel it on expeditions to trade with the Indians where Trenton now stands; but even after improvement had begun it was passable only to foot and horseborne traffic, not to vehicles. When a ferry across the Raritan was established at New Brunswick in 1696 the schedule of fees authorized to be charged, provided only for foot travellers and horsemen.

The New Jersey Provincial assembly considered this road a main artery of travel and taxed the innkeepers of Elizabethtown, Piscataway and Woodbridge, ten pounds a year for its maintenance.

The Lincoln Highway leaders chose this route for the same reason as did the Dutch colonists—it offered the easiest topography between its terminals.

They chose the Gettysburg routing between Philadelphia and Pittsburgh instead of that via Harrisburg because the Gettysburg route offered greater directness plus the advantage of an easier connection to Washington. They went into Fort Wayne because the easiest and best route across Ohio took them there. They took up the Overland Trail at Geneva instead of in Chicago because they realized, even so early, that it was desirable to keep through traffic out of the congestion of cities. They crossed the Mississippi via the Clinton Bridge because that was nearest and the Missouri at Omaha because that was in most direct line with their objective at Great South Pass. From Omaha west their route was dictated emphatically by the topography; they went right up the valley of the Platte as the forty-niners had done, following precisely the route of the Union Pacific railroad as dictated by their highway's illustrious godparent, Abraham Lincoln. They laid down the route to Salt Lake City rather than to Ogden because they meant to go south of Great Salt Lake. From Ely the position of the passes through the Sierra Nevadas dictated location of the route through Reno and so to Sacramento and San Francisco.

While selfish interests, they anticipated, would clamor for a realignment of this route through certain sections, the Lincoln Highway leaders knew that no better could be devised.

With this route on a map, President Joy, Secretary Pardington and Mr. Fisher went west to Colorado Springs where Governor Ammons, host to the conference, had assured them they would be very welcome on the afternoon of August 26, 1913.

CHAPTER VI

PUTTING STEAM BEHIND THE IDEA

AN early record of the Association describes the Lincoln Highway, as presented to the Conference of Governors that August afternoon in Colorado Springs, as "nothing but a red line on a map." In a sense, the description is accurate, for west of Pittsburgh it lacked any semblance of a connected route, and in all its length, from coast to coast, there were but 650 miles of good macadam or stone road. Nor was there any paving on it outside the corporate limits of cities. To that extent it was merely a line, an objective toward which the Association proposed to work even if, as the directors believed, twenty years should be required for attainment.

Yet many sections of it had the backing of history and usage. Part of it, the Ridge Road across Ohio, was an established travel route of the Indians long before the white man came. Other parts, near Bedford, Pennsylvania, followed surveys made by George Washington.

In eastern Pennsylvania, from Paoli to Lancaster, it followed the Philadelphia and Lancaster turnpike, constructed in 1792–94, which in turn was the successor of the old Conestoga Road that had its beginning in 1683. From Lancaster to the Susquehanna, it followed another old turnpike.

The New Jersey section was the Old Plank Road originally laid out by the Dutch settlers Other sections followed the Overland Trail, the Pony Express route, or the path of the '49ers.

And in California, from near Lake Tahoe down through Placerville as far as Folsom, it traversed a road which in the 'sixties was regarded as the very acme of highway construction, the route of the Overland Stages.

The experience of generations had shown that these portions of the Lincoln Highway were the easiest and most direct ways between their several terminals. What the Association now had to do was to procure connections between these various sections and the improvement of the entire route.

"What we really had in mind," said Henry B. Joy, "was not to build a road but to procure the building of many roads, by educating the people.* Beyond question we·did bring about what is known as the Good Roads Movement in America. We knew that a real road across the country would have to come; our problem was to get steam behind the idea."

The governors were to fire the boiler for the first steam. While the state executives looked at the red line on the map, Messrs. Joy, Fisher and Pardington formally asked them to lead their people in support of the Lincoln Highway. They outlined the reasons for choosing the route shown, indicated the fallacy of acceding to

* In a letter to John S. Mitchell, active leader of the Automobile Club of Southern California, dated October 6, 1913, Secretary Pardington amplifies this idea, explaining that the announcement of the route was, in a sense, hurried, in order to forestall efforts at diversion. Mr. Pardington adds:

"This was done to crystallize sentiment on one road first, after which our energies, in the event of our being successful in the one undertaking, would be directed toward the establishmnt of a second transcontinental road, unless the object lesson offered by us should result in activities of the people along the Santa Fe Trail and Old National Road. We are hopeful that this very thing will result."

local clamors for diversion, and appealed for support upon the solid basis of patriotism. "With the authority to plan and the power to execute of the great Napoleon," said their address, "The Lincoln Way might be creditably planned and executed with dispatch from the beginning.

"The idealists who have energetically pressed forward the great project of a Lincoln Highway from coast to coast have accomplished wonders toward crystallizing a nation-wide demand for the consummation of such a great and desirable project.

"A committee of these idealists," they continued, "after energetically and at their own personal expense pressing the propaganda to national fame and interest, decided to increase the force behind their efforts, enlist the financial aid of others, and thus develop a stronger public interest and support of the work.

"After much deliberation they decided to centralize and organize with headquarters at a convenient center.

"Route investigations began," they explained. "All data was studied. Climatic conditions considered. Routes possible and impossible were travelled and details carefully noted as bearing on the ultimate decision which the Lincoln Highway Association was organized to make, as to what route would in its judgment be the most practicable to become the great Lincoln Memorial Highway.

"The Lincoln Way so selected, if done wisely, will become great.

"None know better than those who will assume to select the route, that it is not done with Napoleonic authority or power.

"The force behind the decision will be only the wisdom of it, which it is hoped will give the selection of route the force, because it is believed that the route of the 'Lincoln Way,' wisely chosen, will have behind it the patriotic force of the whole people.

"The appeals of sections have been heard. The arguments of all interests have been and are being weighed.

"Shall the Lincoln Way be marked on the map from large city to large city? Shall it be from point of interest to point of interest?

"Shall it be a highway from New York to San Francisco, as direct as practicable considering the limitations by Nature in the topography of the country?

"See America first!

"With all our force we endorse that sentiment! But a transcontinental highway that wound from large city to large city, from one wonder of nature to another would indeed be a devious and winding journey in this great America of ours.

"It becomes plain that the decision on such a complicated route could not be arrived at in generations. No concentrated effort could be gained for the execution of the work. It becomes plain that the scope of the work must be within the practicable. It must be such as immediately upon presentation to gain your support and mine.

"The decision must be confined to one permanent road across the country to be constructed, no matter how desirable others may be and actually are.

"Such has become the basic principle guiding the Lincoln Highway Association."

Mr. Joy amplified this formal address. "Our object," said he, "is to make a decision. It is clear that to accomplish the building of any road, opinion must be crystallized. So long as we spend our time discussing the merits of one route versus another, we can make no progress. It is with no desire to discriminate against any route that we have made our decision, but to select some route upon which opinion may be crystallized by the broad patriotic views of the citizens.

"That there should be a Lincoln Highway across this country is the important thing; that it should be the most practicable route for the purposes involved is the proper thing."

On this basis the Governors accorded the plan their hearty support. Governor Ammons of Colorado and Governor Hodges of Kansas, both of whose states had been traversed by the Indiana Manufacturers' Tour, and who had confidently expected that the Lincoln Highway would be routed the same way, were bitterly disappointed. But there was no help for it; Nature had not designed the topography in such manner as to make that the logical and direct way to go.

However, the eloquent appeal of Governor Ammons, and the courtesy required toward their host, caused the three Lincoln Highway men to assent to a loop or detour from the Lincoln Highway to Denver. This loop left the main red line at Big Springs, Nebraska, and returned to it at Cheyenne.

No single act of its own ever caused the Lincoln Highway Association quite so much regret, difficulty and trouble as this seemingly proper step.

The next move was to announce the route to the public. This should be done quickly, the Association officials felt, to forestall efforts at diversion, create publicity and bring the Association to the attention of the public. The question was, How could the announcement be made in the most dignified, impressive, and at the same time newsworthy manner? They debated this on the train as they returned eastward and decided that it should be done by proclamation. There and then, in Mr. Joy's compartment, the president wrote, with Mr. Pardington's assistance and Mr. Fisher's occasional comments, the Proclamation of the Lincoln Highway which was to serve the Association as a basic statement of principle ever afterward. This document follows:

PROCLAMATION
of Route of
THE LINCOLN HIGHWAY

WHEREAS: The purpose of this Association is: TO IMMEDIATELY PROMOTE AND PROCURE THE ESTABLISHMENT OF A CONTINUOUS IMPROVED HIGHWAY FROM THE ATLANTIC TO THE PACIFIC, OPEN TO LAWFUL TRAFFIC OF ALL DESCRIPTIONS, WITHOUT TOLL CHARGES AND TO BE OF CONCRETE WHEREVER PRACTICABLE. THIS HIGHWAY IS TO BE KNOWN, IN MEMORY OF ABRAHAM LINCOLN, AS "THE LINCOLN HIGHWAY," and,

WHEREAS: Toward the end of accomplishing this purpose ELABORATE RESEARCH and INVESTIGATION has been prerequisite to crystallization of opinion before wise and intelligent decision could be reached and,

WHEREAS: This Association desires to impress on all people that it FULLY ACKNOWLEDGES that a public declaration by it of a route is of NO FORCE OR EFFECT except as it shall be wise and practicable, and being so meet the approval of the people for such a useful and enduring memorial and WHEREAS: It is obvious that this Association can only aid and cooperate toward the desired end, AND THAT UPON ALL THE PEOPLE, and especially upon the Officials of each State and County and upon the inhabitants thereof, within the borders of which is designated by these Resolutions a section of the LINCOLN HIGHWAY, DOES REST THE PATRIOTIC BURDEN of Establishing, Broadening, Straightening, Maintaining, and Beautifying such HIGHWAY to the end that it may become an appropriate MEMORIAL to the GREAT MARTYRED PATRIOT whose name it bears, and,

WHEREAS: One chief step toward the desired goal is to crystallize in the public mind the PRACTICAL WISDOM of the route selected, therefore, be it recorded here:

First: That in general it has been for nearly a century and is today the main Overland Trail, and that part lying west of Chicago is known by that historic name.

Second: It is the most direct and most practical route as to grades, curves and general topography.

Third: It is to the greatest extent improved and marked throughout its length.

Fourth: It serves the greatest population.

Fifth: It is capable of being established as a fitting Memorial Highway at the least cost, and,

WHEREAS: It is now proper to declare the results of deliberation and inspection, in the HOPE that the wisdom and care in selection may insure united sentiment, and with the prayer that this record will appeal to the hearts of all patriotic Americans to the end that plans and activities toward construction may go IMMEDIATELY FORWARD,

THEREFORE, BE IT RESOLVED: That the LINCOLN HIGHWAY now is and henceforth shall be an existing memorial in tribute to the immortal ABRAHAM LINCOLN;

that the LINCOLN HIGHWAY does extend from New
York to San Francisco over and through the following
States:

State of New York. State of New Jersey. State of Pennsylvania. State of Ohio. State of Indiana. State of Illinois.
State of Iowa. State of Nebraska. State of Colorado. State
of Wyoming. State of Utah. State of Nevada. State of
California.

More specifically, the route is described as passing
through the following cities in the several States, viz:

1. NEW YORK—New York.

2. NEW JERSEY—Jersey City, Newark, Trenton, Camden.

3. PENNNSYLVANIA—Philadelphia, Lancaster, York,
Gettysburg, Chambersburg, Bedford, Ligonier, Greensburg, Pittsburgh, Beaver Falls.

4. OHIO—Canton, Mansfield, Marion, Kenton, Lima,
Van Wert, known as Market Route No. 3.

5. INDIANA—Fort Wayne, Ligonier, Elkhart, South
Bend, Laporte, Valparaiso.

6. ILLINOIS—Chicago Heights, Joliet, Geneva, De-
Kalb, Rochelle, Ashton, Dixon, Sterling, Morrison,
Fulton.

7. IOWA—Clinton, DeWitt, Cedar Rapids, Tama,
Marshalltown, State Centre, Ames, Grand Junction,
Jefferson, Dennison, Logan, Council Bluffs.

8. NEBRASKA—Omaha, Fremont, Columbus, Central
City, Grand Island, Kearney, Lexington, Gothenburg,
North Platte, Ogallala, Big Springs, Chappell, Sidney,
Kimball.

9. COLORADO—Julesburg, Sterling, Fort Morgan,
Denver, Longmont, Loveland, Fort Collins.

10. WYOMING—Pine Bluff, Cheyenne, Laramie, Rawlins, Wamsutter, Point of Rocks, Rock Springs, Green

River, Granger, Fort Bridger, Evanston.

11. UTAH—Echo, Parley's Canyon, Salt Lake City, Garfield, Grantsville, Timpie, Kanaka Ranch, Fish Springs, Kearney's Ranch, Ibapha.

12. NEVADA—Tippet's Ranch, Schellburne Pass, Ely, Eureka, Austin, Fallon Wadsworth, Reno, Carson City.

13. CALIFORNIA—Truckee, Auburn, Tallac, Placerville, Sacramento, Stockton, Oakland, San Francisco.

AND BE IT RESOLVED: That this is an appeal to the State Authorities and to all Officials, to properly dedicate, to re-mark and re-name the said described Highway with the Lincoln Highway Insignia.

And it is finally RESOLVED: That copies of these resolutions be sent to the PRESIDENT OF THE UNITED STATES, to the GOVERNOR of each State, to the MEMBERS OF THE NATIONAL CONGRESS, and to the MEMBERS OF THE LEGISLATURE of each State.

Done by THE LINCOLN HIGHWAY ASSOCIATION, INC.

Directors	By Henry B. Joy, President
R. A. Alger	Carl G. Fisher, Vice-President
Albert J. Beveridge	A. R. Pardington, Vice-President
R. D. Chapin	Emory W. Clark, Treasurer
Emory W. Clark	Henry E. Bodman, Legal Counsel
Paul H. Deming	Frank H. Trego, Engineer
Carl G. Fisher	
A. Y. Gowen	
Henry B. Joy	
A. R. Pardington	
F. A. Seiberling	
John N. Willys	

"Issued from Headquarters Lincoln Highway Association, at Detroit, Michigan, U. S. A., the Tenth day of September, Year One Thousand Nine Hundred Thirteen."

Back in Detroit, they rushed this proclamation to a printer and had thousands of copies struck off. They titled their address to the Governors "An Appeal to Patriots" and had that, too, reprinted by the thousands. Then they spread these documents broadcast to the newspapers of the country, released for publication on September 14, with a well-written news story.

That, however, was but a beginning. They sent the Proclamation and the Appeal to Patriots far and wide to automobile dealers, manufacturers, chambers of commerce, road enthusiasts, anybody and everybody whom they believed would display them and so attract further attention for the route and the Association.

The Lincoln Highway staff was limited; they called, as they were to do many times in the future, on the Packard Company, and Mr. Joy still tells with pride how the entire Packard office staff worked nearly all night so that everyone might receive his copy by September 14.

"They were good sports," said Mr. Joy. "They were just as much interested as I was. The magazines and the newspapers ate up the story and they're the people that really put the Lincoln Highway over."

To give a background of color and interest to the issuance of the proclamation, President Joy issued a personal appeal to all Packard employees, dealers and agents, to decorate their places of business with American flags, Lincoln Way Pennants and portraits of Lincoln and to urge all others in the motor car industry to do likewise.

In addition, he sent a personal appeal, as President of the Lincoln Highway Association, to the owners of all Packard cars, enclosing with each letter a large reproduction of the Proclamation, and urging the recipient to arrange for its display.

All this Messrs. Joy, Fisher, and Pardington did without even consulting the executive committee; then, as ever, what the Lincoln Highway Association wanted was action.

The executive committee's later ratification of their acts was prompt and unanimous and was characteristic of the Association's policy that the man or men in charge of a particular matter should carry it out regardless of specific authorization for its details. Indeed, time and time again President Joy was to say to Mr. Pardington or his successors as secretary:

"Is that the way it should be done?"

"Yes."

"Well, why ask me? Why don't you go on and do it?"

Here, in one sentence, is the secret of the marvelous results attained by the Lincoln Highway, the thing that kept men working day and night, year after year, to make it a success. Each man had his work to do and the man higher up not only let him do it but expected him to do it.

Consider the personalities of its leaders, their various responsibilities, the necessarily limited amounts of time they could devote to the activities of the Association. Carl G. Fisher, who originated the idea, was head of the Prest-O-Lite Company, which rightfully claimed the major portion of his energies. Henry B. Joy, as president of the Packard Company, was responsible for the progress of that corporation. F. A. Seiberling, president of one of the world's largest rubber companies, had responsibilities which he was compelled to place ahead of his highway activities. J. Newton Gunn was not only Vice-

President of the United States Rubber Company but President of its largest and most active subsidiary, the U. S. Tire Company.

In their respective services as head of the Association, Messrs. Joy, Seiberling and Gunn had the assistance and counsel of executive committees, it is true, but the members of these committees were all deeply engaged in the country's economic life. Mr. Joy and his successors could lay down principles and establish policies, but they had no time for details.

It was necessary that there should be active executives. These men the Association found in Messrs. Pardington, Ostermann, Bement and Hoag. From these individuals came recommendations for many of the organization's most notable endeavors. From them came the administrative supervision which carried those endeavors to fulfillment. It is significant that the directors in general approved every recommendation they made, supported them loyally in what they did and, unsolicited, voted them increase after increase in salary.

With such a spirit pervading the organization, it is not surprising that the action of President Joy, in issuing the Proclamation, was immediately approved.

The dramatic manner of the route's presentation, the patriotic appeal of the name Lincoln and the thorough manner in which press material was distributed obtained publication of the story at length almost everywhere.

The public response was tremendous and immediate. Letters, promises of support, checks, poured in with every mail from all sections and all classes. In one mail checks were received from Vancouver, B. C., Florida and Maine, one of them for $1,000. Grand Army men who had been proud to call Lincoln Commander-in-Chief sent in their contributions; farmers who had no automobiles contributed because they said the plan would make for improved roads. Road enthusiasts, to whom Secretary Pardington had entrusted certificates of membership for sale, reported quick disposal of their allotment and asked for more.

Ministers, lawyers, bankers, motorists, notables of all kinds, even the President of the United States, Woodrow Wilson, sent in checks and asked to be enrolled as members. Automobile clubs bought certificates in blocks.

᾽Automobile dealers telegraphed for additional copies of the Proclamation to be posted in their windows. Governors urged their citizens to support the movement and pledged their own cooperation to the Association. Governor James M. Cox of Ohio wrote: "I expect to do all I can to encourage this enterprise and assure you of my hearty sympathy with the movement. Anything we can do for you in this State will be done."

As Edward N. Hines said years later: "The Lincoln Highway crystallized, on a national plane, America's latent sentiment for roads."

Striking while the iron was hot, the Association leaders called for a nation-wide celebration to dedicate the highway to the memory of Lincoln. They asked each state executive along the route to proclaim the day of the dedication, October 31, a legal holiday and call on the citizens to participate in its celebration. The response to this request was quick and cordial. Governor Oddie of Nevada, delayed in issuing his proclamation because of absence from his Capitol, telegraphed it to all newspapers along the line of the highway in his State, to make sure Nevada citizens had sufficient notice to prepare a worthy celebration.

This second major move in the Association's long campaign of propaganda evoked a new series of endorsements, because it brought the name of Lincoln and the memorial character of the highway even more strongly to the fore. Following up this advantage, the Association asked the clergy of the nation to discuss Lincoln in their sermons on November 2, the Sunday nearest the dedication.

This evoked some stirring tributes to the Great Emancipator and was perhaps as shrewd a stroke as was delivered in all the Association's years of arousing public sentiment. Many of the statements from nationally known clergymen were publicized through the Association's press releases, among them one from His Eminence, John, Cardinal Gibbons and others from Dr. Newell Dwight Hillis and Dr. S. Parkes Cadman.

Cardinal Gibbons wrote: "I am greatly pleased to know that success in the undertaking is assured, as I believe that such a highway will be a most fitting and useful monument to the memory of Lincoln."

The statement from Cardinal Gibbons was of special value because of his conservatism and the rarity with which he voiced an opinion on public questions. The Association sent his expression to all Roman Catholic publications in the country as well as to the lay press.

The dedication was a complete success. In some regions the various communities concentrated their activities in a combined celebration, as in northern Indiana, where in line with the Hallowe'en spirit of the season, the Indiana farmers made Jack-o'-Lanterns and set them

on fence posts along the route for miles so that, as Mr.
Fisher said, "It looked like a continuous bonfire and
celebration."

H. E. Frederickson, Lincoln Highway consul for Nebraska, wrote of the celebration at Omaha:

"I have eight large loads of old street car ties and three
barrels of good burning oil for our bonfire, $100 worth
of fireworks and the mayor and others for short speeches.
Most of our retail stores will be decorated in red, white
and blue."

Wyoming gave the highway an enthusiastic welcome.
In fact, to insure that she would do her part, Payson W.
Spaulding, of Evanston, State Consul, drove all the way
across the state and back, a trip of nearly 900 miles.

At Trenton, New Jersey, the good roads enthusiasts
turned out a first class parade with illuminated floats and
the traditional accompaniments.

Naturally, in many of the newspaper articles resulting
from such Association activities, the name of Henry B.
Joy was mentioned as President of the Association. Naturally, also, the newspaper writers mentioned that he was
President of the Packard Motor Car Company. Mr. Joy
promptly ordered that this be eliminated insofar as the
organization's headquarters had power to do it. The less
he personally appeared in Lincoln Highway affairs the
better, he said, "Because it may create prejudice against
the work of the Association in the minds of those who
may feel that I have created it for the purpose of ex-
ploiting Henry B. Joy."

As for the Packard Company, he gave these instructions: "I notice mention is made of Packard. This is

directly against my wishes. It hurts the whole proposition by creating prejudice—and justly so."

And now, with the Association formally launched, the governors' endorsement obtained, the route proclaimed and public interest thoroughly aroused, Secretary Pardington had a little time to devote to other matters which were clamoring for attention. These were the obtaining of additional subscriptions to the $10,000,000 fund proposed by Mr. Fisher; the enrollment of prominent men as sponsors; and the sale of the $5 membership certificates over the preparation of which he had labored long and painstakingly weeks earlier back in New York.

He had also to meet, as best he could, the demands which were beginning to be made for some official of the Lincoln Highway to address good roads meetings held at widely distant points.

Steam had been raised to working pressure; from now on the task was to utilize its energy.

CHAPTER VII

AN OBJECT LESSON IN FINANCE

ALTHOUGH the Lincoln Highway Association received contributions or payments of dues from thousands of persons, the great burden of its operating expense was always borne by a small group of men; rarely as many as fifteen, for many years only six. Much as it accomplished, and rapidly as it brought about the building of roads all over the country, it could have done more and attained its goal in a shorter time had it been amply financed from the start.

On the other hand, it does not seem peculiar that the organization was able to interest and obtain large contributions from some of the nation's most notable citizens. But for the economic dislocation resulting from the World War, it would undoubtedly have obtained a great many more of these in the years from 1914 to 1919, when a larger income would have been of greatest advantage.

When the Lincoln Highway Association swung into full stride in the fall of 1913, after issuance of the Proclamation, it faced two financial problems. One was to bring subscriptions to the proposed construction fund up to $10,000,000; the other was to obtain funds for ordinary operating expenses. Of the two, the latter was the more pressing, for although Messrs. Fisher and Allison had defrayed all preliminary expenses, there had been other expenses since organization was perfected and

ARTHUR R. PARDINGTON, FIRST
SECRETARY AND VICE-PRESIDENT

AUSTIN F. BEMENT, VICE-PRESI-
DENT AND SECRETARY

HENRY C. OSTERMANN, VICE-PRESI-
DENT AND FIELD SECRETARY

GAEL S. HOAG, FIELD SECRETARY
AND EXECUTIVE SECRETARY

there was but $6,000 in hand to meet them; $1,000 each having been advanced by Messrs. Joy, Seiberling, Fisher and Gowen, and the Hudson and Packard Motor Car Companies.

Mr. Pardington proposed that the Association finance itself through the sale of membership certificates, with a minimum price of $5, and very elaborate machinery was set up for selling these. This sales organization was chiefly made up of motor car dealers and good roads enthusiasts all over the country, to whom they sent books of certificates with a request that the receiver sell the certificates and remit the proceeds. They supplemented this with a direct mail campaign for larger contributions.

For a time it appeared the sale of certificates would not only solve the problem of operating finance but produce a balance to be used for construction. Mr. Pardington optimistically even set a goal of $1,000,000 for the first year's activity.

Then small-town residents began to show reluctance to contribute funds for anything but actual construction work in their own communities. He met that with an arrangement for such contributions to be held in their home banks pending use for local construction. This restarted the flow of certificate sales but money that remained on deposit in banks along the line did not help finance the overhead of the Association. The Association's entire effort, as it was recognized later, was too diverse and Mr. Pardington, as the active administrator, had to spread his efforts too thin. In ill health at the time and frequently suffering great pain, it is remarkable that he did not break down.

Instead of collapsing, however, he formed and put

into execution a brand new scheme. By dint of clever letters and a few personal calls, he induced more than forty magazines and automotive trade journals to donate to the Association advertising space in each of their issues for a year.

These publications ranged all the way from The Fra to the Harvard Lampoon. Then he induced Elbert Hubbard, Homer McKee, LeRoy Pelletier, William C. Freeman and other noted advertising men to prepare copy telling the Association's story and appealing to the public for support.

As a result of this campaign, the Lincoln Highway received contributions from places as far off the proclaimed route as Manila, Honolulu and London. Many of the contributions were for sums far in excess of the $5 minimum requested.

They had sent President Wilson Certificate No. 1; now Mary Clark Thompson of Camden, Maine, sent in a check for $1,000 and asked for Certificate No. 2, with the stipulation that she receive no public recognition for the contribution. Number 3 they sent to Robert T. Lincoln, son of the president they were memorializing. They whipped public sentiment with clever propaganda.

Not all their work, however, could alter the fact that the plan was unsound from a business standpoint; the $5 unit was too small in proportion to the cost of selling. In addition, much expensive engraved material was lost through the broadcasting of books of certificates without any assurance that the recipients would make a sincere effort to sell them. It is possible that this also involved some monetary losses. However, in all the annals of the Lincoln Highway Association, involving the handling of approximately $1,250,000, many thousands of dollars of which were collected and sometimes disbursed by volunteer and amateur assistants, there is on record but one case of misappropriation of funds. This involved only one volunteer worker in a small town and but a small sum of money!

Nor was the campaign for subscriptions to the $10,-000,000 fund progressing. The directors, into whose special charge this was given, could not spare the time for personal solicitations. President Joy and Secretary Pardington did make some calls in New York, obtaining several moderate subscriptions, but the anticipated thousands of dollars simply were not forthcoming. Mr. Pardington circularized 3,000 millionaires with but negligible results.

The situation was serious. The Association owed $16,000 for printing and mailing 150,000 copies of the Proclamation and the Appeal to Patriots. To cover this and other matters the directors voted to borrow $19,000. President Joy offered personal guaranty of the entire sum, but the other directors present insisted on sharing it, so that the note bore the endorsements of Messrs. Fisher, Seiberling, Clark, Alger, Chapin, Gowen and Deming.

Nobody was willing to give up the ship, but it was apparent that something drastic must be done quickly. The directors hit on the plan of retaining a man to make contact with wealthy citizens and induce them to subscribe and another man to travel along the highway, stirring up local interest and disposing of certificates. They chose H. J. Larsen to call on prospective subscribers and H. C. Ostermann as a Consul-at-Large to do field work.

Henry C. Ostermann not only was a genius in several ways, but was probably one of the most remarkable persons ever allied with the Association. Ostermann belonged to that charmed circle of personalities who are immediately accepted by all classes of people. Courteous, affable, perfectly poised, cultured, and intelligent, he filled a most exacting position perfectly.

It was not realized at that time that the retention of Mr. Ostermann as Consul-at-Large was to provide one of the main driving forces of the organization in the days to come. His work proved incomparable, his friends became countless, and while he lived, his service to the Association brought untold admiration and respect, not only from his associates in the work, but from all whom he encountered. His accidental death in 1920 was mourned sincerely by thousands of friends.

Just where Mr. Ostermann was born is not known. At the age of six he was a newsboy in New York City, living in a newsboy's home. At nine he became a bell-boy in a hotel, and in turn thereafter, a cash-boy and cigar clerk. At seventeen he was discharged from the Navy following three years' service. He drifted through California, picked oranges, and worked on West Coast steamers. From 1895 to 1897 he travelled with Buffalo Bill's Wild West Show, ranched in Montana and North Dakota, became a flagman on the Illinois Central railroad. He was promoted first to brakeman and then conductor. In 1906 he invented and developed a grain door for freight cars. To promote this, he organized a car-building concern. In 1913, he expanded still further when he started an automotive business in Deadwood, South Dakota. There he

distinguished himself in public service; the Chamber of Commerce of Deadwood adopted formal resolutions of appreciation for certain of his efforts. Just as his future appeared to be established, investments in a smelting concern proved disastrous and he was left with practically nothing.

Such was the man who presented himself for service with the Lincoln Highway Association. His talents, his experiences, his ability as a public-speaker, and his radiant personality were just what the Lincoln Highway needed. From the moment he started from Detroit—and his travels carried him many times across the country— these qualifications lifted him to extraordinary successes, both in contacts with industrial leaders and in those country-store caucuses wherein the fate of the nation has ever been decided.

To Mr. Larsen and to Consul Ostermann, then, the Association committed the work of increasing its income to an adequate figure. However, not even Mr. Ostermann's many qualifications were equal to the task imposed on them, and Mr. Larsen was able to do even less.

Mr. Joy called in Mr. Pardington for a heart-to-heart talk about the entire situation. Mr. Pardington proposed that efforts be concentrated on obtaining 100 founders at $1,000 each, or 1,000 contributors at $100 each, the money to be used in financing the Association's educational work for the next eighteen months by which time he believed business conditions would justify a campaign for large contributions.

Mr. Joy voiced the opinion that the best thing the Association could do would be to arrange for building six sample or "Seedling Miles" of road, one each in the states of Illinois, Iowa, Nebraska, Wyoming, Utah and Nevada.

They combined the two proposals and submitted them to the directors.

"I feel," said President Joy on this occasion, "that the work in which the Lincoln Highway Association has engaged is not the work of a moment; it is not the work of a year; it is not the work even of a decade. It is the work of a generation, and our Association has been thoughtfully devised to be continuous in its efforts and self-perpetuating.

"It seems clear to me that I would prefer to pursue the education of the public and the collection of funds in a small way until the public mind is more saturated with the objects and intent of the Lincoln Highway Association, and until the times may seem more propitious for asking large contributions.

"In groping about in my own mind for some concrete, tangible thing to do which would place the Lincoln Highway more plainly before the communities, I have always had in mind building in each one of the states from Illinois to Nevada inclusive, a sample mile of the roadway. It is quite possible that these seedling mile sections might be made two miles or three miles by the aid of the counties or local communities where it might be decided to do the work. The educational benefit of a sample mile of Lincoln Highway road in each state would be of inestimable value in promoting our work. The work of the Lincoln Highway Association would then become a tangible, feasible, sensible expenditure of the funds being raised.

"I would rather do this tangible work at present than to exert extraordinary effort to raise the ten million dollar fund at a time when the maximum effort would yield the minimum return of any time in twenty years."

It is significant that in four sentences Mr. Joy used the word "work" four times.

Messrs. Larsen and Ostermann were asked to relinquish their salaries, though both remained on a non-salary basis; several other important economies were ordered, and for the first time definite principles were laid down for the Association's educational campaign.

Here is the program they adopted:

1. Encourage the marking of the route throughout its length.

2. Encourage local boards having power to name streets and roads, to designate the route as "Lincolnway" wherever it passed through their jurisdictions.

3. Obtain contributions in sums ranging up to or exceeding $1,000 with the idea of using funds so obtained for constructing demonstration sections, or "Seedling Miles" as they were afterward called, in the six states named.

Probably none of the directors realized that adoption of this plan meant final abandonment of Mr. Fisher's original proposal. The Indianan had contemplated donating material to communities to build roads; the new program meant educating communities, by object lesson, to build roads for themselves.

No one said, and no one can say, that Mr. Fisher's plan was wrong or could not have been put into effect; the new idea merely seemed more advantageous at the time and the progress made under it rendered a return to the original basis unnecessary.

As the organization swung into 1914, President Joy devoted his first attention to lifting the burden of debt it was carrying.

To Messrs. Fisher, Chapin, Seiberling, Gowen and Willys he wrote:

"Our Association, as you know, is in debt $21,700. I want now to clean up this indebtedness. The Packard Company has contributed some $7,000. I do not want to ask my company for any more. In checking over the list of directors I find six interests represented which I feel ought to be able to clean up this debt. These are Carl G. Fisher, R. D. Chapin, F. A. Seiberling, John N. Willys, A. Y. Gowen, and Henry B. Joy. I will give my check spot cash for whatever you think is my share. Won't you please put your shoulder to the wheel and help me clean it up?"

This appeal won the hearty support of those addressed; more, it established the principle of underwriting by which the Association was to be financed to success. The plan was worked out in detail at the end of that year; under it each director contributed what he felt he could, generally a flat sum of $1,000 or $2,000, then the more affluent among them underwrote whatever else was needed.

This underwriting system was placed on a triennial basis at the beginning of 1915 so that, while expenditures were held to strict conformity with the annual budget, complete freedom was always left for planning into the future.

In the earlier years of the Association's activity the secretary spent considerable time and effort in obtaining founders; that is, subscribers who would contribute $1,000 annually for a period of three years, but by far the best results in this line were obtained by the directors.

Thus at the 1915 annual meeting the financial report showed as founders, beside Roy D. Chapin's Hudson Motor Car Company, John Willys' Willys-Overland Company, Carl G. Fisher's Prest-O-Lite Company, A. Y. Gowen's Lehigh Portland Cement Company, Henry B. Joy's Packard Motor Car Company, F. A. Seiberling's Goodyear Tire & Rubber Company, and Messrs. Joy, Fisher and Seiberling personally, the following founders obtained through the efforts of the directors:

Paige-Detroit Co.
E. A. Deeds.
James A. Allison.
A. C. Newby.
H. S. Firestone.
William Randolph Hearst.
Universal Portland Cement Co., of which B. F. Affleck was president.
T. Coleman DuPont.

Besides these, Mr. Gowen had obtained contributions of $500 each annually from the Marquette Portland Cement Co., Chicago Portland Cement Company and Northwestern States Portland Cement Company; and a contribution of $300 annually from the German-American Portland Cement Company. All of these contributions were to run for three years.

At the same time Messrs. Joy, Fisher, Seiberling, Gowen, Chapin, and Willys were guaranteeing a further revenue of $12,000, or $2,000 each, and later they actually contributed that sum in cash.

Thus the organizers of the Association, including Mr. Allison who was not at that time a director, contributed for the year $22,000 as against $8,800 obtained from outside subscribers.

At the beginning of 1916 a new source of revenue was devised—Sustaining Memberships. Sustaining members were persons contributing $5 or more annually. This class of membership was created primarily to assure the continued interest of a large number of people, but it also produced considerable income.

Nevertheless, possibilities for effective work developed more rapidly than revenues.

One director expressed some feeling because the cement manufacturers had not made more substantial contributions; only eight companies had donated cement or subscribed cash. This director suggested that the organization advocate use of some road material other than concrete.

Mr. Joy, however, declined to consider this. "So far as I am concerned," he said, "if the cement people never subscribe, I want to stand pat on the concrete idea."

So they stuck to concrete.

Though the Association was underfinanced, it certainly had good financiers at its head. Austin F. Bement so managed affairs during the few months he served as acting secretary that a bank balance was built up. During 1916, when he was secretary, he increased it, and in the next three years he saved $7,500 from estimated operating expenses.

On three occasions this balance assured continued operation when it seemed as if finances to carry on could not be obtained. Also in 1916 Secretary Bement, aided by Field Secretary Ostermann, built up the sales of maps, guides and other material, and increased the receipts from advertising in the Guide, until the money coming in from such comparatively minor sources more than equalled the contributions received from founders. Still, he did not find it as easy to raise money for the Association as Mr. Fisher said it was.

Wrote the Indianan, enclosing a check for the first year's contribution of a new founder:

"It is perfectly easy to get assistance for the Lincoln Highway Association, if your directors only go after it. I think you are too easy with them. You should first give them a good dinner and then a good cussing whenever you want money. I will dig up another founder within a few days which will fulfill my obligations, after which I will quite probably do nothing, unless you commence to yell."

War conditions materially hampered financing in 1917, and the Association entered 1918 with but limited funds in sight.

However, there was too much to be done and it had embarked too heavily into Utah and Nevada road construction to allow of any slackening of effort or reduction of personnel. Fortunately, the sustaining membership receipts for the year exceeded $9,000 and to obtain what additional money was needed in 1918, they induced five of the founders to pay their 1919 subscriptions in advance.

The annual meeting at the end of 1918 reached no definite conclusions as to financing; the passage of a federal bill for direct improvement of highways appeared imminent and the directors felt that undoubtedly the Lincoln Highway would be one of the first roads to be considered by whatever authority such a bill set up.

"Upon passage of such a bill," said Mr. Seiberling, who had succeeded Mr. Joy as President, "The Lincoln Highway Association could feel that its work was accomplished and that it had successfully achieved the ends for which the organization was incorporated."

Yet he argued that the Association should not discontinue activities until the Lincoln Highway was capable of handling traffic in all weathers and of carrying transcontinental freight with assurance and dispatch. They resolved to continue for two years, which they estimated would be ample for accomplishing this result under the proposed legislation.

Mr. Bement pointed out that continued operations at the current rate would result in a deficit of $15,000 for 1919, and one of $35,000 for 1920, but added that funds due and in hand would finance the organization's activities for seven months. The directors instructed him to proceed with as small an expenditure as possible.

With a free hand, and with the loyal support of Mr. Ostermann, the secretary was able to make the following report to the directors exactly one year later:

"Very fortunately we have no financial problems at this time, which is quite unusual. A year ago today we had only enough money to carry us on a conservative basis for eight months. Fortunately we were able to build up our membership support very materially and gained from that source a much greater income than we had

JAMES NEWTON GUNN, PRESIDENT OF LINCOLN HIGHWAY ASSOCIA-
TION DURING THE WORLD WAR PERIOD. TO HIS EFFORTS ARE LARGELY
ATTRIBUTABLE "THE IDEAL SECTION" IN INDIANA

any reason to figure on at the first of the year. We were also able to secure five more founders and to secure the back payment of $2,000 on an old pledge. We came through a year of unusually heavy expense without having to sell any of the $7,500 worth of bonds which we expected to have to dispose of and use for current expenses, bought $2,500 worth of additional bonds and ended the year with a bank balance some $1,200 over and above all indebtedness."

The obtaining of the additional founders was due to the efforts of the directors; the increase in sustaining membership revenues, which aggregated for that year the highest figure ever reached, $12,260, was almost entirely due to Mr. Ostermann's effective work in the field, but the general success of the year was due to Mr. Bement's skill both in initiating new activities and in carrying out principles which President Seiberling laid down.

For 1920 and succeeding years the most liberal financing plan ever developed by the Association was worked out, though only after the directors had held three meetings, the last one in New York.

W. C. Durant, president of General Motors, and J. Newton Gunn, president of the United States Tire Co., had been elected directors. At the New York meeting, the first time he took his seat on the board, Mr. Durant offered to contribute $10,000 toward a $100,000 fund for carrying on the work during 1921 and to underwrite another $10,000 in addition to this contribution. But $100,000 was more than they needed, so the amount was reduced to $50,000 and contribution of this sum was underwritten jointly by Messrs. Gowen, Durant, Seiberling, Chapin and Gunn.

After a little further discussion they extended this arrangement for two additional years. Later Mr. Fisher, who was not present at the meeting, joined in the underwriting and Mr. Gowen induced the cement Association, which had been contributing to the highway body for two years, to increase its contribution.

No further financial problems arose until late in 1923, when, completion and maintenance of the Lincoln Highway having been assured through passage of the Federal highway act, serious consideration was given to the discontinuance of the Association's major activities.

They still had $30,000 in trust funds on hand. It did not seem sound judgment to terminate their activities until that money had been properly expended or returned to the donors and so they voted to continue for one year. They did not decide whether activities should be prosecuted beyond that time and they made no provision for financing the organization's work.

They did, however, approve a reduced budget subject to the finding before January 15 of enough contributors to cover the $19,000 difference between anticipated income and estimated expenditures. By January 17 they had found $11,000 of this money; $5,000 of it in a contribution which Mr. Gunn was able to obtain from Edsel B. Ford and which was to be continued at the same rate for two additional years. With such a start they felt they would be able to obtain the rest of the needed funds and went ahead on their usual basis. However, the $8,000 was not obtained. The savings Secretary Bement had accumulated again came to the rescue and covered a deficit of $5,540.

Cutting their operations to fit the income in sight, the directors approved for 1925 the lowest budget in the Association's history, $26,000. This represented a reduction of $19,515 from the 1923 budget.

The financing then in prospect carried the organization through 1926 and at the end of 1927 the directors voted to terminate all activities except a project for permanent marking, which was separately financed, and vested control of the Association's activities and policies in the executive committee. The Association ceased active work with a comfortable balance in bank, as Gael S. Hoag, who had succeeded Bement as secretary at the beginning of 1925, had not only conserved but increased the nest-egg of savings Bement left for him.

In reviewing the financial affairs of the Lincoln Highway Association even the most casual observer must be struck by the extremely sound business policies which were followed at all times and by the care which was taken in the handling of all funds. All the moneys it handled were regarded as trust funds and a very strict policy was observed in disbursing them.

The day after the Association was organized, President Joy wrote to Mr. Pardington laying down principles which were followed in letter and spirit ever afterward. Here is his letter:

"I want to impress upon you, particularly now at the beginning of the work, that there shall be no one employed by this Association except strictly on the merits of the service and for value appropriate with the service rendered. There will be no favoritism in connection with the affairs of this Association toward any employe; the outfit must be organized from beginning to end on a basis of efficiency, economy, and straight square dealing always in every way. Every expenditure of money must be on record plain and clear and up and above-board.

"The records of our receipts and disbursements must be kept absolutely plain and clear and open to inspection of any interested party; and disbursements of any character must be made upon the voucher of the Association, properly approved, directly in favor of the party to whom the money is payable. This Association is Trustee for any funds which may come to it to be devoted to the work in question, and the application of those funds to the purposes of the Association must be beyond suspicion and will of course, be audited by disinterested auditing firms of repute from time to time."

Mere care in conservation of funds was not all the Association's handling of its finances, however. It exercised always just such sound business judgment as would be expected from the character of those at its head. For instance, it required all funds, except working balances, to yield revenue, either investing them in government securities, or depositing them at interest in approved banks.

These operations were often on a large scale, trust funds on hand alone amounting to $200,000 over a considerable period. Interest on general funds was used for general purposes; interest on each trust fund was added to its principal and these additions were never expended without the consent of the contributor. In two cases after the object for which funds were contributed had been attained, considerable refunds were made to the donors out of this interest money.

These interest payments, the obtaining of which must be credited solely to the Association's good business management, sometimes ran to large sums. On the Willys-Overland Trust Fund of $50,000, more than $10,000 of interest was accumulated.

The General Motors Trust Fund of $100,000 was so handled as to produce more than $23,000. Most of this fund was expended in improving the highway in Nevada; part was used toward the erection of permanent monuments and several thousand dollars was returned to the donors.

The Fisher Trust Fund of $25,000 was not only made to earn interest prior to expenditure of any money but a balance remaining over was placed at interest and earned a small sum annually for some years.

The United States Rubber Company and United States Tire Company contributions for construction of the Ideal Section and promotion work, aggregating $130,000, were paid out almost as soon as received and so showed no such returns.

Whenever the Association allotted trust funds to a state for highway improvement, it arranged the contract so that the amount donated obtained a maximum of results, donations from the Association being conditioned on allocation of state funds to the work contemplated, and the joint sum being used to procure the expenditure of federal aid moneys which considerably exceeded the total of the two. Thus a comparatively small sum from a trust fund was made to bring about the expenditure of several times its own amount on the road.

Even in the most minor matters the Association carried out strict business practices. During the years of its activities somewhat more than $1,250,000 passed through the Detroit headquarters without the loss of a penny. Its bad debts were negligible, all arising from unpaid bills for advertising in its publications. It never failed to pay a bill, and after its organization period its annual reports seldom showed more than a few dollars in accounts payable. Once or twice when questionable demands were made on it by individuals who fancied themselves its creditors, members of the directorate personally settled the bills rather than pay from the association treasury, funds which they did not believe were fairly due the claimants.

It is rarely that any organization of such scope, operating over so many years, can present so good a record.

CHAPTER VIII

CARRYING THE LINCOLN HIGHWAY MESSAGE TO THE PEOPLE

THE Lincoln Highway received countless thousands of columns of newspaper and magazine space in publications of all sorts, from the *Saturday Evening Post* to backwoods weeklies, hundreds of pages of display advertising, nobody knows how many expressions of approval from the editorial sanctum, the pulpit and the rostrum. It received these because it was working solely and wholeheartedly for the public interest; because it had no private axes to grind, and because none of its directors, founders or other officers, profited from its activities.

With the sole exception of the patriotic and sentimental appeal involved in its name "Lincoln," the Highway Association went before the public on a basis of cold, hard, solid, logical fact. It worked toward education; it never sought to convince anyone except by facts. Every dollar expended by the Association was for educational purposes; even the money spent for actual road construction was used to create object-lesson roads. It bought no advertising, subsidized no publications, paid no printing bills except its own.

The Association thus having absolutely clean hands, the press felt free to treat its activities on the basis their news value justified. This is the secret of its success, for without the press it could not have carried on the educational work that was its very life.

By contrast, many an organization whose doings are otherwise newsworthy fails to obtain press recognition because its activities are for the personal profit of some individual or group; many another which is entirely unselfish and public-spirited fails to gain editorial attention because what it is doing is not of general interest, is not strictly news.

The Lincoln Highway Association utilized with a high degree of intelligence the support accorded it.

Mr. Joy repeatedly gave credit to the American press for the building of the Lincoln Highway; however, the fact remains that what the publishers did was but to print the news. The Association created the news by doing things that were interesting and new, then at the proper time and in the proper way, informed the proper people of what was going on. The natural functioning of the press produced the desired result.

Secretary Bement in addressing the Association's Board of Directors described its attitude as follows:

"Publicity in our lexicon means not merely the continuous supplying of material to the press. It means constructive accomplishments which inspire national public interest. It means the undertaking of projects which command public attention and arouse public enthusiasm and support. It means keeping the name before the public and a never-ending pressure toward the great objective."

From Carl Fisher's first announcement, the power of the press to gain support for the Coast-to-Coast road plan was recognized. The first press releases issued from the Indianapolis headquarters were crude but they carried facts and so the newspapers cheerfully rewrote them.

The real genius of the newspaper educational material came after Mr. Pardington took hold of affairs in Detroit and employed Fred T. Grenell, city editor of the Detroit Free Press, to prepare news articles in news style.

The Association never insisted that its presentation of the Lincoln Highway's news material be used as offered; it simply provided the press with the facts and let them be used according to the newsmen's judgment. At the same time, everything they sent to the papers was news and was prepared in such form that it could be printed without change if desired. This was, of course, the tactful method of procedure and the absolutely correct and proper way to obtain maximum space in every paper.

One thing it did do—for a number of years it kept its news out of the hands of the automobile editors and insisted that it be passed on direct by the city editors or news editors of the different papers. By this means it maintained the status of the Lincoln Highway as a topic of general news value, equally interesting to all classes instead of only to the motoring public.

The first major release of the Lincoln Highway Association was the story of its creation out of the Coast-to-Coast highway organization originated by Mr. Fisher. The second was the trip of the Indiana manufacturers and the third was the proclamation of the route. The first was what might be termed spontaneous news, arising in the normal course of events; the second was a news-creating activity; however, with the third, art steps in. The story was spontaneous news, but by sending out the large type placard reproductions of the proclamation, they created a spot-news local story in every community where these placards were displayed, and so obtained more publicity than could have been gained by any other method.

With its fourth big news release, the celebration, the Association stepped into the plane of pure creation. There was no reason back of the immense amount of news mention which that event received except the celebration itself, which the Detroit headquarters had initiated and carried through. Thus the Association actually made this news. The same was true of the Lincoln observances in churches throughout the country.

The Association created news, too, when it produced many of the letters endorsing the road which it used in accelerating sales of membership certificates, and also made news in obtaining some of the checks it photographed for similar purpose. President Wilson's letter of endorsement, for instance, was obtained through the intercession of his cousin, John A. Wilson, vice-president of the American Automobile Association. His $5 check for a certificate of membership was obtained through Congressman Doremus. These were roundabout steps, but the news so created were well worth the effort.

However, it is not to be supposed that every item the Lincoln Highway obtained in the press was so created; on the contrary, practically everything it did or said had news value because the plan was new, bold and dramatic and the people were interested in it. Mr. Pardington and Mr. Grenell recognized this fact and made use of the routine of the Association's operation as a source of news items.

These formed what an advertising man would call the sustaining or institutional campaign; whenever it wanted something special, the Association directed special publicity toward that particular object. For instance, as a feature of the campaign to sell membership certificates, they reproduced in halftone President Wilson's No. 1 certificate and offered the reproduction as an illustration to every newspaper which would print it. They did the same with checks sent in by Governors of states for purchases of certificates, with Thomas A. Edison's check and with those of other notables and with letters from outstanding persons endorsing the movement.

They were very careful to make their appeals as timely as possible; if there was some event already in the public eye, they connected the name Lincoln Highway with it wherever and whenever possible. The Association's publicity files for 1913, 1914, and 1915, when the Panama Canal was a general topic of conversation, are full of references to that enterprise. They interviewed newsworthy personages about the comparative costs of the Lincoln Highway and the Canal and about the relative values of the two projects to the country; they issued stories about the relative lengths of time each had been talked of and about the relative periods which would be required for completion of each.

When the World War began, they issued stories about what the Lincoln Highway would mean to national defense. They appealed to Major General Hugh L. Scott, chief of staff; to Major General Leonard Wood, and to other military notables, for statements on the value of France's good highways to her mobilization, they contrasted the French speed with the slowness of Russian maneuvering; they suggested the worth of the Lincoln Highway as a means for transporting war materials and for assisting in concentrating troops. And whatever comment they received was promptly made into a news story and sent out.

When business conditions threw men out of work, they suggested employing them on road construction, particularly construction of the Lincoln Highway. When universal military service was being discussed in the United States, they issued articles about that, with the Lincoln Highway adroitly mentioned. One such, appearing under President Joy's signature, drew this cordial comment from Theodore Roosevelt:

"Dear Joy: That's a crackerjack article of yours about universal service. I am very glad you wrote it and hope it will be circulated everywhere."

Still later, when American unity was a subject to be stressed, they prepared news items and magazine articles on the function of highways, and particularly the Lincoln Highway, in creating national solidarity.

That, too, won Colonel Roosevelt's approval:

"Dear Joy: Your monograph on National Highway is admirable. I am particularly interested in it, and pleased with it. I particularly liked your phrase 'Tightening The Union.' You use exactly the words to express the idea."

On the other hand, not everything was favorable all the time. There were critics who did not hesitate to express themselves freely. Yet the Association adroitly turned even the criticisms to its own benefit.

The editor of a small Nevada newspaper asked one day in 1914:

"What have you done with the money?"

To him Secretary Pardington replied:

"The Lincoln Highway Association is seeking to interest the people of the east in the states of the west, in the hope that touring will increase, a general knowledge of the conditions in the west be disseminated and the population of your state be increased.

"It will probably interest you to know that at this writing a total of $265 from the citizens of your state has been contributed to the Lincoln Highway and yet Nevada is the state, because of its topography, its isolation, etc., most to benefit because of the educational work which we are carrying on.

"We sincerely trust that you will get out and get under and help us make attractive the route across your state."

This letter won such hearty support that the editor was later appointed a Lincoln Highway consul!

There never was a time when they wasted effort trying to persuade any newspaper to print their material. Everything they offered rested squarely on its own merit as news.

On the other hand, they rarely, even in the organization days before a press representative was employed, missed an opportunity to extract the full value from every circumstance that developed. While Theodore Roosevelt was running for the Presidency on the Progressive ticket, Mr. Fisher was elected to office as a county commissioner on the Republican ticket. Roosevelt telegraphed him congratulations. Mr. Fisher responded, thanking the Bull Moose and urging his support for the transcontinental highway!

And they kept everlastingly at it!

"Whatever results the Lincoln Highway Association

has secured," says one of its very early annual reports, "and whatever effect its efforts are having on public opinion on the subject of roads, must be attributed to its policy of constant, consistent, educational appeal to the reason, the sentiment, the patriotism of the American public.

"This work, while incidental to the main ends of the Association, is in reality the means by which the continued efforts of the organization are kept before the public and continued support secured."

Publicity work of this caliber was extremely rare in those days; it would rank with the best even today. Once an effort was made to cut down postage expense by utilizing the contributed services of several advertising agencies to distribute material. But the press saw in this a hint of pressure and failed to respond so readily as it did to the forthright offering of the material direct from Association headquarters. The plan was quickly abandoned.

If the organizers of the Lincoln Highway Association were alert to the value of newspaper publicity they were equally alert to the worth of magazine publicity. Mr. Fisher early interested Elbert Hubbard in writing about his proposed road. When the Sage of East Aurora printed an article about it in The Fra, Mr. Fisher bought thousands of copies and mailed them to potential subscribers.

One of Mr. Pardington's earliest efforts to gain editorial notice of any kind was directed toward the *Saturday Evening Post*. The Association approached George Horace Lorimer, the editor of the *Post*, through several channels before they at last obtained his assent

NEVADA COMMEMORATES FINANCIAL AID GIVEN BY THE LINCOLN
HIGHWAY ASSOCIATION

to the publication of a story on the Lincoln Highway, but when he did agree, he gave hearty cooperation. Senator Beveridge, a director of the organization, was the man selected by Mr. Lorimer to write the article. He produced a work which did much to increase public interest in the highway.

The Association obtained permission from Mr. Lorimer to reproduce this article, which it circulated widely. In fact, for many years reprints of it were sent to all persons seeking information as to the history and purposes of the organization.

However, between first suggestion of the article to Mr. Lorimer and its publication, two years passed, and when the *Post* did publish the Beveridge discussion of the project, the Lincoln Highway was already an old story to magazine readers. Shortly after the Proclamation was issued Harold W. Slausson, editor of *Leslie's*, asked for an article. Secretary Pardington wrote it and it was published December 11, 1913. Ewing Galloway, conducting a good roads department for *Colliers*, also asked for material which Mr. Pardington provided, writing later to Mr. Fisher:

"Buy last week's *Colliers* and read the article appearing over your name which I wrote at their suggestion. I hope it meets with your approval."

Mr. Pardington could do such things with Mr. Fisher because of their long friendship and his accurate knowledge of Mr. Fisher's viewpoint.

"The *Independent*, the *Outlook*, *Scribner's*—in fact, all the big magazines—are asking us for signed articles," he wrote a few days later. "This to my mind is a very good sign as it evidences the fact that the Lincoln Highway movement is sinking in."

The trade press and the magazines devoted to motoring were glad to print Lincoln Highway articles as often as the Association could prepare them. Many technical periodicals asked for material, even such strictly one-class publications as Case and Comment, the law magazine, and Bit and Spur, devoted to equestrian sports. The latter sent a representative from New York to Detroit to obtain an article on the highway.

Mr. Pardington, in August, 1914, commented in a letter to President Joy, "The financial publications of the country are practically the only class which up to this time has not treated the Lincoln Highway as it should be treated."

The statement was true at the time, but not for long, for the financial periodicals soon joined the procession. This avid appetite for Lincoln Highway material remained with the periodical press for a long time. Even the Canadian and European magazines developed it. Such a demand naturally called for prolific writing at the Detroit offices. Many years later Austin F. Bement, successively publicity man, secretary and vice-president of the Lincoln Highway Association, was to estimate his output over ten years at 300,000 words a year, a thousand words every working day, all on the subject of the Lincoln Highway!

Even the National Association for the Advancement of Science invited papers from the Association and one of them, on the economic and strategic value of the highway, written by Mr. Bement, was published by the Scientific Monthly.

Encyclopaedias also asked for articles on the highway

and the Association.

That the magazines really valued these contributions is proved by the size of the checks they sent in payment, just as though the Association were a regular contributor in the usual sense. As much as several hundred dollars was often paid into the treasury for an article which Mr. Bement produced as a part of his regular activities, perhaps in a single day, though as a writer he was more painstaking than rapid.

Messrs. Grenell and Bement, working under Secretary Pardington's direction, and later Mr. Bement working alone, produced scores of articles which appeared under the signatures of various directors. Mr. Joy, who understood better than most how to get maximum results from a subordinate, frequently suggested an article and left its details to be worked out by Mr. Bement; generally, however, revising with a vigorous pencil before it was sent out for publication.

So well did these two cooperate in such authorship that it is virtually impossible to differentiate between articles produced by Mr. Joy unaided and articles produced by Mr. Bement along lines suggested by Mr. Joy.

The men directing this work were no dry-as-dust distributors of commonplace material; when they turned out a magazine article it had life and verve and color and drama in it. They used every opportunity to make their material interesting. For instance, Frank H. Trego, the Association's official engineer, was a student of the history of western roads and trails; they asked him to write on this subject, on the Pony Express and on the Overland Stage line and also to supply material which they used freely in articles.

Colonel Waldon was an enthusiast on outdoor life; several times they obtained telling articles from him on the charms of travelling the long road west to the top of the Rockies and down to the Pacific. President Joy himself wrote vigorously and Mr. Bement had the gifts of observation and colorful description; Mr. Joy was more likely to be stirred into personal authorship by some controversial subject; Mr. Bement did more descriptive writing, though he was equally apt at arguing a case. They made one trip over the highway together which produced a quantity of highly acceptable magazine material. The quality of their output may be judged by the following letter to Mr. Joy from Charles A. Munn, of the *Scientific American:*

"From an advance copy of the automobile issue of the Scientific American, I had the pleasure of reading your interesting account of your trip across the continent on the Lincoln Highway. I found the article was very interesting, and I was surprised to find how much juice could be squeezed out of what I feared might be a somewhat dry subject."

Besides writing magazine material of their own, however, Mr. Pardington and the other Lincoln Highway men realized very early that the interest of independent writers was extremely desirable and set about to cultivate it. They did everything possible to direct these authors and if possible, their writings, toward the highway. Dr. Frank Crane was one of the first of those to be so converted to the Lincoln Highway faith, and wrote many a sermonette on the subject for the chain of magazines and newspapers to which he contributed.

Like Senator Beveridge's, his pen was ever at the service of the Association: one of the finest pieces of work he ever did is the foreword to a booklet the Association published in the interest of its Memorial Miles plan, entitled "Two Memorials." He wrote:

"One thing that distinguishes man from other animals is that man is a tomb builder. The most ancient relics of the race are from tombs.

"Some of the most amazing structures are memorials to the dead; such as the Pyramids, the Taj Mahal, the Tomb of Napoleon, and the Washington Monument.

"What is a monument? It is some sort of work of a permanent character designed to perpetuate the name and fame of a person.

"Most monuments have been constructed with an eye to display, and to attract the attention of the curious. But the real monument should be for the use of the living.

"Then the memory of the dead would be interwoven into the continuous interest of those who live."

One of the Crane sermonettes so pleased a Lincoln Highway contributor that he reproduced 65,000 copies of it in artistic form and sent them broadcast at his own expense as an aid to the Association's efforts.

Some of the ideas used for publicity came in from outside editorial sources The Association subscribed liberally to clipping bureaus and the bundles of clippings always received attention. One thought which was picked up and amplified in publicity was that of a western agricultural editor who described the Lincoln Highway, named in memory of the Great Emancipator, as the emancipator which would free the farmer from the thralldom of bad roads.

Akin to this magazine educational material were the pamphlets and booklets which the Association used freely, its annual reports, and its touring guides.

Two small booklets, hardly more than leaflets, were issued before the formal organization; a third was issued ·soon afterward and several were published in connection with various phases of the Lincoln Highway work. Sometimes, when it seemed such sales literature was needed, funds in hand would not warrant its publication and, to provide needed literature large automobile manufacturing concerns issued complete editions of their house organs as Lincoln Highway booklets.

Similarly, the Goodyear Tire & Rubber Co. printed and supplied to the Association 65,000 copies of a booklet called "Hints to Tourists," mainly devoted to a list of equipment for the transcontinental trip, a great adventure in those days. Demand for these far exceeded the supply and when the organization began to publish touring guides, the "Hints" were incorporated in those volumes.

Besides what it gained from the printed word, the Lincoln Highway Association had the benefit of a long campaign of carefully organized word of mouth advertising.

This advertising proceeded very largely from the volunteer workers of the Association. These men, state consuls, county consuls, local consuls, were selected because of their enthusiasm for road improvement, and this enthusiasm not only led them to talk about it informally but, in scores and scores of cases, to devote practically all their time outside of business hours to its work.

It was nothing unusual for a Lincoln Highway consul to travel many miles at his own expense to address a good roads meeting, or to make four or five such addresses in a week. In fact, much of the support obtained from the farmers and small town residents can be attributed directly to the efforts of these men.

Nor were these volunteer speakers the only active ones in the field; even before the Lincoln Highway Organization had been fully perfected, invitations were pouring in to Detroit for Mr. Joy, Mr. Fisher, Mr. Pardington or some other representative of the highway project to appear and address congressional committees, conferences, the American Highway Congress, the American Automobile Association, and any number of sectional or state or city groups all over the country.

Try as they would, and valuable as they knew the results of such public appearances to be, the officials of the Lincoln Highway never could attend all the meetings to which they were invited, though one of Secretary Pardington's reports tells of his appearance at thirty-eight, from York, Pennsylvania, to Omaha, between January 30 and May 14.

The value of such activities was that they brought home the Association's message in a more effective way than the printed word could do and that they very often reached a class of persons difficult of access through the press. This value was recognized in eventual appointment of Mr. Ostermann as field secretary, with appearance at such meetings a large part of his duties.

In the beginning, those addressing these meetings had no easy time of it. The sentiment for highway building was not strong; there were great numbers of farmers and others who regarded improved roads as of value only to automobile owners; thousands of taxpayers saw in them only another means of increasing their tax burdens; the Lincoln Highway workers were often heckled unmercifully.

Speedily, however, sentiment became more favorable, and when states and counties began to advocate bond issues for road construction, appeals for a Lincoln Highway man to visit the community involved and explain the good roads idea, were many. It was one of the Association's boasts that no bond issue for improvement of the Lincoln Highway ever failed to receive the voters' approval when the organization had been able to send a representative to discuss the matter with the citizens.

In these meetings, the appeal was adroitly adapted to the interests of its auditors. Bankers were told what the highway would mean to banking; small town merchants were shown how it would improve their business; manufacturers were shown the effect of good roads on distribution, deliveries and sales.

One of the great supports of the Lincoln Highway was its friends, and it was in meetings such as have been described that these friendships often did greatest service.

In 1916, while Woodrow Wilson was President of the United States, he spoke at exercises held to stimulate interest in the highway at Princeton, New Jersey, and planted a tree at the roadside to aid in its beautification.

Governor Frank B. Willis of Ohio, addressing a Lincoln Highway celebration in his home town of Ada, gave signal aid when he told Ohio farmers they were wasting $4,700,000 a year by failure to build improved roads. This speech did a great deal toward putting the highway improvement idea into practice in Ohio. The Association picked it up and distributed it in full to newspapers all over the country.

How many other notables made addresses of this or other character in support of the Lincoln Highway movement will probably never be known. All, of course, were the direct result of the organization's efforts to create favorable public opinion, though very few were directly solicited by the Detroit headquarters.

The four forms of publicity here discussed were far from being all those in which the Association engaged. Messrs. Pardington and Bement both regarded Lincoln Highway educational work as a sort of snowball which automatically increased its volume as it went along; their task was to keep it in motion and they developed a whole category of additional means to this end.

CHAPTER IX

THE Lincoln Highway Association was always active in encouraging motor touring, not because it had any interest in promotion of travel, but because it recognized that increased motor traffic brought about increased demand for improved highways. Its methods were two —the provision of maps and similar material to make things easier for the long distance motor traveller and the sponsorship of newsworthy events to arouse touring interest and show the practicability of automobile touring over the Lincoln Highway.

Some of the events it sponsored had effects of nation-wide importance. The trip of the First Army Transcontinental Motor Convoy in 1919, which was arranged by the government at the instance and with the assistance of the Lincoln Highway Association, had a large part, perhaps the determining part, in obtaining passage of the Federal Highway Act.

This trip followed the Lincoln Highway from Gettysburg, Pennsylvania, to the Pacific Coast. It obtained a tremendous amount of publicity for the highway and for the cause of highway improvement. It stimulated a vast amount of motor travel, and it demonstrated forcibly the economic value of highways in general. It also served to develop important military information and valuable data on road construction requirements. The Association itself regarded this trip as "establishing for

A VISTA OF DISTANCES—A SECTION OF THE LINCOLN HIGHWAY BETWEEN ELY, NEVADA, AND WENDOVER, UTAH. THIS ONE HUNDRED TWENTY-FIVE MILE STRETCH IS FREQUENTLY REFERRED TO AS ONE OF THE MOST DELIGHTFUL DRIVES IN THE NATION

all time the correctness of the carefully chosen route of the Lincoln Highway, both from the standpoint of strategic utility and of efficiency and directness."

The Association's knowledge of the military aspects of highways naturally led it into cooperation with the army during the war. Mr. Ostermann spent most of the winter of 1917 piloting convoys of government trucks along the eastern section of the highway and the other officials of the Association, especially Mr. Chapin, were very active in developing highway transportation to relieve the railroad congestion. Mr. Joy and Colonel Waldon were already in military service.

During his work, Mr. Ostermann conceived the idea of sending a military truck train over the entire Lincoln Highway. He and Secretary Bement took this up with the military officials but conditions prevented it from being done until the summer of 1919.

In the literal sense of the word, this trip was pioneering, for the longest trip previously undertaken by a military motor train was only 900 miles and this was to be nearly four times that distance. It was the first transcontinental military expedition. Moreover, it was to involve the traversing of a great variety of roads, through practically all the conditions, except snow, which a truck could encounter, and the army men prepared for it with great care.

The army's main purposes in making the trip were:

To make an extended performance test of motorized equipment.

To contribute something to the good roads movement, for the development of through highways as a military asset.

To demonstrate the practicability of long-distance motor transport, and the necessity for federal aid for highways to make this possible.

· To collect detailed data for the use of several branches of the military service.

To exhibit to the public the development of motorized military equipment.

Two full motor transport companies, plus observers, engineers, signal corps men, medical detachment, and much additional equipment were assembled into one motor train so that, all told, 79 vehicles, 260 enlisted men and 35 officers made the trip. The convoy included 65 trucks and special-purpose vehicles of all the standard types in use by the army. Their average weight, with load, was 8 tons. Some weighed as much as 14 tons. There were 4 mobile kitchens, tank trucks for oil, water and gasoline, two spare parts trucks, two machine and blacksmith shop trucks, one searchlight truck, two artillery tractors, one pontoon trailer, an office work truck, four ambulances, four staff cars, two reconnaissance cars, four motorcycles, and Mr. Ostermann's big white official Lincoln Highway Packard.

Through arrangement by President Seiberling, the Goodyear Tire & Rubber Company's 15 piece band accompanied the convoy in one of the company's motor trucks.

Under the command of Lieutenant Colonel Charles W. McClure, an overseas motor transport officer, the convoy started from the Zero Milestone in Washington on July 7, 1919, having been officially dispatched by Newton D. Baker, Secretary of War, and arrived in San Francisco 62 days later. Field conditions were observed throughout the journey.

Because of the unusual weights of the heavier vehicles, the engineers were kept busy rebuilding or reinforcing bridges. Between Cheyenne and Evanston, Wyoming, alone, there were 47 structures which required their attention and on the entire trip nearly 100 were either strengthened or rebuilt.

The trucks almost tore to pieces some of the light road constructed in the west, which had been intended to provide for tourist travel only, and thereby demonstrated that highways must be constructed with more solid roadbeds and heavier, stronger surfacing.

This same destruction of roads also showed plainly the need for federal aid in constructing adequate highways across the sparsely settled western states.

Military information of great importance was developed. The army purposely drove the trucks hard, maintaining a schedule of 18 miles an hour. The trip showed exactly what could be expected from the various types of trucks under severe day after day operation, and many changes and improvements were recommended as a result.

The progress of the train was one of hard work on the road and entertainment at the stops. The hospitality steadily became warmer as the convoy proceeded. Partly this outpouring was due to the traditional cordiality of the west; partly it arose from the fact that the westerners saw in the trip an important means of increasing the aid they hoped to receive from the federal government, and which they so sorely needed.

Crowds turned out everywhere. At Salt Lake City the governors of 17 western states greeted the convoy officially; and in many other of the states traversed the governors met and welcomed the personnel of the train.

Two destroyers escorted the ferryboats on which the convoy crossed the bay to San Francisco, where, led by an escort of cavalry from the Presidio, it passed up gaily decorated streets and between cheering lines of people to Lincoln Park. There formal exercises celebrating completion of the expedition were held at the End of the Trail Marker at the western terminus of the Lincoln Highway.

In the course of these exercises medals, struck off by the Association in honor of the convoy's exploit, were presented to the officers and men who had participated, the presentation being made by Colonel Robert N. Nobel, under special authority of the War Department.

That this convoy could pass over the highway was a tremendous demonstration of progress. In 1913, the Lincoln Highway had been but a red line on a map, with less than one-third of its total length improved. Yet, in 1919, the government was able to send over it a motor train more than twice the weight recommended by officials of the Association, on a schedule half again as fast as the highway body felt it wise to attempt.

The army record of studies developed from this expedition is a book of many hundreds of pages. The publicity obtained for the highway, and for the cause of highways improvement generally, would have filled one of many thousand even larger pages. Much additional good was done through the good roads meetings held at every noon and night stop along the route. The farmers of the country for many miles north and south of the highway took advantage of these opportunities to inspect the motorized military equipment. In many towns whose total population was less than 2,500 crowds of 5,000 assembled for these meetings.

Association records indicate that the passage of the convoy, and the good roads messages delivered at these meetings, were responsible for favorable action on many county bond issues for highway building, especially in Iowa, which was then just beginning highway work.

On the ground that high-speed trips demonstrated the condition of the road and stimulated touring, the Lincoln Highway Association cooperated with many drivers endeavoring to make transcontinental records.

The history of such drives dates back very far. As early as 1908 a large part of the Lincoln Highway was used by racers in a New York to Paris contest. It was run for a joint prize offered by the New York *Times* and Paris *Matin,* in which six started and three finished and attracted much attention. The starters included an American, a German and an Italian, and three French drivers. Gael S. Hoag, later secretary of the Association, attributed to this race the awakening of his interest in highways.

In 1916 Bobby Hammond set the motoring world agog with a trip from San Francisco to New York, in an Empire roadster, in 6 days, 10 hours, 59 minutes. The Association boasted: "It's a real road which will permit a traveller to average 21 miles an hour each hour of the 24, day and night, day in and day out, for practically a week running."

But there were to be more records and far faster times made that year. A Marmon automobile was driven from San Francisco to New York in 5 days, 15 hours. A Hudson Super-Six was sent across in 5 days 3 hours 31 minutes.

That record stood for four years and then was broken by the Hudson Motor Car Company with an Essex, which crossed from San Francisco to New York in 4 days 14 hours 4 minutes. With the exception of one airplane record, this was the fastest time made across the continent up to that date by any single moving vehicle.

After the post-war spurt in highway improvement much faster runs were made and the man who has attained greatest prominence as a long-distance driver came to the fore. He was Louis B. Miller, a San Francisco business man who had never been connected with the automobile industry.

Mr. Miller made his first drive across the continent in 1925 when he was 51 years old, using a Wills-Sainte Claire. He left New York City at 1 a.m. July 14 and arrived in San Francisco at 4:45 a.m. July 18. His time was 102 hours 45 minutes.

The next year, Ab Jenkins and Ray Peck of Salt Lake City, professional drivers, jointly drove a Studebaker from New York to San Francisco between 2:07 a.m. June 14 and 12:27 p.m. June 17—86 hours 20 minutes.

A few weeks later, using the same car in which he had made his former mark, Miller set a new one of 83 hours 12 minutes for the run from San Francisco to New York. This included 45 minutes lost when a traffic officer held him up within 20 miles of his goal.

Road conditions having been further improved, Miller went after a round-trip transcontinental record in 1927. In a Chrysler Imperial "80" he drove from San

Francisco to New York in 79 hours 55 minutes, paused in the metropolis exactly one minute and finished the round trip in 167 hours 59 minutes, just one minute less than a week.

Miller did not try the trip again until 1931. Leaving San Francisco at 5 a.m. on August 4, he was checked in at New York at 1:33 a.m. August 7, started back to the west at 2:45 a.m. and arrived in San Francisco at 5:09 p.m. August 9. This drive was made in a Plymouth. The elapsed time was 5 days 12 hours 9 minutes. This was almost exactly twenty times as fast as sturdy Tom Fetch had been able to make the trip in 1903!

In contrast to these high speed runs were numerous tours made by parties of motorists at more leisurely rates.

One of the most important was a transcontinental trip made by representatives of the Republican National Committee campaigning for the reelection of President Coolidge. Another event of this class was a demonstration of motor freighting made by a convoy of Goodyear Tire & Rubber Co. trucks transporting airplane tires from Boston to San Francisco on a pre-arranged schedule.

To hammer home to the individual tourist the message it was broadcasting through its other educational efforts, the Association provided the motoring public liberally with maps, logs, guidebooks, and road information of all wanted sorts.

One of its first activities was the sponsoring of a small folder, on "Lincoln Highway Route, Road Conditions and Directions." This contained directions which seem ludicrous today but at the time were valuable and necessary, such as "pass in front of saloon buildings and turn left around shearing pens."

This was issued in October, 1914. The first official guide was issued March 30, 1915. Beside the actual log of the road, occupying more than 100 pages, it gave directions for meeting numerous emergencies likely to be encountered by the tourist of that day.

The next guide followed this volume by a year and was dedicated to Mr. Pardington in a touching tribute written by President Joy.

"It is not too much to say," he wrote, "that the Lincoln Highway insignia stretching from Jersey City on the Hudson to Oakland on the Pacific, is more his work than that of any other man. Thousands have given dollars to the cause; Pardington gave himself."

The third edition of the guide was issued in the spring of 1918 and was dedicated to Lieut.-Col. Henry B. Joy, who had resigned the presidency to enter military service.

The fourth followed it by three years. This volume was dedicated to Mr. Ostermann, who had been killed in an automobile accident near Tama, Iowa, June 8, 1920.

The fifth edition was published in 1924 and was by far the most elaborate the Association issued. Its 536 pages offered a wealth of historical and informative material, maps of routes to western scenic spots and other items of value to those interested in the general subject of highway improvement as well as to the tourist. It was dedicated to Carl G. Fisher as "The Father of the Lincoln Highway."

All these guidebooks contained advertising; without

this support they could not have been published.

They served as the earliest, and for a time, the only handbooks on highway improvement. National educational authorities recommended them for classroom use. Educational publications gave free space to advertising them to teachers, at special rates arranged by the Association. Many thousands were purchased for use as textbooks.

The Association also compiled and published a variety of maps for its guidebooks and for general use.

As another aid to the tourist, it prepared detailed telegraphic reports of road conditions which were supplied free to press and public. These were the only reports ever to cover completely any transcontinental route.

As a basis of these reports, selected Lincoln Highway Consuls, state, county and local, sent in telegrams on a given night each week, giving up-to-the-minute information on the condition of the highway in his jurisdiction. State consuls' reports were more or less general; those of the county and local consuls were detailed and explicit. Weather information was included whenever pertinent to the condition of the roads and their availability for motor travel. This information was supplemented by telegrams from selected automobile clubs, a few chamber of commerce officials and certain other very carefully chosen sources.

Every one of these sources was interviewed personally by Field Secretary Hoag and instructed carefully as to what was wanted.

The information was consolidated in the Detroit headquarters of the Association on the morning following its dispatch, and immediately released to the local press for telegraphic transmission, local publication or reference in the individual newspapers' information departments. Copies were also mailed to numerous automobile clubs, both on and off the highway, to newspapers all over the country, to all Lincoln Highway consuls and to other individuals and organizations who held it available for the use of the traveller over the highway. The entire cost was borne by the Association and no charge was made for the reports.

The system, actually less complex than it appears, worked very smoothly, chiefly because every member of the dispatching organization was chosen with such care and instructed so thoroughly. These road reports were issued through the touring season for some years, until the general improvement of the highway rendered the traveller virtually independent of weather conditions except heavy snow in the mountain passes.

The news importance of the Lincoln Highway and the value attached to everything concerning it is evidenced by the fact that newspapers hundreds of miles distant from its route frequently published these reports in full. The reports thus were an extremely valuable means of keeping the Association's name and objective before the public.

The cumulative effect of this and other educational effort put forth by the Association can easily be seen from the figures on tourist travel for the several years covered by its activities.

Mr. Bement estimated that the 1913 tourist travel across the continent on the route, or approximately the route, of the Lincoln Highway was about 150 persons.

In 1916 D. E. Watkins, secretary of the California State Automobile Association, estimated that year's motor traffic into his state at 25,000 parties. Most of these cars, Mr. Watkins said, had reached California over the Lincoln Highway.

Mr. Bement estimated the 1924 traffic at 20,000 to 25,-000 cars; the Automobile Club of Southern California, basing the statement on actual records, said that 26,431 automobiles from other states arrived in California that year. California and Colorado each estimated their tourist traffic for that year was worth more than $40,-000,000 to their local business men.

Ten years later the number of cars from other states reaching California was in the hundreds of thousands. For 1933, official state records show 577,852 cars from other states entered California of which 80,027 came over the Lincoln Highway.

Activities in encouragement of touring, however, formed but one phase of the Association's educational effort for highway improvement.

It procured the renaming of several state roads and many city streets, traversed by its route, as "Lincoln Highway" or "Lincoln Way." It produced radiator emblems bearing its insignia and gave them to all who subscribed. It induced motor car manufacturers, contributors to the Association, to place the Lincoln Highway insignia on their products. It sold miniature Lincoln Highway insignia made up into lapel buttons, thousands of which were bought and given away by the larger automobile companies. It produced Lincoln Highway pennants for decoration of tourists' and members' motor cars after a fad of that day. It produced stickers bearing

its insignia which were pasted on store windows, correspondence and windshields; hotels used thousands of
these on their stationery. It sold portraits of Lincoln
and framed copies of the Lincoln Highway proclamation. It induced contributors to insert in all their advertising the phrase "Contributor to the Lincoln Highway."

One of its cleverest moves was to solicit penny contributions from school-children, in return for which it
gave certificates of membership to schools.

The revenue from this was small but the plan produced the best human interest story of the organization's
twenty years of campaigning. This was the contribution
of eleven cents in copper coin by the native children at
a remote school in Alaska. A very simple and sincere
letter accompanied this contribution. Pictures of the
coins and facsimile reproductions of the letter were
printed all over the land.

While the Association's object in this educational
work was improvement of the Lincoln Highway in particular and other highways in general, a corollary effect
was the establishment of the organization as an authority
on highways and a center of highway information. Promoters of other highway organizations wrote for copies
of its by-laws, articles of incorporation and similar material; probably only the federal Office of Public Roads
was more frequently called on by engineers and roads
officials of this and other countries.

The Federal Bureau of Education mentioned the
highway prominently in a bulletin entitled "Main
Streets of the Nation" which it prepared in 1924 for the
use of school teachers. The highway was made a subject

of study in many schools from the standpoints of arithmetic, geography, history, economics and transportation. Thousands of students wrote to the Association for information. Houghton Mifflin & Co., Boston publishers, asked for Lincoln Highway material to use in preparing textbooks.

The Association was compelled to maintain large files of printed matter, sometimes exceeding seventy items, for use in answering inquiries, and to do much original work in developing material for special cases.

"It will surprise you to know," Mr. Pardington wrote in 1915 to the directors, "that we have been asked to furnish the verbatim text for state highway laws in Texas, Oklahoma and Iowa, and we have been asked for advice in Nebraska. This Association today is the big factor in the good roads movement of the country."

The Association also cooperated with the State of Wyoming in drafting its highway law and with Pennsylvania in drafting the measure abolishing toll roads in that state. The State of New Jersey obtained information from it on roadside beautification.

At first, when funds were limited, the Association used few pictures. An expense of $100 to provide pictures estimated as likely to produce 40 pages of publicity was once a serious consideration.

Later, it used pictures by thousands, in its annual reports, in its guides, in the newspaper press sheets and as illustrations for magazine articles.

To provide the photographs needed for this work it levied on all available sources, but the best one was the cameras of the Association officials whose work took them out along the route. Even after eliminating duplicates and undesired subjects, there remained in the files, when the organization ceased active functioning, more than 3,000 negatives, mostly from this one source.

These protographs practically comprise a history of the Lincoln Highway. They show every condition ever encountered on the road, from President Joy's automobile sunk hub-deep in the mud of an Iowa town's main street, to the fine concrete highways which Iowa eventually built; from flooded roads and ungraded alkali desert of 1913, to elevated, drained and concrete-paved thoroughfares of 1933 able to accommodate 40,000 vehicles a day.

While the Association derived revenue from many items of its promotional material, its greatest profit was obtained from a motion picture of the entire highway which it produced in 1915.

This picture was Mr. Pardington's idea. To finance such an undertaking, however, was beyond the Association's means and so it was decided that the communities along the road should be asked to share the expense in return for the picture's advertising value to them. Messrs. Joy, Fisher and Pardington underwrote the expense.

The Stutz Company contributed a car for the use of Mr. and Mrs. Ostermann, the official cinematographer, Leon Loeb, and Edward A. Holden, Ostermann's secretary.

The Studebaker Company furnished a car which was used by J. Meinzinger, research engineer and R. C. Sackett, a publicity man.

The Packard Company also sent a car for the use of governors, mayors and other dignitaries. This was in charge of T. A. Stalker, a technical expert. Other mem-

FRANK A. SEIBERLING, PRESIDENT OF THE ASSOCIATION DURING TWO-
THIRDS OF THE PERIOD OF ITS EXISTENCE

bers of the party were Mr. and Mrs. O. P. Canaday and C. M. Reiling, statistician. The Stutz was painted in Lincoln Highway colors; the other cars bore enamelled metal emblems of the Association.

The start was made from New York, May 15, 1915.

Everywhere elaborate preparations were made to show each city at its best. Acting Governor Edge of New Jersey greeted the party at Trenton and Governor Willis of Ohio was chief speaker at two meetings held in its honor. The travellers were guests of honor at a meeting in Fort Wayne, Indiana, where Thomas R. Marshall, Vice-President of the United States, was the principal speaker and lauded the Lincoln Highway.

Automobile parades, scenes of road improvement, dedications of bridges and of newly constructed sections of highway, processions of school-children, every sort of function, celebration and activity connected and unconnected with highway building was arranged for them to photograph. So much local patriotism was evinced that Mr. Pardington was constrained to write letters to the various communities asking them to forego the fire apparatus, police departments and brass bands and to show instead "scenes having a real interest, scenes tending to make it safe, easy, and pleasant to come your way and call on you."

Between cities, the party busied itself taking photographs of scenery, historic sites, road construction, maintenance, improvement, and anything else tending to interest the traveller and stimulate touring.

The film was completed in time for exhibition at the Panama-Pacific Exposition that year. After the Exposition closed, the picture was started eastward on a long series of one-night stands, with exhibitions in every community which had participated in its financing. It met with high enthusiasm everywhere.

One of the sponsors in a remote Nevada town wrote: "We had intended giving three shows, commencing at 8:30 in the morning, but the house was packed at 8 o'clock and we started in. At 11 we started the second show and at 3 o'clock the third, and a fourth in the evening. It was a tremendous success."

"We made a great mistake in not getting a larger hall to show the picture," wrote another. "There were hundreds of people who wished to see it that could not get inside. If we could have shown it before we voted on the county road bonds, I am sure the election would have carried overwhelmingly in favor of the bonds."

Later the film was placed on general exhibition. The Federal Bureau of Education borrowed it for display to the National Conference on Rural Problems. An educational film service took over a copy on a royalty basis and paid several hundred dollars for its use. Including the cost of the camera and all other expenses connected with the enterprise, a clear profit of $1,361.82 was derived.

Verily, as propagandists these men left nothing to be desired!

CHAPTER X

"SEEDLING MILES" CONVERT THE SKEPTICS

WHEN the Lincoln Highway Association held its first meeting on July 1, 1913, its only asset was an idea. Yet such was the force of this idea, and such the driving power and genius of the men who advanced it, that within a bare fourteen months one of the most remarkable feats of road-building history had been accomplished.

This short period witnessed the transition from mud road days to the era of the modern concrete highway. Within this short time the Association had successfully launched the idea of concrete highway construction, had convinced the public of the soundness of its plans, obtained the support of industrial leaders and was actually giving away thousands of dollars' worth of cement for construction of Seedling Miles.

It had virtually brought about a revolution in transportation.

Consider for a moment the conditions the Association had overcome. When it was formed the general public was apathetic, even antagonistic, toward road construction. Of those who did favor highway building, a great many had not lifted their ideals higher than a good gravel road. Rounded dirt and the split-log drag applied after each rainstorm were in several states regarded as providing an entirely satisfactory highway. Many influential men opposed the expenditures necessary to con-

struct hard-surfaced roads. Of the few who approved
these outlays, many favored materials other than concrete. Worst of all, there was official inertia to be overcome.

And yet, in this short space of fourteen months, the
Lincoln Highway Association had converted communities from Pennsylvania to Wyoming to the belief that
improved roads were a necessity and that concrete was
the best and most economical material for construction.
It even raised enthusiasm to such a pitch that private
citizens contributed thousands of dollars for building
concrete roads. Indeed, it is doubtful whether, without
some such financial inducement, certain conservative
officials would have dared appropriate public funds for
building highways with a material which many of them
considered an experiment.

By any standards, it was a remarkable accomplishment. It was rendered more remarkable by the fact that
the Association also convinced individual cement companies that it would be to their interest to donate their
product for use in demonstration miles. It was with such
cement that construction work was begun early in October, 1914, on the first "Seedling Mile," near Malta,
Illinois.

The fact that the negotiations with the Portland Cement Association had dragged to such a length was not
due to any unwillingness on the part of that body to contribute to construction of the highway. A. Y. Gowen's
contact with Mr. Fisher in 1912 and his position as a
director of the Lincoln Highway Association resulted
from the efforts of the cement group to assist in this work.
The cement association was purely a trade group and

did no manufacturing; there were many different mills in the country and conditions which were agreeable to one were unsuited to another, rendering it virtually impossible to work out a plan of contribution on which all would agree.

A solution of the problem was found in donations of cement, obtained from individual companies through the influence of Mr. Gowen, for the specific purpose of building Seedling Miles. The Association having suspended its efforts to obtain the $10,000,000 subscription planned by Mr. Fisher, these individual donations answered its needs admirably.

The first donation was made by the Atlas Portland Cement Company on April 20, 1914, and comprised 6,000 barrels. It was closely followed by others of 5,000 barrels each from the Northwestern States Portland Cement Company of Mason City, Iowa; the St. Louis Portland Cement Company of St. Louis; the Sandusky Portland Cement Company of Sandusky, Ohio; the Chicago Portland Cement Company and the Marquette Cement Manufacturing Company of Chicago; and one of 2,000 barrels from the Crescent Portland Cement Company of Wampum, Pennsylvania; a total of 33,000 barrels, the value of which at that time was approximately $40,000. However, when much of this cement was used its worth had appreciated so that it represented a much larger sum.

Not all this cement was utilized.

No sooner was definite word received that cement would be available when needed than Secretary Pardington, acting under Mr. Joy's instructions, began active negotiations to select the places where it should be used.

It was to the interest of the Association, no less than to the interest of the cement industry, that such highway as was built with donated cement should be first class in every respect and to that end strict conditions were laid down. These conditions were soon made more exacting. Whereas at first the Association was glad to obtain construction of even a ten foot highway, it soon revised its demands to a minimum width of sixteen feet, and in 1918 to a minimum width of eighteen feet, which is as wide as some states were building even main route highways many years later.

The Association's objective was to obtain as much concrete construction as possible in return for cement sufficient to build one mile of highway and to have this road built on the open highway where mud had been the rule, so local traffic would have opportunity to note the striking difference between the demonstration section and the unimproved road at either end.

For the first mile, Mr. Pardington called together all the county and local consuls of Illinois in a meeting at De Kalb, under the chairmanship of State Consul J. W. Corkings He had 8,000 barrels of cement available for use in Illinois, enough for four miles of highway.

He had therefore proposed that the route of the Lincoln Highway across Illinois be divided into four equal sections and that the townships in each section compete for enough cement to build one mile. This proposal was heartily approved and the consuls went back to their homes to see what they could do, while Mr. Pardington went on to Iowa.

There he announced that 8,000 barrels of cement were available for construction of four miles of concrete

A TYPICAL WYOMING BRIDGE NEAR GREEN RIVER, WYOMING

highway in four different counties of that state. The offer established the good faith of the Lincoln Highway Association, Mr. Pardington said afterward, in a way nothing else could have done; unfortunately it developed that there were legal obstacles in Iowa state laws and the gift could not be accepted.

While Mr. Pardington was in Iowa, the Illinois communities began their competition. Consul Corkings, a real giant in highway promotion, led the struggle in his home town of De Kalb and surrounding territory, and not only distanced all competitors in his section but did it so quickly that his community won the first allotment of cement.

He raised $2,000 in cash from public subscriptions and induced the county supervisors to appropriate another $3,000. With free cement this was just enough to build one mile of road on a grade which the state had partially prepared west of De Kalb. The state donated the use of its road machinery and assigned engineers to supervise construction. Of course this took time and more time was required to allow other communities, if they could, to outbid De Kalb for the cement. But none did, and on September 26, Mr. Corkings was almost ready to initiate the laying of the first concrete paving in Illinois.

"We have only enough money to build a road 10 feet wide and that made us go some," he wrote to Mr. Pardington. "The state highway commission is building all of the roads in Illinois 10 feet wide except between big cities. The grading will all be done next Wednesday. Kindly start two cars of cement at once so we will not be holding them back."

Then a hitch developed. Mr. Pardington asked one

of the mills which had donated cement to supply the allotment. They were unable to ship it immediately and Mr. Pardington, unwilling to see the fine edge of De-Kalb's enthusiasm dulled, appealed to the Marquette Company. They answered by wire:

"Your letter twenty-sixth. Can ship cement for De-Kalb County road beginning at once."

Secretary Pardington wrote to Consul Corkings:

"The ball is opened and you are the leader of the first dance. I have just received word from the Marquette Company that they are shipping to you 2,000 barrels of cement."

So was built the first of the Lincoln Highway Seedling Miles. It lies between 6.2 and 7.2 miles west of the De Kalb post office and the builders did a good job, for 20 years afterward it was still part of the state highway.

It was not until December that Nebraska, the next state to show interest, began serious negotiation for an allotment. This application came from Fred W. Ashton of Grand Island, Hall County consul. There were on deposit in Grand Island banks $1,170, proceeds of membership certificate sales, and this money he thought, would be a fine nucleus for a seedling mile fund.

He proposed that it be used to buy additional cement to make the road 16 feet wide instead of 9 or 10 and reported to Mr. Pardington that the county board and city council would assume all details of construction.

To give some practical help, Mr. Pardington sent him estimates on quantities of sand and gravel required; copies of the specifications used for concrete roads in

Illinois and other information regarding concrete highway construction. The Lincoln Highway Organization frequently was called on to perform like service for many county and even state governmental bodies.

Unfortunately, local jealousies delayed appropriations of public money for the seedling mile until the next May and even then, to insure the appropriation, Mr. Ashton had to guarantee that the cost would not exceed the estimate.

The Lincoln Highway Association, in addition to the cement, offered to Hall County and other counties in Nebraska whatever steel culverts were necessary on seedling miles; E. E. Placek, president of the Nebraska Culvert Manufacturing Company, having agreed to provide culverts for any Nebraska miles. It also, through the Portland Cement Association, provided engineering consultation and through the American Institute of Architects, who had donated its services for the purpose, provided advice on architectural treatment of bridges.

Through his business connections, Mr. Ashton enabled the county to purchase sand and gravel at very favorable terms.

The mile was completed November 3, 1915, and Mr. Ashton very proudly telegraphed the Association late that afternoon:

"Seedling Mile at Grand Island completed today."

Two days later he was applying for more cement, to build two more seedlings.

Meanwhile the virus of highway improvement with which the Association had inoculated the country was taking hold vigorously.

News that Grand Island citizens were agitating for a seedling mile was noised about, as the Association had anticipated and hoped, and the county consul at Kearney, Willard F. Bailey, was soon negotiating with the Association for cement for a mile in his jurisdiction.

The Kearney Commercial Club voted to finance the construction and named a strong committee to raise the money. They did not, however, look with favor on a narrow roadway and asked for 3,000 barrels instead of 2,000, promising to make the road 15 feet wide.

The inevitable delays were ended when W. L. Stickel personally guaranteed a shortage of $3,000 and in spite of their later start, the Kearney mile was completed only three days later than that at Grand Island. This mile borders the grounds of two state institutions, just west of the city limits of Kearney.

Back in Illinois, Whiteside County, of which Morrison is the county seat, had been ready since the preceding September to build its seedling mile. Delay in starting work was charged by the county consul, Will F. Miller of Sterling, to the tardiness of state officials. In justice, however, it must be said that Illinois' new state highway commission was very busy getting a general program of work started and preparing standard concrete highway specifications which were later used as a model in many states.

Mr. Miller's county appropriated $16,600 for concrete paving on the Lincoln Highway. This was more than any other section in his district would put up, easily winning the 2,000 barrels and, as a sort of extra award, earning the county an allotment of like amount from state funds. Then the county authorities voted to match,

LINCOLN HIGHWAY OFFICIALS, ENGAGED IN FIRST HAND INVESTIGATION OF DESERT CONDITIONS IN 1917, ENCOUNTERED DIFFICULTIES

dollar for dollar, any sum the state would allow for road work and to spend it all on the Lincoln Highway!

This was fine, from the Association's viewpoint, but better was the news that Whiteside County's example had so stirred neighboring counties that they, too, were anxious for allotments of cement. Farmers were offering to haul road materials free, and both urban and rural residents were contributing funds for improving the Lincoln Highway.

Strictly speaking, the Whiteside County mile was not a mile at all as the cement contributed for one mile was increased by use of county funds and three miles were built, partly west and partly east of the town of Morrison.

That same year, 1915, the Indiana legislature approved an issue of bonds by St. Joseph County, the proceeds of which were intended to build 16 miles of Lincoln Highway of concrete 18 feet wide. However, Warren Township voted for more bonds than its legal bonding limit permitted. To help them out, the Lincoln Highway Association donated 2,000 barrels of cement and had one mile of the stretch in that township arbitrarily marked as a seedling.

In the midst of all this activity, Mr. Pardington succumbed to the illness against which he had struggled so valiantly for years and negotiations which he had initiated were interrupted.

Over 22,000 barrels of the cement which had been donated had not been applied for. Therefore at the annual meeting at the end of 1915, the Association revised the conditions for donation of cement and offered 3,000 barrels to any community that would build one mile of concrete road on the Lincoln Highway, the offer being limited, however, to one mile in any one county. Mr. Bement, as Mr. Pardington's successor, was instructed to allot the remaining cement on hand to counties preferably in Iowa, Nebraska and Wyoming, but to Indiana and Illinois if necessary to assure its use at an early date. Consuls along the route of the highway in the states named were notified and urged to induce their communities to accept.

Then a curious situation arose. Because of limitations placed by certain donors on the states where their cement might be used, and the slowness of counties in those states to apply for this material, the Association found itself with cement available which it could not utilize. At the same time, its own activities brought in applications for 9,000 barrels of cement which it could not supply.

Although highway improvement always resulted from the efforts of Lincoln Highway consuls to induce their counties to apply for cement, many applications lapsed because of legal or financial difficulties. Others were abandoned when strikes in the mills, congestion on the railroads or wartime demands for the product prevented the Association from arranging prompt delivery. Yet some communities accepted the offer, waited until Secretary Bement could fight down all delays, and built important sections of the road with the cement.

One was Cook County, Illinois, where Ralph E. McEldowney, consul at Chicago Heights, induced officials to arrange for construction of a 4½ miles section.

One of the most remarkable seedling sections was that near Fremont, Nebraska, where not merely one but six miles of concrete highway were built as a direct result of contribution of 3,000 barrels of cement. This six-mile stretch was the largest immediate result ever obtained by Lincoln Highway cement contribution.

Negotiations for it began in 1914, when County Consul George F. Wolz, later state consul for Nebraska, so enthused the Fremont Commercial Club that it subscribed $8,000. Delays, chiefly due to the war, interfered and it was not until 1918 that actual shipment of cement was started. The work was finished in 1919. It was the second piece of construction to be done anywhere under the Federal Aid law. It began at the northern boundary of Fremont and extended westerly for six miles.

This job was one of the first to use some of the methods later generally employed for highway construction, including the moving concrete mixer, piping of water to the mixer, and batch delivery in trucks.

In 1918 another seedling mile was built in Linn County, Iowa, near Cedar Rapids, the cement came from the Northwestern States Portland Cement Company of Mason City, Iowa. The donation of cement by the Association induced the county officials to build immediately one and three-quarters miles of additional concrete road, and also had a bearing on the securing of federal aid for the county. The efforts of Edward Killian, county consul, and William G. Haskell, eastern state district consul, were responsible for this construction. It was the first concrete road in Iowa.

Late in 1917, Mr. Ostermann met Clinton Cowan, state highway commissioner of Ohio. They discussed the status of the Lincoln Highway in Paulding County, Ohio, where but one mile of the route is located, remote from centers of local interest and consequently neglected. They agreed this would be a fine location for a demonstration section. Mr. Cowan promised that if the Association would supply 3,000 barrels of cement, the state would do the construction. It was completed in 1919.

The efforts of W P. Graham, Ogle County consul, State Consul J. W. Corkings and S. E. Bradt, then state highway commissioner and later state consul, led to the construction in Illinois of what were virtually six seedling miles with which the Association had only a remote connection.

In 1916 several counties in Illinois, Ogle among them, were anxious to obtain Lincoln Highway cement. Conditions of various natures interfered and the whole matter went into abeyance though Mr. Corkings' continued active efforts for the paving of the Lincoln Highway across Illinois. As part of his program he sought donations of sufficient cement to build one mile of concrete road in each of six Illinois counties. With the assistance of Mr. Gowen, this cement was obtained through T. G. Dickinson, president of the Marquette Cement Manufacturing Company.

Of value comparable to a seedling mile was a stretch of concrete road 18 feet in width, three-quarters of a mile in length, constructed on the Lincoln Highway by the Loyal Order of Moose, directly in front of their children's home at Mooseheart, Illinois. This construction cost nearly $12,000 and was a free gift by the order to the public.

No seedling miles were constructed after 1919. By the spring of that year the heavy traffic of munitions-laden trucks rolling over the Lincoln Highway to the Atlantic seaboard had so thoroughly demonstrated the value of hard-surfaced improved highways that the cement manufacturers felt it unnecessary to make further donations toward such missionary work. At the same time, the Lincoln Highway Association had seen the results of the seedling mile construction spread so far, and the value of the concrete road become so generally accepted, that it felt further activity of this character was not needed. It accordingly turned its attention toward improvement of those western sections where the states were financially unable to bring the highway up to the standard desired.

Several times makers or sponsors of other surfacing materials criticized the Association for having espoused cement in its proclamation and for its continued advocacy of this product. Its invariable answer was that it had named this material because it believed concrete best for use on highways as it visualized the traffic of the future. On at least one occasion, the Association suggested to the sponsor of a very excellent material that he construct a sample mile adjacent to a concrete mile and let the future decide their relative values. The challenge was not accepted.

CHAPTER XI

ALL Lincoln Highway men were public-spirited. The local consul in the smallest community on the route and the president of the organization alike were enthusiastic, able to visualize what real highways could be and willing to labor endlessly and unselfishly to create them.

Having material of such temper available, it is not surprising that President Joy and Secretary Pardington fashioned from it one of the most effective organizations ever created. In this organization local rights were protected and local questions were administered by local officials; questions affecting the highway as a whole, or interrelationships of different communities, were administered by the national authorities. At the same time there was no bureaucracy through which policies were handed down from the top; national headquarters was just as close to its minor officials as it was to a state consul. Business was handled directly and efficiently. The national headquarters was always ready to suggest, advise, direct, and assist, but it acted as a coordinator, not as a dictator, and many a suggestion from an obscure member was received with gratitude and put into national effect with benefit.

Most of the consuls, who did the real work, were able to work as individuals, to plan and to execute on their own initiative, and frequently did so. At the same time they all understood cooperation and could work as a unit

WILLIAM C. DURANT, FORMER PRESIDENT OF GENERAL MOTORS CORPORATION. THROUGH HIS INTEREST THAT CORPORATION DONATED A HUNDRED THOUSAND DOLLARS TO ASSIST CONSTRUCTION OVER WEST-ERN DESERT SECTIONS OF THE LINCOLN HIGHWAY

in carrying out the policies of the organization as a whole.

Many of these consuls were the leading men of their communities, professional men, bankers, clergymen, attorneys, doctors, merchants, editors. Many others were of less conspicuous vocations. But they all had the faculty of leadership and they all labored mightily for the public good.

Had the local representatives been able only to carry out orders, no matter how loyally, the Lincoln Highway Association could never have attained the success which it achieved. No group of men sitting in Detroit could have administered as wisely, as effectively and as quickly, the multitude of matters which were handled by the consuls themselves.

On the other hand, had the consuls not been able to subordinate personal views to general policy, success would have been even less possible.

The consular organization numbered from 245 to 285, the number increasing as the need for closer local attention developed at more points. At the head of the body were State Consuls, responsible for the welfare of the Lincoln Highway movement in their commonwealths. Each county had its County Consul and in each community there was also a Local Consul. Later, District Consuls were appointed to aid several state leaders.

Many consuls served for long periods; a few served practically throughout the 14 years of the organization's greatest activity. Not one of them ever relinquished his post, whether from ill health, removal to another city or the pressure of individual affairs, without real and deep regret.

The first consuls were named by the directors in September, 1913. They were:

Horace E. Fine, Trenton, for New Jersey:
H. O. Smith, Indianapolis, for Indiana:
F. E. Edwards, Chicago, for northeastern Illinois:
J. W. Corkings, De Kalb, for western and northwestern Illinois:
W. F. Coan, Clinton, for Iowa:
H. E. Frederickson, Omaha, for Nebraska:
Payson W. Spaulding, Evanston, for Wyoming:
C. L. Newcomb, Jr., for Colorado:
Gael S. Hoag, Ely, for Nevada:
E. P. Brinegar, San Francisco, for California:

A little later H. B. Lewis was named consul for New York, Charles Tyng, of Salt Lake City, was made consul for Utah and John Hopley, of Bucyrus, consul for Ohio. Shortly thereafter Frank B. McClain, Lieutenant-Governor of Pennsylvania, was made Lincoln Highway consul for that state and W. M. Griffin, of Fort Wayne, succeeded Smith as Indiana state consul.

Two of these first state consuls were destined to rise to prominent positions in the Association's work. Mr. Coan was elected an honorary vice-president in 1914; Mr. Hoag, some years later, became successively Field Secretary and Managing Secretary.

The first county consuls and many of the first local consuls were named on the recommendation of these state representatives. Some of the recommendations were not good, as was to be expected, but men who could not or would not work for the Lincoln Highway on broad, impersonal, public-spirited lines soon eliminated themselves.

Very few of the consuls were politicians, or holders of public office, though all were intimately acquainted with the politicians and the politics of their own communities.

The duties of a consul were honorary and onerous. He was, so far as his own community was concerned, the Lincoln Highway Association. The headquarters at Detroit looked to him for information, advice and suggestions, as well as for energetic execution of its general policies. He was required to base his actions on the principles laid down in the Lincoln Highway Proclamation, but so long as he acted for the carrying out of those principles the Association supported him fully.

The consuls were the contacts between the Association and the public officials who were to do the actual road construction. They were the chief means of enlisting support, moral and monetary, from the communities along the route; the turners of local political wheels, the schemers and organizers of plans, in the execution of which the influence and prestige of the national body were frequently called into play effectively.

Where special circumstances required, the Association appointed consuls at points not on the route; as witness the naming of a local consul in Hawaii in the very early days; appointment of Fred L. Baker, of Los Angeles, as consul for southern California in 1919; and the much earlier appointment of Col. William G. Edens as Chicago Consul, which post he still holds. Once a state consul, John S. Fisher of Indiana, Pennsylvania, was chosen from a city not on the route of the highway.

Consuls were generous donors of their time and money; something has already been told of their activity in holding and attending meetings to stimulate public spirit for highway improvement, but they were active in dozens of other phases of the Lincoln Highway movement. They often turned their hands to propaganda work with excellent effect. A. A. Moore, district consul at Marshalltown, Iowa, wrote a booklet called "The Road Boosters' Wrangle" which played a large part in converting Iowa farmers to the good roads idea.

Too much cannot be said for their public spirit in the furtherance of what, after all, benefited them no more than it benefited many others. There are innumerable instances where each really carried on Lincoln Highway work at considerable personal cost. In at least one case a Lincoln Highway Consul sacrificed a political career to uphold the integrity of Lincoln Highway policy.

They had the will to do, and in the final analysis, they probably accomplished as much as any other single force to make the Lincoln Highway, and the present highways of the United States, a reality. They certainly accomplished more than any other agency except the press; in a very large degree they and their activities influenced the press.

In the beginning, the consuls were almost entirely lacking in direct contact with the Association's executives; Mr. Joy saw them when he drove along the route; some of them came in to Detroit for conferences; Mr. Pardington saw as many of them as he could when he attended good roads meetings, but it was not until Mr. Ostermann was retained as field representative that each consul was brought into close personal touch with what the Association was doing.

From the time of his appointment in 1914 the Field Secretary endeavored to see each consul at least twice each year, as he drove the round trip, coast to coast.

The trip usually required seven months, for he stopped everywhere, heard everything threshed out, gave advice on the spot or referred the matter to Detroit, as needed, and often remained in one place several days to help solve local problems.

This work was of enormous value. The Field Secretary held meetings in the interest of highway improvement, kept the national headquarters in touch with local developments, brought a fresh viewpoint to local matters, and stirred up the interest of communities wherever and whenever activity lagged.

A part of his work was to make and revise the Association's logs of the road; the log Mr. Ostermann made in 1916, covering the whole length of the highway, is said to have been the most complete ever made of any road. Besides ordinary information valuable to the tourist, it gave a vast amount of data intended for the Association's use in working for improvements, such as the type and extent of each piece of construction; the width, capacity and type of all bridges; the locations of all streams, the number and location of railroad crossings; the width and character of surface for every mile of the distance.

He studied new construction, so that valuable ideas might be passed on to other communities, and examined the locations of improved routings. It was largely through this latter phase of his activity, in which he was often assisted by local consuls, that the mileage of the highway was reduced from its initial 3,389 miles in 1913, to 3,101.8 miles in 1933.

Here is a summary of his work for a typical year, taken from the minutes of the annual meeting for 1918:

"Twelve states and ninety-six counties were visited; every state and county official was interviewed and no less than 300 road meetings were held. Stops at each of the 400 cities, towns and villages on the route were made at least twice, and conferences held with the State, District, County and Local Consuls. Many additional meetings were held with Commercial Clubs, Boards of Trade, Automobile, Rotary and Kiwanis Clubs. The following matters were taken up at these meetings; road improvements, Seedling Miles, bridge and culvert construction, marking the route, sustaining memberships; state, county and city line markers; elimination of dangerous railroad crossings; straightening bad curves. Photographs were taken for the Association's records and a complete record of road improvement, with expenditures, compiled. Over 200 newspaper editors were also visited and the Association's activities discussed. Inspection of the Goodyear (Seiberling) and Fisher Sections was made a number of times during August, September and October."

One very important part of his work which Mr. Ostermann did not mention in this report was the selection of consuls. After the first group of county and local representatives had been named by the State Consuls, appointments were made by the Field Secretary on the recommendation of the Association's representatives in the region. Many times some man suggested for consular appointment was interviewed, studied, and found wanting without ever knowing he had been considered for the post. Care always was exercised and a man's actions in behalf of highway improvement determined the selection.

Sometimes, also, the Field Secretary studied possible

MESSRS. SEIBERLING, OSTERMANN AND HOAG STUDY THE UTAH DESERT
SOIL

UNIMPROVED NEVADA ROAD. THIS WAS CONSIDERED A "GOOD" NEVADA
ROAD WHEN THE LINCOLN HIGHWAY WAS LAID OUT

appointees for state consular posts and reported what he learned to the directors, for appointments of the state representatives were always made by the national authorities and the aptitudes of the men chosen for this work were studied even more carefully than those of prospective county or local representatives.

The Association did everything possible to emphasize the fact that the consul was an essential part of its organization. To maintain contact with the consuls and morale in the consular organization, it sent the consuls its press sheets, and before the press sheets were instituted, sent them special circulars, just as it regularly sent bulletins to directors and founders. In April, 1917, it began publishing for them a separate folder, called the Lincoln Highway Forum, which was sent also to sustaining members.

Sometimes state consuls assisted general contact work by calling their county and local consuls together in state meetings; at other times they made trips across their states to do locally what the Field Secretary was doing nationally.

The leaders of the organization were quick to acknowledge their debt to the consuls. One of the very earliest records of the Association is a faded copy of a greeting sent them over the signatures of Messrs. Joy and Pardington on the First Anniversary of the Proclamation of the Route.

In 1914, Senator Beveridge wrote to Secretary Pardington:

"I have been much impressed by the progress of the great enterprise, the Lincoln Highway. The results already achieved are plainly due to cooperation. In the last analysis, the consuls of the Association must be given the credit. I believe the keynote of our success is the personnel and the fidelity of the good, patriotic citizens who so ably supplement the work of our directors. The most we can do is to plan and to keep the work before the nation. The burden of doing things rests upon the Association's representatives—the consuls."

In 1917, the organization established three classes of service awards, symbolized by bronze, silver and gold medals, which it mounted as watch fobs and distributed to Lincoln Highway workers.

With the medals was sent a certificate of award, stating that the Association was not awarding the medal or expressing appreciation for any activities the recipient might have carried on in its behalf but rather that it was acting for the general public in extending recognition for his efforts to benefit his fellow citizens.

The medals were awarded in limited numbers only. The first year only six silver ones were awarded: to State Consuls Horace E. Fine, W. F. Coan, John E. Hopley, J. W. Corkings, Geo. F. Wolz, and Gael S. Hoag.

At the same time twenty bronze medals were awarded. Some months later, twenty-two more medals were bestowed. The practice was not continued beyond this second group of awards, though every year the Association sent the consuls a special greeting of some kind. One such read:

"The advent of 1923 finds the Lincoln Highway Association well along in its tenth year of endeavor. *You* are one of those who have been directly instrumental in making it what it is today, truly 'The Main Street of the Nation.' On behalf of our directors and myself, I here voice our appreciation.

GAEL S. HOAG, Field Secretary"

Less prominent than the consuls, but invaluable when mass action was required, were the Sustaining Members. These men contributed a considerable part of the organization's financial support but what the Association sought most in establishing this type of membership was interest. As Mr. Joy said:

"We sold 'em stock in the Lincoln Highway and then they had to keep active to take care of it."

Sustaining Members were the rank and file of good roads supporters. It was they who attended the good roads meetings, who were assigned by the consul to carry out the details when some special event was in prospect, who served on delegations to county boards. Time after time individuals from their ranks were called on to bring pressure to bear or to make personal appeals for some special cause.

There was never any direct return to these public-spirited men; the compensations were always of the intangible sort—a certain prestige, an opportunity for real service, the knowledge of a worth-while work done. It was loyalty to a great idea that kept these men active.

Such loyalty could not have been obtained if the Association's leaders had been less high-minded or less able to meet men face to face and talk to them man-fashion. Personality played a tremendous part in enlisting this great volunteer force for highway improvement. Only the personal magnetism and obvious sincerity of a Carl Fisher, for example, could have obtained more than $4,000,000 in subscriptions to the original transcontinental road plan, or enlisted the whole-hearted support of the shrewd industrial leaders who organized the Lincoln Highway Association.

The ability of Mr. Joy, who had spent years in the west as a mining engineer, to meet and talk to westerners in their own idiom was unquestionably important in enabling him to gain the information on which the route was laid out, while his clear-headedness and vision were vital in formulating the principles on which the Association built to success.

The genius of Mr. Pardington for organization was essential to set the Association on its feet.

The wonderful morale built up among the consuls and other supporters along the route could not have been created so readily nor so quickly without the vitalizing influence of Mr. Ostermann, or maintained without the sincerity and forthrightness of Mr. Hoag. Certainly the Association could not have obtained the thousands of columns of publicity which it did obtain had it not had the benefit of Mr. Bement's amazing ingenuity; nor could it have operated through several lean years without the business genius displayed by him and by his successor, Mr. Hoag.

Everyone gave of his best. This explains how such great effects could be brought about through the activities of so small an organization. The largest number of sustaining members the Association ever had was not far from 3,000. Its consuls never numbered more than 285. Even in 1918, a year of peak activity, when the Association had more than 1,500 newspapers on its mailing list and was handling almost 1,500 pieces of mail every working day, the staff at Detroit comprised only Secretary Bement; Field Secretary Ostermann; two stenographers, a bookkeeper-cashier and a girl who looked after the mailing. For a long time after Mr. Hoag became secretary, the headquarters personnel included, besides himself, only one stenographer and a part-time officeboy.

The headquarters organization and directorate was a marvelous team, each contributing some special talent peculiar to himself and, by some means more definite than chance, it appeared that each assumed an ascendancy at the exact time necessary for his particular contribution to make itself felt to the greatest advantage.

Modestly omitting to mention the very important contributions made by himself, President Seiberling in 1933 said:

"The fact is that without Fisher and Joy we would have no Lincoln Highway; without the money furnished by Durant and Willys the work could not have been carried along; and without the very high class service of all our secretaries it might easily have been a half-way job."

Mr. Joy's assumption of the presidency came precisely when it was necessary that some very clear-headed and energetic man take over direction of Mr. Fisher's ambitious plan and press it forward through practical channels.

The personnel of the committee which Mr. Joy drew around him was similarly hard-headed and practical. There were Russell A. Alger, Albert J. Beveridge, Roy D. Chapin, Emory W. Clark, Paul H. Deming, Carl G. Fisher, Albert Y. Gowen, Arthur R. Pardington and F. A. Seiberling. With Mr. Joy, they formed the first board of directors.

Consider, too, the form of the organization they set up. It was self-perpetuating, because they all anticipated that the work they were undertaking would require a generation. Its powers were so balanced between the active membership and the board of directors that it could hardly get out of control of the original group. It was not for profit because they all realized the work could only be done by voluntary contributions; it was aptly designed for the work.

This work exercised a tremendous fascination on all who were associated with it. Of the original board, Messrs. Clark, Seiberling, Joy, Chapin and Fisher have served continuously since the Association was formed.

Mr. Joy's administration continued for five years; that is, until 1918, when he resigned to become one of America's war-time industrial staff as a "Dollar-a-Year" man, a post in which his services were recognized with a commission as lieutenant-colonel. All his original directors, except Mr. Pardington, who died, remained on the board throughout his administration. John N. Willys was added in 1914; the vacancy caused by Mr. Pardington's death was filled by election of Mr. Bement in 1915; Colonel S. D. Waldon, James A. Allison, and Henry F. Campbell, secretary-treasurer of the Stutz Motor Car Company, were added in 1916.

During Mr. Joy's administration the Association dropped the Fisher plan of raising $10,000,000 and focussed its efforts instead on a program of education and building of seedling miles. The first marking of the highway and the establishment of a very active service for the benefit of tourists also belongs to this period.

When Mr. Seiberling was chosen to pilot the Association through the difficult last year of the war, the directorate was further enlarged by the addition of Alvan Macauley, president of Packard Motor Car Company, and of Mr. Ostermann.

At the end of 1918, Messrs. Ostermann and Bement were elected to vice-presidencies in recognition of their services.

Mr. Beveridge resigned because his literary work required all his time and Mr. Alger resigned for business reasons. To replace them the Association chose W. C. Durant, then head of General Motors, and J. Newton Gunn, president of the United States Tire Company, and enlarged the Board by restoring Colonel Waldon, who had been off it while serving in France. Both Colonel Waldon and Mr. Durant have remained on the directorate ever since and Mr. Gunn was a member until his death in 1927.

Mr. Seiberling's administration saw the completion of the Seedling Mile program and the beginning of the Association's long series of efforts in aid of sparsely settled western states, which could not finance high class highways.

While Mr. Seiberling was president, too, plans for construction of the Ideal Section were begun and the first army transcontinental motor convoy trip was made. These were all important achievements, but to them Mr. Seiberling added a careful and conservative management of Association affairs which enabled it to live through war-time difficulties.

Mr. Seiberling gave up the presidency in 1920 because of the increased requirements of his business. The directors chose Mr. Joy to replace him but the original leader of the Association held the reins for less than half the year; his health would not permit him to bear the burden.

Mr. Seiberling was re-elected and served out the year, then asked the directors to relieve him of presidential responsibilities. The Board heeded his plea and named Mr. Gunn to succeed him.

In 1920 Mr. Ostermann lost his life, Messrs. Deming and Campbell offered their resignations. W. O. Rutherford, vice-president of B. F. Goodrich Co., and Edsel B. Ford, president of the Ford Motor Company, were elected directors and Mr. Ostermann was succeeded as Field Secretary by Gael S. Hoag.

In 1923 C. S. Mott, vice-president of General Motors Company, and G. M. Stadelman, then president of the Goodyear Tire & Rubber Co., were elected directors. Both concerns had contributed heavily to the western construction work but were now without any representation on the Board because of changes in their own corporate organizations.

At the 1924 annual meeting, Mr. Bement resigned his secretaryship, though retaining the vice-presidency, and entered business for himself. The directors chose Mr. Hoag to succeed him. This year also, E. S. Evans, of Detroit, who had long been a founder, was elected a member of the Board. A year later, B. F. Affleck, president of the Universal Portland Cement Company, was elected. Since that time the Board has been unchanged.

Mr. Gunn's administration was largely occupied with a struggle for retention of the approved alignment in Utah and Nevada and with construction of the Ideal

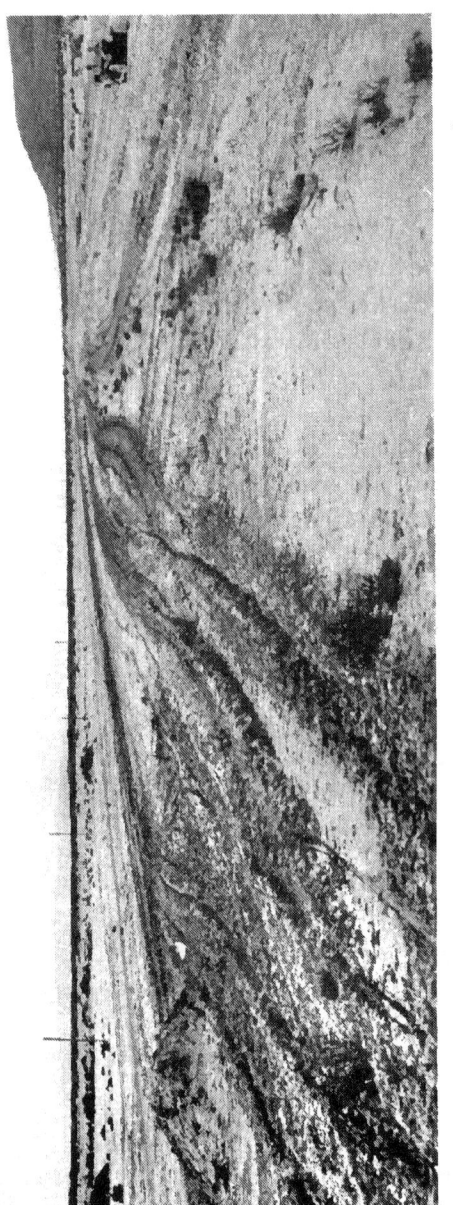

BEFORE IMPROVEMENT—THE FALLON FLATS, IN CHURCHILL COUNTY, NEVADA, IN 1916

Section. He was ill through most of 1927, Mr. Seiberling acting for him, and in December when it appeared he never again would be able to participate in Lincoln Highway affairs, the Association elected Mr. Seiberling for a third time. The rubber magnate has held the office ever since.

The chief activity of the Association in this third Seiberling administration was the placing of concrete monuments along the highway from coast to coast. With completion of this work, the Association attained the last of the objectives announced in its proclamation.

This marking was carried out after the actual closing of the organization's offices on December 31, 1927, and the suspension of all other activities. It is doubtful whether any great purpose could have been served by continuing operations. The sentiment for highway improvement which it sponsored for so many years had become so strong, and the country had come to regard highways as so essential, that there seemed no need for further stimulation of public opinion in this regard.

The road had been constructed, they were about to give it as permanent a marking as could be devised, and all other objectives laid down in the Proclamation had been attained.

Permanent maintenance of the entire route was provided for under the states' Federal Aid contracts with the national government. The last toll gate had been removed from the route years before. What more, then, was to be done?

The directors could see nothing that justified continuance of the work.

Yet, in case some occasion should arise for its services,

they kept their organization intact and as such it remains, a legal entity, still led by the men who organized it and the associates they gathered about them, ready to resume operations quickly if needed.

CHAPTER XII

ADHERING TO THE DIRECT ROUTE

PRESIDENT JOY once likened the Lincoln Highway traffic to a vast river, flowing westward in a single great and increasing stream until it reached Wyoming and Utah and then dividing into smaller streams as though it were passing through a delta, some north to the national parks, some south through the wonders of southern Utah, some northwest toward Portland or Seattle and some southwest toward Los Angeles.

That stream was a river of gold to the country through which it passes—tourist gold—for the hotelkeeper, the garage operator, the sellers of gasoline and oil and food.

Cities and towns contended for this wealth, seeking by all fair and some unfair means to divert the whole stream, or at least a larger portion of it, into that channel where it would profit them most.

While some communities labored to attract traffic by extolling the advantages of their scenery, others sought to control the situation through diversion of the route or construction or nonconstruction of roads. This was particularly the case in the west, where the issue of construction of one section of the Lincoln Highway, or construction of a different route, determined whether traffic should have free flow into both northern and southern California, or whether San Francisco should have a dominant position in the tourist business.

The stake in this contest was a large one and involved

advantages in priority of settlement and priority of development as well as the direct advantage of trade. The Lincoln Highway Association's brief to Henry C. Wallace, secretary of Agriculture, in 1923, expressed the situation thus:

"The vast distances to be traversed by highways in the west, together with the relatively meager road funds, naturally make possible the opening of but one first road between any two important main points. Which will be selected to be opened first with the funds available is, therefore, a question vital to large areas west of the Rockies; a question which can well mean hundreds of millions of dollars in new money, as well as a very large 'head start' in development and settlement, before the gradual completion of a general system of highways puts all sections on a relatively equal basis to bid for the tourist traffic."

In view of this great prize, it is not remarkable that the competition became bitter, or that cities and towns and even one whole state should become blind to the fact that topography fixed the route of the Lincoln Highway just as surely as it fixes the course of rivers on their way to the Sea. They could never understand that mountains and contours, not scenery and historic associations, controlled the situation.

This desire to profit from tourist dollars lay at the bottom of all the numerous requests for inclusion in the route which showered on Will Dobyns in the pre-organization days. It brought further similar requests to Secretary Pardington later on. There were, perhaps, two exceptions—the Kentucky town near which Lincoln was born and Springfield, Illinois, where he lived, sought to have the highway come their way for sentimental reasons.

Some of these requests would have drawn the route very far from the direct line. Cleveland, Ohio, wanted the highway and some Cleveland interests attempted to discredit the project when a different routing was chosen. Another, which was pressed vigorously for some years, would have taken the highway into Los Angeles instead of into San Francisco. Even after the official designation of the city by the Golden Gate as the western terminus, Los Angeles interests led by the Automobile Club of Southern California continued their effort to have the road connecting Los Ángeles with the Lincoln Highway at Ely, Nevada, declared an alternative route, equal in prominence and importance with the section from Ely into San Francisco. This probably would have been done had the automobile club and the highway association been able to agree upon southern California's share in the cost of improving this connection.

Characteristic of the southern California attitude toward the Lincoln Highway is the fact that most of the support accorded the Association by California came from this southern section, though in truth it may be said that all the monetary assistance the Association ever received from the whole state of California does not equal that received from any one of several mid-west towns.

Several other efforts for variations in routing were made in California, notably one which would have brought the highway through Beckwith Pass, along the route favored by Peter Lassen in the emigrant days. Still another would have swung it southward, to make Yosemite and other scenic points more accessible to the tourist.

Powerful interests in Iowa sought to have the highway pass through that state on a line south of that selected.

A bitter local struggle over the routing between Laramie and Rawlins, Wyoming, was finally settled only when Governor Joseph M. Carey issued a formal proclamation establishing the route as the Association laid it out and as it now stands.

Even after the route had been proclaimed by the Association and fixed in detail by the action of the state governors, there were persistent efforts for revisions. Most of the arguments in favor of these changes cited the fact that the Association had once varied from its declared principle of directness. This was in the case of the Colorado loop, or alternate route.

The directors, however, quickly recognized the error that had been made and in the spring of 1915 formally withdrew sanction of the Denver loop as a part of the Lincoln Highway. This action evoked a storm of protest in which Governor Ammons and Senator Charles S. Thomas of Colorado were leaders. The Association stood its ground.

However, the damage had been done and the Association soon found itself engaged with potent interests, including no less a personage than Woodrow Wilson, President of the United States.

People in Baltimore, Washington, Wilmington and Frederick had sought a place on the highway beginning soon after Mr. Fisher announced his original plan. When they saw the red line on the map taking an

AFTER IMPROVEMENT—THE LINCOLN HIGHWAY ACROSS THE FALLON FLATS AFTER IMPROVEMENT
MADE POSSIBLE BY GENERAL MOTORS DONATION

alternate route down to Denver, they redoubled their efforts though the loop they proposed would add 172 miles to the highway. The civic interests of Baltimore urged their senators and representatives to bring pressure for inclusion of the national capital in the highway's routing.

The commissioners of the District of Columbia passed a resolution toward the same end. So did the Automobile Club of Maryland. Then leading Baltimore and Washington citizens, with the Maryland Senators and Congressman J. Charles Linthicum, called at the White House and asked President Wilson to use his good offices in the matter. Meanwhile the Baltimore press was active in agitating the issue and strong representations were made to Mr. Pardington when he attended a dinner in Baltimore.

On June 19, 1914, President Wilson wrote to Mr. Joy:

"I am sure that the whole country is interested to see to it that there should no longer exist a North or a South in this absolutely united country which we all love and that the imaginary Mason and Dixon line should be made once and for all a thing of the past, and as a small contribution to that end I earnestly suggest that the Lincoln Highway Association should grant permission to place the official Lincoln Highway markers on the macadam roadway running from Philadelphia to Washington, through the properly selected streets of the latter city to the Lincoln Memorial now under construction, and from thence along the roadway through Frederick, Maryland, and from Frederick to Gettysburg."

The directors regretted that, because of the principles stated in the proclamation, they were unable to comply with Mr. Wilson's request. They authorized Mr. Joy to inform the President of their decision and here are the salient paragraphs of his response:

"I am under the necessity of stating to you that the work of the Lincoln Highway Association, no doubt greatly assisted through your recognition of its work in its early stages, has progressed so favorably that there scarcely remains along the entire Lincoln Highway any section of the route which has not been marked and to a very great extent renamed. Especially is such the case between Philadelphia and Gettysburg, where in the counties traversed and also in the cities of York, Lancaster, Coatesville, Columbia, Downington, the official adoption by the local authorities of the name Lincoln Way and the marking thereof and the betterments and beautifications in process make the changing of the route in accordance with your suggestions, if for no other reasons, outside of and beyond the control of this Association.

"The Lincoln Highway Association has committed and entrusted the Lincoln Way to all the people, and especially to the States. Counties, Villages and Cities through which its route extends. It is not possible to undo this wonderful work of the communities whose loyal patriotic efforts are making, have indeed made, the Lincoln Highway a part of the map of our country.

"The Lincoln Way is the shortest, most direct and practicable route consistent with the topography of the country from New York on the Atlantic to San Francisco on the Pacific, and to change from that basic principle and extend its length by devious windings from city to city, or from point of interest to point of interest, would insure its failure as a permanent useful Memorial Way.

"It is not within the power of our Association to alter the already painstakingly selected and actually adopted route."

The Association had declined the request of the President of the United States; in a little while it was to decline the request of the man who was to be his successor, Warren G. Harding. More, it was to convince Mr. Harding that its position with regard to routing was absolutely correct, and Mr. Harding was to say as much in writing!

The Harding episode arose from a correction in the alignment across Ohio. The original route, as laid down in the Proclamation, ran through Canton, Mansfield, Marion, Kenton, Lima and Van Wert. This routing, involving a southward sweep from the direct line, was taken on account of the existence of a practicable road along it and the absence of such a road on a directionally preferable routing to the north. However, on September 29, 1913, the route was revised to a line west from Mansfield through Bucyrus.

The revision shocked the people of Marion and other communities thus left off the Lincoln Highway, and they quickly began energetic efforts for restoration of the original routing. They offered as inducements a pledge that the Marion-Kenton road should be completely improved by the end of 1916, that a three-mile mud section west of Lima should be improved, that any faulty places in existing pavement on the route should be repaired, that a beginning would be made on paving either with concrete or brick, and that the Marion-Kenton section should be, in general, "a credit to the great national highway, what the Lincoln Highway should be." They promised active work to obtain publicity for the Association and agreed to hand the Lincoln Highway Association a certified check for $5,000 instantly upon its agreement to reroute the highway, this check to be in the nature of an underwriting for 1,000 memberships in the Association. To cap it all off, they handed the Association a letter from Senator Harding, in which the following passage appeared:

"Being a resident of Marion myself, I am very much interested in seeing the original route re-adopted, and I hope I may be able to do something in promoting the consummation of this great plan through reasonable and rational federal aid."

When the Association failed to approve the proposal for rerouting, the Marionites sent a delegation to Detroit to urge their case. Senator Harding was its head.

President Joy asked Mr. Harding to sit as arbiter over the discussion.

"I let the Marion gentlemen present their entire case," said Mr. Joy, "then I undertook to explain to them the situation, with the aid of a state map showing the roads through the district in question. When I had finished the gentlemen from Marion had in no way changed their opinion that we were acting unfairly and that there had been a gross injustice done them. They stated that they were going to mark their route Lincoln Highway and were going to do a lot of things, rampantly and furiously.

"Senator Harding, however, stated they should take no such course, that they should cooperate with the Lincoln Highway Association, that the Lincoln Highway Association was right in its attitude in the case and in its general principles, and he gave the Association a complete clean bill of health notwithstanding that he was a senator from Ohio and those gentlemen were his constituents."

Several adherents of the Lincoln Highway were in that meeting. One of them, Edward N. Hines, summed up what happened thus:

"We told the delegation that we were from Detroit and we were putting up the money to build the road, but that instead of running it through our home town, Detroit, we were running it where we thought it should go. That settled the question of the route so it could never be budged."

"The whole matter goes to show," Mr. Joy wrote to Mr. Seiberling soon afterward, "how valuable the Lincoln Highway is growing to be regarded. It shows how utterly hopeless it would have been to do anything in the premises except to take the czar-like attitude which we did take originally of formulating the route in its completeness and proclaiming the same."

The Marion people went home breathing fire and brimstone. For several years they continued their efforts for a rerouting, even going so far as to prevent expenditure of road money on the Lincoln Highway in Ohio by procuring the expenditure of all available funds on their own route. But Senator Harding wrote to Mr. Joy:

"I am frank to say that I am quite in sympathy with your policy as you explained it to me on the occasion of my recent call upon you in Detroit.

"I was very glad to make the trip to Detroit and speak to you in behalf of my home city, Marion, and it would have pleased me very greatly to have had Marion restored to the official route; but I have no difficulty in recognizing the merits of the arguments you advanced and I must say that I quite agree with you in the position you have assumed. Had I known that your position was such as you then stated it, I should not have troubled you to give us a meeting.

"I certainly wish you the most triumphant success in pushing along the progress of the great work which you have undertaken."

The Association kept up its effort for improved highways, and when a hard-surfaced road was eventually constructed across Ohio, that road was the Lincoln Highway.

Meanwhile, bitter struggles were being waged in the far west. In Utah, Ogden and Salt Lake City were contending for the routing and the tourist traffic of the Lincoln Highway. In California, San Francisco was resentful of Los Angeles' favorable connection with the highway as a great part of the westbound traffic was going over this connection and not coming into the city by the Golden Gate.

These jealousies were baseless; topography compelled the routing of the Lincoln Highway. (See Map in back of book.)

Having chosen Great South Pass as the best place to traverse the Rockies, the men who laid down this route were confronted next by the wall of the Wasatch range, just east of the Great Salt Lake. There was one feasible place to cross it—the vicinity of Salt Lake City. Other passes lay either far to the north or to the south, involving passage of difficult and barren country.

When the Lincoln Highway men met with the governors at Colorado Springs they favored, and Governor Spry approved, a routing which led the highway through this pass, directly into Salt Lake City. But when the governor returned to his home, he decided that a routing which led the highway into Ogden and thence south to Salt Lake City was preferable. He asked the Association to revise its designation and in accordance with the policy of accepting the dictates of state executives in such matters, the Association acceded to his request.

Ogden people favored a western highway routing which would pass north of Great Salt Lake, following the original line of the Southern Pacific Railroad, and a certain amount of traffic was diverted over this routing. This action was attributed to jealousy of Salt Lake City. Partly because of this diversion and partly because the route through Ogden was some 36 miles longer than that direct to Salt Lake City, the Association in 1915 reverted to the original line.

The rivalry between Los Angeles and San Francisco was complicated by the self-interest of Utah people.

Just west of Salt Lake City, and extending in a generally north and south direction from deep into Mexico to beyond the Canadian boundary, is an arid belt. The Great Salt Lake lies in it and in Utah this desert takes its name from the lake. Any road to the west must cross this desert somewhere, and obviously the location of such a road must determine what section or sections of states farther west shall benefit from the traffic it carries. The Lincoln Highway officials elected to cross this desert not far south of the Great Salt Lake, at a point where its greatest width is less than 60 miles, narrower than anywhere else in Utah.

The logical next point west of this crossing was Ely, Nevada, and one of the fundamental reasons the Lincoln Highway Association selected this southerly crossing of the desert, was that at Ely the motorist was practically the same distance from Los Angeles that he was from San Francisco, with a feasible road connection ready to take him to the southern California metropolis if he desired. Thus by going south of Great Salt Lake and touching Ely, the Lincoln Highway could be made to serve two of the great Pacific Coast Cities, and be more valuable to the motorist and more efficient as a highway. Moreover, on this routing, the building of but one road across this great desert barrier would serve all California traffic.

In planning the construction of the Lincoln Highway, Mr. Joy and the others foresaw that for many years funds for road improvements in this area would not be plentiful. They anticipated that to construct even one road would require a long time and absorb all available money. For these reasons they tried to make their road serve as much traffic as possible, and they sought the concentration on it of all available funds. By such means they felt it would the sooner become the national object-lesson highway which it was their purpose to construct.

These aims did not comport either with the selfish activities of Utah people or the intercity jealousies in California.

There existed no good road west from Salt Lake City nor much road of any kind in Utah west of the Great Salt Lake. Nor did Utah desire one, for on such a road a motorist travelling west would pass quickly beyond her borders, without stopping in any town overnight or spending much for supplies; whereas if he could be diverted instead to a route leading south from Salt Lake City toward Los Angeles, his travel for the next several days would be within the borders of Utah, and he naturally would leave more of his money within that state. Moreover, western Utah is admittedly not a fair sample of the state. Utah people felt the traveller who saw no more of their state than he would observe coming into it from Evanston and going on west to Ely would receive an unfavorable impression. Therefore, on two counts, there was strong reason for sending the motorist south toward Arizona rather than west toward Nevada and the Pacific coast. What happened to him after he left Utah they cared not.

There was a whole chapter of reasons why traffic intending only to go to California should not take the road south. For San Francisco bound traffic it was many hundreds of miles longer. Even for Los Angeles bound traffic it was considerably longer than the route via Ely. It involved about 220 miles of travel across the Mojave Desert, where motoring conditions were severe and even hazardous.

But if Utah must build a road west to connect with Nevada's section of a transcontinental route, then the

Utah people generally were in favor, they said, of building a road directly west across the Great Salt Lake Desert, considerably north of the Lincoln Highway— a task which for many years appeared to be an impossibility. So long as they argued for this and built no other road, then the best road out of Salt Lake City was that to the south, which suited Utah purposes exactly. In fact, Utah interests for many years did all they could to divert westbound transcontinental travel to this southerly road, on which also, they concentrated much of their highway improvement energies.

Because the Lincoln Highway would afford a western outlet for traffic reaching Salt Lake City, whether it was destined for San Francisco or for Los Angeles, Utah as a whole never gave the highway association the support it received in other states.

Utah selfishness blocked improvement of the Lincoln Highway and even after $125,000 had been contributed to Utah, through the Lincoln Highway Association, for betterment of the route to the west, the state failed to live up to its written contract and complete the road. Instead, after some years, and three abortive efforts, it did build the present road west from Grantsville to Wendover, which lacked a connection with the Lincoln Highway.

Utah's attitude in this respect suited southern California very well, for it tended to divert travel south at Salt Lake City and into Los Angeles; for the same reason it was not satisfactory to northern California. Northern California never was very anxious that the Lincoln Highway in Utah be completed, on account of the easy connection which that route afforded for

MEMORIAL BENCH ADJACENT TO THE "IDEAL SECTION" IN WESTERN INDIANA ERECTED AS A MEMORIAL TO THE LATE HENRY C. OSTERMANN, VICE PRESIDENT AND EARLY FIELD SECRETARY OF THE ASSOCIATION

southern California at Ely, but it did earnestly desire
that there be some road west from Salt Lake City so
that northern California could enjoy the tourist business which would naturally follow such a route. Further, San Francisco urgently desired a road west from
Salt Lake City which would have no connection whatever with southern California, so that traffic once embarked on it would have no alternative but to continue through to northern California.

And while Utah dallied and delayed in fulfilling its
contract to construct the missing section of the Lincoln
Highway west, San Francisco and allied interests seized
the opportunity to exploit another route, north of the
Lincoln Highway, and to urge and promote its early
completion.

This route had no feasible connection or branch
leading to Los Angeles. Travel embarking on it must
come into San Francisco, and so long as the Lincoln
Highway remained without an adequate connection
between Salt Lake City and Ely, it gave San Francisco
a dominant position with regard to tourist traffic reaching Salt Lake City on its way west.

Both California and Utah largely ignored the interests of Nevada in the solution of this vexing question.
The southern and central sections of Nevada stood to
profit well from completion of the Lincoln Highway;
northern Nevada would profit if the alternative route
sponsored by California interests were built. Nevada
had spent money on both routes, but which was to be
developed ultimately to a high-type highway depended
absolutely upon what Utah did. If Utah would consent
to only one road west from Salt Lake City, Nevada had

southern California at Ely, but it did earnestly desire that there be some road west from Salt Lake City so that northern California could enjoy the tourist business which would naturally follow such a route. Further, San Francisco urgently desired a road west from Salt Lake City which would have no connection whatever with southern California, so that traffic once embarked on it would have no alternative but to continue through to northern California.

And while Utah dallied and delayed in fulfilling its contract to construct the missing section of the Lincoln Highway west, San Francisco and allied interests seized the opportunity to exploit another route, north of the Lincoln Highway, and to urge and promote its early completion.

This route had no feasible connection or branch leading to Los Angeles. Travel embarking on it must come into San Francisco, and so long as the Lincoln Highway remained without an adequate connection between Salt Lake City and Ely, it gave San Francisco a dominant position with regard to tourist traffic reaching Salt Lake City on its way west.

Both California and Utah largely ignored the interests of Nevada in the solution of this vexing question. The southern and central sections of Nevada stood to profit well from completion of the Lincoln Highway; northern Nevada would profit if the alternative route sponsored by California interests were built. Nevada had spent money on both routes, but which was to be developed ultimately to a high-type highway depended absolutely upon what Utah did. If Utah would consent to only one road west from Salt Lake City, Nevada had no choice but to build at least its main east-west route to connect with the Utah construction. Eventually, at heavy cost, it connected both the Lincoln Highway and the northern route to Utah's one road at Wendover.

With no prospect of the early construction of an Ely-Salt Lake City road along the line it had selected, the Lincoln Highway Association accepted this Ely-Wendover connection, and the Utah construction between Wendover and Salt Lake City, as part of its official route.

Had Utah carried out her contract and completed the Lincoln Highway road across the desert, the country would have had a complete, connected, well improved transcontinental highway many years earlier, with added benefits which cannot be estimated.

JOHN N. WILLYS, PRESIDENT OF THE WILLYS-OVERLAND CO. A FOUNDER
AND DIRECTOR OF THE LINCOLN HIGHWAY ASSOCIATION

CHAPTER XIII

AIDING WESTERN CONSTRUCTION

WHEN Field Secretary Ostermann passed through Ely on his way home in 1915, after supervising the Lincoln Highway motion picture, Nevada State Consul Hoag suggested that the routing of the Lincoln Highway could be very materially improved by crossing the Great Salt Lake Desert on a different location.

Mr. Ostermann, characteristically, gave an open ear and open mind to the plan, and when Mr. Hoag pointed out that it would shorten the highway by 48 miles, became highly enthusiastic. Together they drove over the proposed relocation. Mr. Ostermann noted it in detail as the most important item on a map he had prepared which he said represented "bad roads to be sold to the Lincoln Highway directors."

The new route was from Salt Lake City over existing state highways south and west through Tooele to Clover, thence westerly over a road which Mr. Hoag suggested the Association should construct, in part, to strike the existing Lincoln Highway route at the entrance to Overland Canyon, not far from Ibapah. The construction required was six miles in Johnson Pass and approximately 18 miles across the desert, from the northern point of Granite Mountain to the mouth of Overland Canyon. Mr. Hoag and Mr. Ostermann thought the people of Tooele County, Utah, in which all the proposed new route lay, would contribute toward improvement of the road and that some assistance could be expected from the State of Utah.

The dramatic idea of saving 48 miles of travel by building 24 miles of road fired the imagination of the directors. They discussed it eagerly and when Mr. Ostermann said he thought that the work could be done for not more than $3,000 a mile, or approximately $75,000, Mr. Seiberling promptly offered on behalf of the Goodyear Tire & Rubber Company, to give that amount for the work.

Thus the man who had been first to respond to Carl Fisher's call, before the Lincoln Highway Association was organized, now was first to come to the aid of the institution when it embarked on what was to be its greatest physical accomplishment—the building of roads in the west.

The directors accepted the offer and instructed Secretary Bement to obtain accurate data on which an efficient and proper expenditure of the money could be based, file on a spring of water which Messrs. Ostermann and Hoag had found at Granite Mountain, obtain necessary rights of way across public lands and in general prepare for the enterprise.

Then Mr. Ostermann pointed out that all the points he had listed on his map as requiring improvement were in western states, with sparse population, light local traffic and little revenue to spend on trans-state highways. He proposed to obtain this assistance by appealing to those who had subscribed to Mr. Fisher's project, but who never had paid anything because of lapse of that plan.

The directors approved and Mr. Ostermann took a

train to Miami to call on Mr. Fisher. In just a few days he was back with Mr. Fisher's pledge of $25,000 to finance the building of the road through Johnson Pass. Mr. Fisher also suggested that the field secretary call on his partner, James A. Allison. Mr. Allison agreed to contribute $25,000 to the work. Conferences between Mr. Ostermann and Mr. Seiberling resulted in the rubber man's agreeing also to increase his contribution to $150,000, provided the work on which it was expended was permament in character.

Mr. Ostermann also called on John N. Willys, president of the Willys-Overland Company, and obtained from him assurance that his company would donate $50,000 for improvement of the highway in some other section.

With all the funds deemed necessary for Utah improvement thus in hand, and funds promised for a start on improvement in Nevada, Mr. Ostermann returned to Utah to see Governor William Spry and State Highway Commissioner Morgan, arrange for designation of the new route as state highway, and see how much cooperation could be obtained from the state and from Tooele County.

In order that there might be no possible doubt that the Association was in earnest in offering funds to Utah, $15,000 was obtained from Mr. Fisher as a first payment on his pledge and deposited in a Salt Lake City bank as a trust fund.

Not even this, however, convinced Governor Spry that the Association knew what it was talking about when it proposed building a highway on the chosen route. He suggested instead that its project be aban-

doned and its funds expended on a road from Grantsville directly west across the Great Salt Lake Desert to
Wendover, on the Nevada-Utah line. (See Map in back of
book.)

This road had been projected first by the Salt Lake
City Rotary Club, taken up by the Commercial Club
and since then had been pressed forward by all the
powerful interests of the community. This was the road
favored by San Francisco. About $13,000 had been ex-
pended in grading work on it and the civic organizations were then soliciting additional funds. Salt Lake
leaders estimated about $40,000 more would be re-
quired for its completion.

The advantage of abandoning the Lincoln Highway
routing and constructing the Wendover road, from the
standpoint of the Utah people, was that such a procedure would make Salt Lake City, instead of Ely,
Nevada, the diversion point where travel bound for
Los Angeles would turn southward from the Lincoln
Highway.

The points which were most to Utah's advantage
were most to the disadvantage of the Lincoln Highway
and also, the Association felt, were to the disadvantage
of the traffic on the highway. Mr. Ostermann, after a
personal inspection, gave it as his opinion that it would
cost $250,000 to build an acceptable desert crossing on
the Wendover alignment, and even when built, such
a crossing would not serve so much traffic as the Lincoln
Highway's routing. For these reasons, he refused to
recommend acceptance of the Governor's proposal. He
reported these facts to headquarters and President Joy
came west to make a personal inspection of both routes.

In Salt Lake City, Messrs. Joy, Bement and Ostermann met Mr. Hoag and a delegation of leading
citizens from Tooele, and drove down over the route
to Tooele. There they were promised by county officials that if they would route the Lincoln Highway
as proposed, Tooele County would aid in the needed
construction. Then they drove on through Johnson
Pass and, in spite of the fact that Governor Spry had
stated to Mr. Ostermann that this pass was impassable
for a man on horseback, the Lincoln Highway president drove it with ease in spite of the snow, except for
about 100 feet of the steepest and most difficult part
where the trail was obscured.

Descending the western side of the mountains to
Skull Valley, they based at a remote ranch owned by
the Orr Brothers and set out to explore the valley.
However, snowstorms prevailed day after day, obscur-
ing all landmarks and leaving them, in a virtually trail-
less land, to find their way as best they might.

Morning after morning they would drive out, steer-
ing by blind sense of direction, until the whirling snow
confused them and they had to turn back, following
their own wheel-tracks to the ranch. Several times the
wind obliterated even these, and then the party had to
get home by the instinct of Mr. Hoag or one of the
Orrs, long-time residents in that section and desert-wise
road men. Evening after evening they would eat roast
turkey with the ranch folk and plan anew for the morrow.

They were six days finding their way across the
thirty-five miles of desert which separated them from
Granite Mountain, the end of their inspection tour.

Then they lost another day repairing one of the cars, so that they "suffered," as one member of the party expressed it, "seven turkey dinners besides the danger of getting lost in the snow."

Then the Lincoln Highway party returned to Salt Lake City and made an inspection of the Wendover route.

As Mr. Ostermann had done, Mr. Joy declined to favor it. He told a meeting of Salt Lake City business men he was hesitant to face construction of the new Lincoln Highway Desert crossing via Granite Mountain, twenty-four miles in length, with no more than $200,000 in sight: and he wondered how the Wendover route's proponents expected to construct their road, forty miles in length, in a much more difficult terrain, with but $40,000.

Neither the Salt Lake City men nor the Lincoln Highway officials would yield. Mr. Joy and his associates returned east, the Salt Lake City men did nothing, and the citizens of Ely promptly showed their resentment of the Salt Lake attitude by boycotting the Salt Lake City business houses from whom they normally bought practically everything they ate, wore, or used. They even succeeded in getting the Nevada Consolidated Copper Company, the biggest industry in eastern Nevada, to join them. The economic pressure thus applied, was quickly effective. A meeting was arranged in Ely and a gentleman's agreement drawn up which terminated the boycott but actually did very little to relieve the situation.

Meanwhile, the proposed new Lincoln Highway route had been surveyed. The Association had had pits

THE "IDEAL SECTION," SITE BEFORE IMPROVEMENT

A COMPLETED PORTION OF THE "IDEAL SECTION"

dug to test the desert soil for stability and to locate the water table. It had also filed on the spring at Granite Mountain to assure a water supply for construction work and for motorists and had located a fine supply of gravel adjacent to the site of the work. After a very careful analysis of conditions and consultation with various engineers, it had determined that concrete construction was not feasible for this section of the route at that time. This necessarily reduced Mr. Seiberling's contemplated contribution to its original size, $75,000.

And meanwhile, as they were often to do again, the spring winds and high flood waters in that part of the Salt Lake Desert had washed away most of the grade constructed on the Wendover route. The Lincoln Highway men were more than ever convinced that they were right in refusing to adopt that alignment.

That summer, 1916, by dint of much urging, Mr. Ostermann induced Mr. Seiberling to break a hurried business trip through the west and drive into the desert to inspect the route over which he had promised to build a road. The rubber magnate met Messrs. Bement, Ostermann and Hoag in Salt Lake City on September 10, 1916. He was far behind his schedule and asked that the desert trip planned for five days be compressed to one. They persuaded him to extend that limit to a second day; more he would not yield.

That night they camped at the north point of Granite Mountain, starting point of the section which Mr. Seiberling had agreed to finance.

Next day, they started across the desert and, more than ten miles out, the heavy cars sank through the dry surface and mired down. Mr. Seiberling had to reach Wendover that night to catch a train; they were greatly distressed that he should receive such a sad impression of the desert, and they feared that he would be so disgusted as to withdraw his offer. Consul Hoag particularly was depressed, because if this were done, it seemed Ely and the other Nevada cities on the Lincoln Highway route would lose all share of the profitable tourist business to enjoy which they had worked so long and so earnestly. While he set off to walk the rest of the way across the desert to a ranch for help, the others continued their endeavors to dig out the cars.

Mr. Seiberling always insists that his most vivid impression of this trip was when he saw Mr. Hoag disappearing in the distance; the mirage caused curious effects; the further away Mr. Hoag got, the taller and slimmer he appeared to be until finally he faded out in the haze, lost somewhere between earth and sky. He wondered whether he would ever see Mr. Hoag again.

The day was terrifically hot, there was not a piece of vegetation in sight in any direction and they were on a practically trackless desert. They urged Mr. Hoag to take water with him but he did not wish to be encumbered with that weight and he knew that supplies were none too sufficient for the men who would be left behind. He was too much of a "desert rat" to share their apprehensions because he had travelled that desert many times and knew his landmarks. He did finally consent to stick two oranges in his shirt front and, coatless, he headed for a ranch which he knew was about twelve miles distant. As soon as he reached the western edge of the desert, he marked his course by pieces of rag tied up wherever possible, so that they could follow him if they were able to get either of the cars extricated.

Mr. Hoag relates an interesting incident he encountered on his walk. When he reached the far edge of the desert where clumps of grass were beginning to appear in the hummocks, he noticed an antelope standing close to the line which he was following. He continued his walk without stopping or making any unusual movements and the antelope stood his ground while Mr. Hoag passed within about fifty feet of it. After he had progressed about two hundred yards from the animal, it trotted off toward the hills.

"We were there six hours," said Mr. Bement, "and Mr. Seiberling had ample opportunity to study the desert situation and the nature of the soil, which covered us all plentifully."

To cap things off, they ran out of water in this blistering heat.

Weary beyond words, sleepy, begrimed and thirsty, the little party finally reached Wendover at midnight. Mr. Seiberling's train left at 1:20 a.m. They went into the railroad lunchroom to appease their hunger and there, after a belated dinner, all sat with downcast eyes; Mr. Seiberling evidently deep in thought, the others deeper in dejection. Nobody talked or smoked. Messrs. Hoag and Ostermann thought sorrowfully that now Mr. Seiberling could do nothing but condemn their project as visionary and go back east with a tale of wasted effort, impossible routing and unwarranted hardship.

After a long time Mr. Seiberling swung round on his stool. They braced up. The blow was coming!

"Boys," said the tire man, "I've decided that $75,000 won't do it. Let's call it a hundred thousand, and if Goodyear won't put up the other $25,000 I will."

And then wasn't there rejoicing!

Still, Utah would not accept the money. The rest of 1916 slipped away, and so did 1917. Spry was succeeded as governor by Simon Bamberger. Mr. Seiberling succeeded Mr. Joy as president of the Association. The war increased prices until it seemed the cost of construction would be more than could be covered by the Association's gifts and any funds that might be available from Utah sources.

Then someone revived the idea suggested years before by Warden James J. Tynan of the Colorado State penitentiary and suggested that convict labor be used. If the Association provided the cash, and the state used its already employed engineering staff for survey and supervision work, and convicts were utilized for labor in Johnson Pass, it seemed just possible Mr. Fisher's $25,000 would build the Johnson Pass section and Mr. Seiberling's $100,000 would build the desert crossing; the remainder of the new route could be left for improvement by Tooele County with such state assistance as could be obtained.

The Association laid this plan before Governor Bamberger. The governor expressed himself favorably. He added that he had had his engineers investigate the Wendover route and that not another nickel of state money would be expended on that road with his consent.

The governor visited Mr. Seiberling at his home in Akron late in April, 1917. They reached a complete understanding which Mr. Fisher, who was not present, approved a few days later. This understanding was reduced to contract form and submitted to the Utah State road commission. The attorney-general of Utah, a member of the commission, made a few slight revisions in this draft and the commission then approved it, formally accepting the highway association's proposals on behalf of Utah and binding that state to fulfillment of the contract provisions.

This contract acknowledged that the highway construction involved would "accomplish a work of greatest benefit, not only to the State of Utah but to the United States," formally accepted the Seiberling and Fisher gifts, provided for the renaming of Johnson Pass as Fisher Pass, and bound the state to begin construction not later than September 1 of that year and to complete it by July 1, 1919. In this contract Mr. Seiberling also bound himself to pay to the state the cost of maintaining the desert section for five years, provided this cost did not exceed $5,000 annually.

Mr. Seiberling handed direct to Utah officials checks for $100,000. This money was not handled by the Association in the trust fund manner that other western contributions were. Shortly afterward, Mr. Fisher forwarded the remaining $10,000 of his contribution and this was deposited in trust in a Salt Lake City bank, subject to the order of the State of Utah.

All necessary further survey work was quickly completed, state equipment was mobilized and work begun. It is interesting to note that in surveying this route, the

heat during the daytime caused such mirages the sur-
veyors could not work; they ran their lines at night,
using lanterns for sighting points.

The work in Johnson Pass, or Fisher Pass, as it was
now to be known, was pressed forward to conclusion,
and the Seiberling Section across the desert was brought
to grade.

The State failed to complete the desert section by
July 1, 1919, as agreed but as work was progressing,
and some thousands of dollars of State funds were being
used to further the construction, little was said. Some
seven miles of the section had been finished with gravel
surfacing when, on September 27, 1919, Consul Hoag
discovered that work had been suspended and all the
State's machinery was being taken to the railroad point
at Gold Hill for shipment. He promptly reported this
to Mr. Seiberling.

The report threw consternation into the Lincoln
Highway councils. So confident had the Association
officials been that the road would be completed at an
early date that they had already arranged for its formal
dedication, and had actually purchased gold watches
to be presented to the engineers in charge. Far more
than this, on the strength of Utah's contract to complete the work, they had arranged for thousands of
dollars' worth of construction in Nevada. Mr. Seiberling
in great amazement wrote to Governor Bamberger,
for the cessation of work was a direct violation of the
Association's contract with the State.

Two weeks later, Governor Bamberger replied that
the suspension was due to the necessity of repairing the
road machinery. Some months later, on February 3,

THE "HIGHWAY" ELEVATED BETWEEN JERSEY CITY AND NEWARK, NEW JERSEY

1920, further inquiry elicited the statement from the Governor that the State was willing to continue the construction but lacked funds.

Mr. Seiberling replied with an offer to purchase at par sufficient Utah State bonds to finance completion of the work. No definite answer was ever returned to this offer.

Mr. Joy, who was again President, telegraphed to Governor Bamberger for information but got none.

The Ely people, incensed at what seemed to them discrimination and the result of influence brought to bear by Salt Lake citizens, began planning another boycott. Mr. Seiberling heard of it and urged them not to employ such methods, expressing confidence that Utah would not dishonor her plain contract but would finish the work as agreed. Nevertheless, they arranged the economic pressure and, as before, it shortly brought a request for discussion. This time the meeting was held in Salt Lake City.

B. L. Quayle, now Nevada State Consul, acted as spokesman for the Ely delegation. An agreement was reached providing for immediate improvement of the desert section to the point where it would be easily passable and for its completion as a permanent road as soon as Utah's financial condition permitted. The Salt Lake City leaders promised enactment of a bill for this work at the 1921 legislative session.

No such bill, however, was passed, nor was anything further ever done by the State of Utah toward completion of the Seiberling section.

The directors characterized Utah's failure to finish the road as "rank repudiation of contract which could fairly be stigmatized as dishonorable." Utah officials, however, contended that they had performed everything required by their agreement with the Lincoln Highway Association. The Association endeavored to bring legal action and compel the State to complete its part of the contract but found that under Utah law the State could not be brought into court.

The contract in full is printed as Appendix F of this volume.

While the Association was still hoping that Utah would complete the construction, a new factor entered the entire western situation—federal aid. The law under which this was to be dispensed provided that each state should select not to exceed 7 percent of its highway mileage as a system on which federal funds would be expended as they became available, and a strong effort was begun at once to assure that both Utah and Nevada included the Lincoln Highway in this designation.

Tooele County was willing to tax itself heavily for construction of the Lincoln Highway though unwilling to levy more than a minimum amount for financing the Wendover route. The Association appropriated $15,000 and offered it to Utah to be used, with Tooele County funds, in obtaining the necessary Federal Aid money to complete the route. Utah refused this added money as she had in previous years refused the original offer of $75,000 for the desert crossing.

The Association shifted its efforts to the Federal Bureau of Public Roads, the administrative agency for Federal Aid money. A careful and detailed report was prepared for the bureau's use, urging that if but one road were to be built west from Salt Lake City, the

Lincoln Highway should be that one.

Meanwhile, volunteer maintenance work, largely by one K. C. Davis of Gold Hill, Utah, was keeping the Lincoln Highway in fairly good condition across the desert, and traffic over it was estimated at 40 cars a day. To assist him and make maintenance easier, Colonel Waldon bought and contributed for his use a combination tractor and grader and the Association paid for construction of several small wooden bridges at important points.

Although the Lincoln Highway was then by far the better route, Utah insisted that the Wendover route be designated as its only road west from Salt Lake City to receive Federal Aid. Nevada, which could have forced its neighbor state to designate the Lincoln Highway instead, or go without a connection to the west, fell into line and agreed to make a connection with Utah either at Ibapah on the Lincoln Highway or at Wendover on the more northern route. Nevada's action was a compromise, an effort to satisfy both the people who favored the northern route, which included Reno citizens and Californians from whom she hoped to obtain contributions for highway improvement, and people favoring the Lincoln Highway, on which she had spent a heavy proportion of her highway funds for several years past.

The pressure exerted by California in favor of the northern route was really severe, and in an effort to alleviate it, by educating the public, Mr. Hoag, who had become Field Secretary, induced several California newspapers to send representatives, at their own expense, over the Lincoln Highway to Salt Lake City, returning over the northern route by way of Wendover and down the Humboldt Valley. Mr. Hoag led the party and a representative of the California State Automobile Association accompanied it. In Salt Lake City, the group, with the exception of the field secretary, met with Governor Charles R. Mabey, the new chief executive of Utah. W. D. Rishel, secretary of the Utah State Automobile Association and chief proponent of the Wendover route, accompanied them from Salt Lake City to Wendover and was the target for much chaffing when the party mired down on his favorite road. Afterward he wrote all who had participated a letter of which this is the salient paragraph:

"Any road across the western section of our state is valueless to Utah. We do not need a road over any of the various routes suggested. It will not serve the population of our state whatever. Any road or roads that are built will be built with one purpose alone, and that is to connect up with Nevada and connect up with northern California. We are really helping you out and are not benefiting Utah by the construction of one road or more from here west. We have a good route to California at the present time, by the way of the Zion Park Highway or Arrowhead Trail. From a selfish point of view this route will better serve Utah in the tourist travel. It will give the eastern tourist a chance to see the best sections of our state and it will serve the more populated sections of our state."

Shortly the engineers of the Bureau of Public Roads who had investigated the feasibility of the Wendover Route as a project for Federal Aid reported, recommending its approval. The Association's officials were permitted to see this report, and in reply to it they compiled and submitted to Henry C. Wallace, Secretary of the Department of Agriculture, the most comprehensive study of western road strategy, conditions and economics that was ever prepared.

This was a book of 172 pages, entitled "A Brief for The Lincoln Highway in Utah and Nevada," and containing maps, illustrations, engineering data and a point by point consideration of the routes. It also contained a digest of the negotiations between the State and the Association. In summing up it said:

"We do not feel that the people of Utah will wish to forever rest under the stigma which attaches to having coldly repudiated a state contract. Of no less importance is the question: Does the good faith of a sovereign unit of these United States mean anything? May a state government, hedged about by laws forbidding legal redress—which imply that honor is sufficient guarantee—with impunity ignore such guarantee?"

The book cost nearly $4,000. Mr. Joy footed the bill as a contribution to the Association. The Brief was presented at a hearing in Washington in the office of Secretary Wallace of the Department of Agriculture, on May 14, 1923, which brought together a galaxy of highway notables such as has seldom been assembled.

They included J. Newton Gunn, president of the Lincoln Highway Association, Messrs. Joy, Seiberling, Bement, Hoag, Nevada State Consul Quayle, Senator Oddie of Nevada, George W. Borden, state highway engineer of Nevada; Senator King, Governor Mabey and ex-Governor Spry of Utah, with a delegation including the Utah state highway engineer, road commission chairman and the former attorney-general, Shields; C. C. Cottrell, head of the road bureau of the California State Automobile Association, also accredited as representative of the California State Highway commission; Robert Newton Lynch, head of the San Francisco Chamber of Commerce, Thomas H. MacDonald, Chief of the Bureau of Public Roads, and nearly 100 other persons. Secretary Wallace presided.

The Lincoln Highway Association based its case on the relative merits of the two routes as to service of traffic, cost and time required for completion, precisely as outlined in its brief, copies of which were provided for all present. The State of Utah relied mainly upon the recommendation of the government engineers. The Californians supported the Utah contention. For the people of Nevada, Mr. Quayle argued the necessity of the connection from Salt Lake City to Ely via Ibapah.

No decision was rendered at the time. The Lincoln Highway Association officials conferred with Senator Oddie, who, as former governor of Nevada, was familiar with the conditions, and with Senator King. A call was also made on President Harding. Senator Oddie promised and gave warm support to the Association's argument that the Lincoln Highway should be completed west from Salt Lake City regardless of any other roads.

Secretary Wallace rendered his decision on June 6, approving the designation by Utah of the Wendover route as a Federal Aid highway. As he pointed out in a letter to Mr. Joy, under the law the only issue before him was approval or disapproval of this designation; he could not initiate any other project, or take any action toward establishment of the Lincoln Highway route as a Federal Aid highway because Utah had not designated it as such.

Although Secretary Wallace's statement of the law and the issue was admittedly correct, Mr. Joy appealed to President Harding. The Chief Executive made inquiry of Secretary Wallace, who replied in much the same terms he had already used to Mr. Joy:

"I had the authority to reject the project they (the State of Utah) submitted, but my authority does not extend so far as to permit me to initiate some other project in place of the one rejected."

Then Secretary Wallace wrote to Mr. Joy urging that the Association adopt the northern crossing as part of the Lincoln Highway. The executive committee considered the proposal carefully and at length. Mr. Joy replied:

"We can see neither logic, wisdom nor justice in accepting your suggestion which would now require us to abandon our wise basic principles, to abandon our cooperators in Nevada and Utah, to repudiate our chief supporters, the press and the public. The present administration of the state of Utah has withdrawn Utah's support for the Lincoln Way cordially given by two preceding administrations; it is not impossible that the next administration may again have a different viewpoint.

"The Association is not seeking new possibilities for routes. All possible connections we have long ago investigated and the establishment of the present Lincoln Way and our large investments thereon were made only after not only we, but the two states of Utah and

Nevada, were fully convinced that it was the only right and proper route and the one which would stand as the ultimate one. The present attitude of the state of Utah does not change the existing facts one iota. Utah's present desire to abandon the Lincoln Way does not make the Lincoln Way incorrect. We are not seeking the easiest way but the right way."

Presently construction was begun on the Wendover route.

Still the Lincoln Highway Association kept up the fight. They considered raising private funds and completing the Seiberling section anyway, but abandoned the plan when they could find no means of assuring maintenance after the work was finished.

Meantime, central Nevada was without any connection with Salt Lake City, its natural supply point. The popular demand for action that would open some road to the east was growing heavy.

Nevada had reserved enough mileage from her 7 percent Federal Aid designation to assure federal assistance for the Lincoln Highway from Ely east to the Utah line; now there came a demand that this designation instead be extended to a route—there was no road —from Ely to Wendover to connect with the road into Salt Lake City.

If she yielded to this demand she would be unable to obtain Federal Aid for the Lincoln Highway route later, in case Utah should relent and fulfill her obligations; on the other hand, if she designated the Lincoln Highway and it were not completed, she would be unable to obtain Federal Aid for the Ely-Wendover connection.

She laid her problem before the Lincoln Highway officials.

While it was being considered, the Utah legislature passed a bill, over the protest of Governor Dern and the Utah Highway Commission, and over the protests of various Nevada and California interests, removing the Lincoln Highway in western Utah from the state highway system. The effect of this was to prevent expenditure of any state money on it.

To consider the whole matter, a conference was held in Reno early in March of 1927 and a committee of fifteen appointed to attempt a solution Six members of this committee were from Lincoln Highway counties of Nevada; the remainder came from other sections of the west, including California. Pending report of this body, the Bureau of Public Roads declined to approve any further Federal Aid designations in Nevada.

The committee held several meetings, concluded that nothing could be done for completion of the Lincoln Highway in western Utah, and in September brought in a report which read in part as follows:

."The committee has endeavored to its utmost to find a means that would enable the construction of the Lincoln Highway. The committee believes that the selection of that route would best serve the people of not only Utah and Nevada, but of the whole United States and be a fitting tribute to the Lincoln Highway Association which has done so much to foster the good roads movement all over the country.

"We find conditions such, however, that we see no possibility of having that route constructed for many

years and have, therefore, come to the following conclusion:

"We are of the opinion that the difficulties of every
nature are fewer on the Wendover route than any other
and consequently endorse that route as the one to which
all agencies should immediately lend their support."

Direct personal representations, including some from
high federal officials, were made to the Lincoln Highway Association urging its acceptance and endorsement
of this report, and at a special meeting of the executive
committee, October 20, 1927, the Association gave limited acquiescence to the proposal.

Some weeks later, on December 2, after a very full
discussion, the directors agreed to designate the Ely-
Wendover route, when constructed, as a formal part of
the Lincoln Highway. At the same time, they reaffirmed
their belief that eventually a highway would be constructed along the alignment they had laid down so
many years before and on which they had expended so
much money.

The road from Salt Lake City to Wendover was not
opened for travel until 1925. The government found
the work extremely costly. Several times specifications
were relaxed, in order to permit completion with the
funds available, until they actually were below the
minimum required on Federal Aid projects.

Theirs was the fourth construction for many miles of
this road, which had been built three times by the state
of Utah, or with funds contributed by Salt Lake City
interests. Each time the experience was the same—the
grading work done in one summer was washed away, or
almost washed away, before the next. Spring thaws

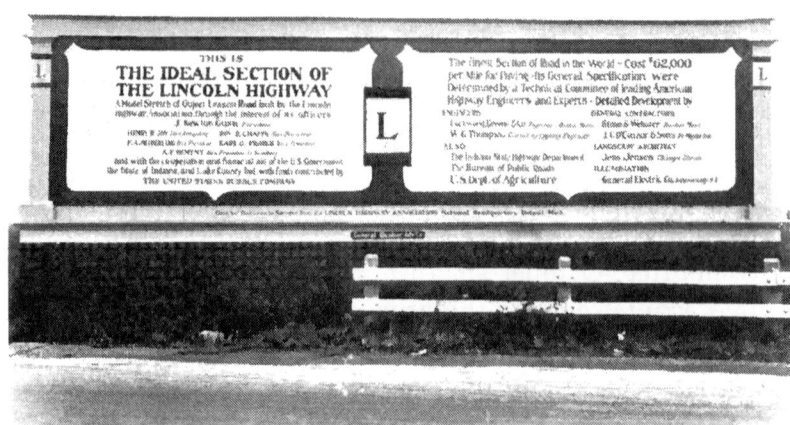

A BILL BOARD ERECTED ADJACENT TO THE "IDEAL SECTION" TO EX-
PLAIN THE EDUCATIONAL LESSONS OF THAT CONSTRUCTION

A FOOTPATH BORDERING THE "IDEAL SECTION"

brought water down into the flat salt beds of the desert bottom and spring winds raised waves of heavy salt water which literally tore and battered away the earth fill.

The Utah constructors never had attempted to build across the section where the salt beds lay thickest; there they had simply let the motorist run over a short wooden bridge from earth fill to firm salt bed and drive ahead. The salt was amply able to sustain an automobile, but if a driver got a little off the road and ran into breaks in the salt he promptly sank. This means of crossing the salt beds was quite feasible even in wet weather, as the water was shallow, except that the salt water, getting into parts of his automobile was likely to ruin it by corrosion. At least one Lincoln Highway car was ruined in this way.

When the government engineers reached this section, they cut through the salt beds at a small distance to one side of the proposed road and brought up earth from beneath the salt to build an elevated grade.

To withstand the battering action of the heavy salt water, however, they were compelled to build the shoulders of this grade with a four-to-one slope, instead of the ordinary one-to-one or one-and-a-half-to-one.

This section of highway is remarkable in that all culverts used are of wood, put together with wooden pins, as the salt water soon eats away metal.

It was gravelled very lightly at the start and has required heavy maintenance ever since.

The connection from Ely to Wendover was finished in gravel construction in 1930 and promptly marked and designated by the Lincoln Highway Association. It has since been improved with a bituminous surfacing.

While for years the Seiberling Section received much of the Association's attention, it was by no means the only, or even the largest, section of western highway construction for which the organization supplied part of the funds.

Nevada and Wyoming, as well as Utah, received this aid, the contributions aggregating $218,267.10. Incidentally, the Lincoln Highway Association was the only highway or trail organization ever to spend money for actual construction of highways.

Mr. Ostermann, in urging construction of the Seiberling Section, characterized the road it would replace as the worst section on the entire highway, but he also said that the Fallon Flats, in western Nevada, were the next worst. On them he proposed that the Association expend the $50,000 donated by the Willys-Overland Company. The directors were determined to administer this money in such a way as to produce the greatest possible amount of construction. At first they offered only a portion of it to Nevada and made the proffer conditional upon state and, where possible, county participation. To show good faith, they placed $20,000 in escrow in Nevada banks.

However, legal difficulties interposed, and it was not for several years, until after a constitutional amendment had been adopted, that Nevada could accept the money.

When it became apparent that Nevada would be unable to use all the Willys-Overland donation at once, the Association placed the other $30,000 of the fund in escrow in Wyoming banks and offered it to that state for improvement of the highway between Medicine Bow and Rock Springs, in Carbon and Sweetwater counties.

Actually, $20,000 of this Willys-Overland gift was expended in Wyoming before any Lincoln Highway money was expended in Nevada. As a result of its offer, the Association had the satisfaction of seeing $139,-000 worth of improvement made on the highway in Sweetwater County and $115,000 in Carbon County, a return of more than twelve for one on its gift.

Meanwhile, it developed that Nevada, once she swung into action, would be able to use considerably more than the $30,000 remaining in the Willys-Overland Fund. Early in 1919, the directors asked several leaders in the automotive industry to talk the matter over with them. At this gathering, Field Secretary Ostermann was called upon to name the points at which he felt outside aid would be needed to bring the entire Lincoln Highway in Nevada up to the standard demanded by the traffic.

One by one the field secretary told them off, with mileages and other data.

"What will it cost to take care of them all?" demanded W. C. Durant, president of the General Motors Corporation.

"A hundred thousand dollars," was the answer.

"All right; we'll take that," snapped the motor magnate. "What's the next order of business?"

And so it came about that instead of Willys-Overland money being used in Nevada, the Association in 1919 offered that state a total of $104,000, including the $100,000 General Motors Trust Fund. Nevada accepted

and used during the ensuing six years $75,296.60. As a
result of this contribution Nevada was able to construct
103.0 miles of road, costing $1,299,732.93.

The construction projects were:

Across the Fallon Flats, in Churchill County.
Across Frenchman's Flat, in Churchill County.
Over Carroll Summit, in Lander and Churchill counties.
Between the Eureka-White Pine County line and the
Devil's Gate, twelve miles west of Eureka.

Later, part of the unexpended balance of the General
Motors donation was used for the establishment of permanent monuments on the highway. Nearly $20,000
was returned to the General Motors Corporation.

Half the unexpended balance in the Willys-Overland
fund was used for marking the eastern portion of the
highway in 1920; the remainder was used in establishing the permanent monuments in 1928.

CHAPTER XIV

EXEMPLIFYING THE COMING HIGHWAY

THE first Federal Aid bill, requiring states to establish highway departments and stimulating a flood of money for construction, completely transformed the chief problem of the Lincoln Highway Association. Whereas in the beginning the organization had concerned itself most with creation of an enlightened sentiment for road building, only six years later the problem had become one of demonstrating proper methods of construction.

The need was urgent, for moneys allocated to road improvement in 1919 were nearly $600,000,000, those in sight for 1920 were almost twice as much and, despite the best of intentions, highway authorities were unavoidably wasting a great proportion of the funds available.

Traffic was increasing by leaps and bounds; motor freight transportation had begun and was proceeding no one knew whither; no one knew what burdens the roads would have to carry even a few years in the future.

No standard existed by which highways could be designed with reasonable assurance that they would stand up until they were paid for.

Obviously, determination of such a standard was an activity in which the leadership of the Lincoln Highway Association would have tremendous value. Its standing with the public, its prestige in engineering and professional circles, its experience in economic, technical and practical aspects of highway construction, together with its freedom from political influence, made it preeminently the organization to undertake this work. Mr. Bement was confident that the Association could find the desired standard but it lacked finances for the necessary study and for construction of an object-lesson section of highway which would make its findings widely known.

To this end, he approached C. B. Seger and J. Newton Gunn, respectively president and vice-president of the United States Rubber Company. Both gentlemen were interested and together they induced the rubber corporation to offer $100,000 for the purpose of determining an ideal standard and constructing an ideal section of highway.

The Lincoln Highway directors unanimously accepted the offer and the rubber company made $10,000 available for preliminary work.

The first step was to gather information. Mr. Bement sent nearly 4,600 questionnaires to public and private engineers concerned with highway construction in all parts of the country and compiled their replies as a basis of discussion. There was agreement on only two things —that the surface of any highway subjected to continuous traffic should be hard, and that the subgrade should be well drained.

Some of the engineers favored concrete, some brick, some bituminous material and one sheet steel. Several argued for macadam or gravel for lanes on which trucks would travel and harder material for passenger traffic lanes. One wanted separate eight-foot lanes for east-

THE STANDARD LINCOLN HIGHWAY STATE LINE MARKER

MR. JOY, ON ONE OF HIS EARLY PILGRIMAGES, CAREFULLY STUDIES PIONEER ROAD SIGNS

THIS IS THE TYPE OF MEMORIAL MONUMENT ERECTED IN OHIO BY THE BROTHERS JOHN AND FRANK HOPLEY

bound and west-bound traffic; another wanted a single four-lane highway forty feet wide; one suggested 18 inch strips of concrete, separated by a 24-inch gravel space, for each of as many traffic lanes as were required. Some suggested curbs and some did not.

To digest the suggestions made and frame basic specifications, the Association called together seventeen of the country's foremost highway engineers and economists. This technical committee met in New York City December 17 and 18, 1920. The technical men honored Mr. Bement by electing him their chairman. The personnel of the committee follows:

T. R. Agg, Prof. Highway Engineering, University of Iowa, Ames, Iowa;

Arthur H. Blanchard, Prof. Highway Engineering, University of Michigan, Ann Arbor, Mich.;

H. Eltinge Breed, Consulting Highway Engineer, New York City;

Edward N. Hines, Chairman Wayne County Highway Commission, Detroit, Mich.;

A. R. Hirst, State Highway Engineer, Madison, Wis.;

Major Mark L. Ireland, Q.M.C.U.S.A. Fort Eustis, Virginia;

Elmer C. Jensen, Chairman, Lincoln Highway Committee American Institute of Architects, Chicago, Ill.;

Jens Jensen, Landscape Architect, Ravinia, Ill.;

Prof. A. N. Johnson, Dean Engineering College University of Maryland, College Park, Md.;

Clifford Older, State Highway Engineer, Springfield, Ill.;

Major J. M. Ritchie, Chief of Operations, Motor Transport Division U.S.A., Washington, D. C.;

A. R. Taylor, late State Highway Commissioner, Co-
   lumbus, Ohio;
W. G. Thompson, late State Highway Engineer,
   Trenton, N. J.;
H. E. Hilts, State Highway Engineer, Harrisburg, Pa.;
Col. Sidney D. Waldon, President Detroit Automobile
   Club, Chairman Detroit Rapid Transit Commis-
   sion, Detroit, Mich.;
L. H. Wright, Director, Indiana State Highway Dept.,
   Indianapolis, Ind.;
F. R. White, State Highway Engineer, Ames, Iowa.

The preliminary questions before the committee were:

1. How far it was wise to look into the future in
anticipating developments of vehicles, speeds and traffic
densities.

2. Whether the cost of certain types of construction
was justified.

3. What difficulties were likely to be presented by
advances in motor freight transportation.

4. Where the law of diminishing returns would begin
to operate as between original cost and cost of maintenance.

It is surprising that even so able a group, faced with
such difficulties, was able to solve most of them in so
brief a meeting. However, it did, and in addition decided on a number of fundamentals, most of which con-
form very closely to present accepted practices. In summary, its decisions were:

A standard right of way 110 feet wide.
An anticipated traffic of 15,000 passenger automobiles
and 5,000 motor trucks. It is interesting to note that
Colonel Waldon dissented from this recommendation,

holding that the traffic of 1940, for which they were planning, would be much heavier than this on any main through trunk route such as the Lincoln Highway— as indeed it already is on a number of highways; though in general the proportion of truck traffic is less than they anticipated.

Average speeds of 35 miles an hour for passenger cars and 10 miles an hour for trucks.

Drainage should be by submerged tile and catch-basins.

The paving material should be concrete, 10 inches thick.

Reinforcing steel should not be considered as adding strength to the concrete surfacing but rather as tying the parts of the slab together in case of cracking.

The section should have earth shoulders.

The section should be lighted.

Adequate permanent maintenance should be provided.

No curves should have a radius of less than 1,000 feet and all curves should be super-elevated for a speed of 35 miles per hour.

A footpath should be provided for pedestrians.

Guard and warning signs should be provided and all embankments protected by guard rails.

Grade crossings should be eliminated.

The specifications should be predicated on maximum loads of 8,000 pounds per wheel.

Comfort stations, park sites and ideal campsites should be provided.

Advertising signs should be prohibited along the right of way.

Vision at intersections should be clear for 500 feet to both sides.

At a second meeting in Chicago on February 12, 1921, the committee recommended that, to afford opportunity for object lesson treatment, a 90-degree curve should be embodied in the Section if possible.

At the same time, it decided unanimously in favor of a concrete pavement 40 feet wide, to accommodate four lanes of traffic, laid in the middle of the right of way, and recommended that provisions be made for widening the right of way in future.

This gave the Association a framework of basic principles upon which definite specifications could be erected for any particular piece of highway it chose to develop as an Ideal Section. The site was the next consideration.

Many communities sought to have the section placed within or near their borders. One city, near but not directly on the highway, offered to contribute $50,000 toward construction of the section if the Association would locate it near that municipality.

However, the Association had ideas of its own. Secretary Bement and Field Secretary Ostermann had studied the matter exhaustively. The choice narrowed down to four possible locations and the directors authorized a detailed inquiry into the advantages offered by each.

It was essential that whatever site they chose should be a part of the Lincoln Highway and eligible for federal aid to insure permanent maintenance.

The second requirement was availability of a wide right of way.

The third was convenience. The Association wanted the section built at some central location where it would carry a maximum of traffic and have the greatest object lesson value.

Fourth, it desired that the location chosen should not present unusual difficulties, because it wanted the road, when built, to be just such a highway as might be constructed anywhere.

It also desired that whatever location was chosen should afford the greatest possible contrast between the existing roads and the projected ideal construction.

On these principles, and after an exhaustive study of other suggested locations, the directors decided on a portion of the Lincoln Highway in Lake County, Indiana, commencing at Dyer on the Illinois-Indiana boundary, 33 miles south of Chicago, and extending easterly to the town of Schererville.

With the money available, the basic specifications outlined and the site chosen, the Association retained Lockwood, Greene & Co., engineers, to draft the final specifications and W. G. Thompson, former State Highway Engineer of New Jersey, as consulting engineer. Jens Jensen, of Ravinia, Illinois, an outstanding landscape architect, was entrusted with the landscaping of the right of way.

Agreements were made with the state of Indiana and with Lake County for their cooperation and the U. S. Rubber Company generously increased its gift to $110,-000; that is, $100,000 for actual construction in addition to the money already given for preliminary expenses.

The state pledged $33,000 and the county $25,000; these sums representing what they would have to spend on an ordinary 20-foot concrete road on the chosen location. Later $20,000 of Federal Aid money became available, but the state insisted that most of this be used as a credit toward its contribution. The Association fi-

nanced the purchase of additional ground for the widening of the existing narrow right of way.

The Association placed actual construction in the
hands of Stone & Webster, noted engineers and contractors. It was desired that an Indiana firm receive the
contract for the work. So in cooperation with C. Gray,
state highway engineer of Indiana, bids were obtained
from three Indiana contractors of high repute, covering the entire construction of the section except landscaping and lighting.

Then on July 7, 1922, Stone & Webster took the contract for the work at the price bid by the lowest of these
bidders, J. C. O'Connor & Sons of Fort Wayne, and on
July 8, sublet the work to that company at the same
figure.

Work proceeded rapidly and actual paving was completed in December, 1922. The landscaping, installation
of the lighting equipment, and some smaller items were
completed the following year.

The Ideal Section of the Lincoln Highway is 7,161.7
feet, almost exactly a mile and a third, in length. Its 40-
foot concrete surfacing is 10 inches thick and contains
80 pounds of reinforcing steel per 100 square feet. Ex-
pansion joints are spaced 75 feet apart and are filled
with bituminous compound. There is one longitudinal
joint in the center of the slab This slab was designed to
withstand stresses five and one-half times as great as the
maximum wheel-load and impact expected.

Owing to the type of drainage employed, there are no
ditches at the edges of the paving. Shoulders are broad
and firm. The section includes one bridge and one culvert.

The Ideal Section was the first piece of highway of its type ever built. True, in and near some cities there had been other sections of 40-foot concrete road, but they lacked one or more of the other features which made the Ideal Section outstanding; that is, the wide shoulders, the wide right of way, the fine drainage, the underground wiring arrangements, the landscaping, or the lighting. Nowhere, on any rural highway in the world, was anything comparable to it. It has served as a model for construction of several sections since.

The methods used in construction were as highly advanced as was the section itself. Extreme care was taken to assure a smooth surface, to prevent vibration and shocks to the slab from vehicles. Heavy side forms were used, on which was operated a mechanical tamper and finisher. This was followed by several beltings with a heavy canvas belt, and these in turn followed by floating with long-handled broadfaced floats. Work was continued until a 10-foot straight edge laid on the surface revealed no departure from true grade greater than $\frac{1}{8}$ inch.

In order that the subgrade might not be disturbed after finishing, handling of materials on it was prohibited. An industrial railroad of 24-inch gauge was installed to haul materials from a nearby railroad siding to the working point. Trains were made up of twelve cars, each carrying two tip-over batch boxes. Each batch box had separate compartments for cement, sand and gravel. Gasoline locomotives of six tons' weight hauled the trains.

Sand and gravel arriving at the siding were unloaded by locomotive cranes and dumped into loading bins straddling the tracks of the industrial railroad. Materials were fed from these bins to the batch boxes, then a trainload of material hauled out to the mixer at the workplace. The mixer was mounted on caterpillar treads and moved as necessary.

Batch boxes were handled from cars to a mixer-hopper by a boom on the mixer. The method insured great accuracy and uniformity in the mix and avoided waste of materials.

After pouring and smoothing, the concrete was allowed to set for a time, then covered with wet straw and cured wet for two weeks. No traffic was allowed on the slab for 30 days after pouring.

The Ideal Section of the Lincoln Highway was one of the first, if not the first, urban sections of highway in the world to be lighted.

The General Electric Company contributed the equipment, which was of the Novalux type, then new but since familiar on a number of highways and bridges. The lights were carried on artistic and graceful concrete standards of original design, 35 feet in height, 250 feet apart and alternated on opposite sides of the road. All wiring was carried underground in conduits. Such was the arrangement of reflectors that the entire road was lighted, very little light was wasted on illuminating areas outside the paved section, and there was no glare. This lighting system was designed and installed under direction of W. D'Arcy Ryan, chief illuminating engineer of the General Electric Company.

Motorists were surprised and delighted to find they could drive this section at night, without headlamps on their cars, as fast and as safely as in full daylight, having full view of the road and of approaching cars at all times.

Through arrangements with the Northern Indiana Light & Power Co., the lighting on the section was maintained in nightly operation for some time after its opening but later this was discontinued, neither the state, the county nor the towns at the ends of the section being willing to assume the expense involved.

Under Mr. Jensen's direction, the right of way on both sides of the paving was beautifully landscaped. The Association had arranged with the telegraph and telephone companies to move their poles and wires back to the edge of the widened right of way, out of sight behind the numerous trees native to the section, and the landscape engineer made the most of his opportunity. His artistic ability was especially evident in the laying out of the footpath. This curves through the trees on the south side of the road so that the pedestrian, though only a few feet from the concrete, has constantly in view a delightful vista of timber and shrubbery.

In fact, so beautiful is this section that, in 1926, the directors decided there was no more fitting or suitable place on the entire highway for the erection of the memorial to Mr. Ostermann, for which his friends had contributed funds some time before. In a tree-banked nook, looking out on the highway, a simple and beautiful memorial bench was erected. This bench, designed by Mr. Jensen to harmonize with the surroundings, carries a simple bronze plaque with memorial inscription.

After completion of the section, much attention was given to the development of an ideal campsite. The Association acquired a seventeen-acre area of rolling, wooded land, adjacent to the Ideal Section, for this purpose and Mr. Gunn, who had been elected president, interested Edsel B. Ford in financing its development. Mr. Ford donated $5,000 for preliminary expenses, but by the time designs had been completed and other arrangements made, the trend of motorists away from open-air camping rendered the plan unnecessary.

The cost of the Ideal Section, including lighting installation, landscaping and other items pertaining to the road proper, but excluding expenses in connection with the campsite, was $166,655.16. It is significant of the difficulty and engineering importance of the project that the engineering expenses connected with it amounted to $18,620, exclusive of supervision.

One hundred twenty thousands dollars of this sum came from the United State Rubber Company—$10,000 for preliminary expenses, the $100,000 originally donated for construction, and $10,000 additional given when more funds were needed. In addition the rubber company afterward donated $10,000 for disseminating information concerning the section and the standards of highway construction which it exemplified.

Long before this had been given, in fact before the selection of the site had been commenced, the Association was deep in educational work dealing with the project.

The plan had many features which rendered it attractive to editors. One article which appeared in *Collier's* asked the public for suggestions as to what should be incorporated in the section and where it should be located. This evoked much interest.

The technical press gave the project many pages. The Bureau of Public Roads issued special bulletins about it, as Thomas H. MacDonald, chief of that bureau, desired to give wide circulation to the engineering data developed by the Association. Engineers read papers about it before meetings of technical societies both in this country and abroad. Numbers of engineers visited the site during construction or inspected the section after its completion, as did highway authorities by the score. Sunday supplements and magazine sections of newspapers gave it pages upon pages of space.

All through the various stages of planning, design and construction, Mr. Bement kept up a running fire of newspaper and magazine articles, dealing with each phase as it came up. The lighting particularly came in for a great deal of attention, as it was of so novel a nature, and the idea of lighting a rural highway was so unusual and spectacular, that well nigh everyone was interested.

There never was a road in whose behalf the spotlights of propaganda were burned so brightly.

The result of this twin effort in construction and education was exactly what the Association had anticipated. The standards developed have been adopted for the highest types of construction everywhere.

CHAPTER XV

DEVELOPMENTS IN HIGHWAY MARKING

THE Lincoln Highway was marked four separate times, each time on a better system. Except the old National Pike, it is the only American highway throughout whose length monuments of permanent character have been placed.

In the beginning, marking was necessary to link into one recognizable highway the many roads comprising the route. It was necessary as a means of establishing the highway physically, so that selfish interests could not divert it from its proper alignment. It was important as a service to the traveller and as a means of stimulating travel.

"Any motorist would prefer to follow a thoroughly marked route where he is at all times sure of his direction and the correctness of his course," says the 1916 report of the Association, "even if that route be in some instances inferior to other parallelling routes not so marked.

"A mediocre road, perfectly marked, is preferable to a perfect road on which the traveller is always in doubt as to his direction."

Standish L. Mitchell, secretary of the Automobile Club of Southern California, said in 1917:

"We invariably find that signing increases travel and following the increase of travel comes the betterment of the road."

TYPE OF SIGN ERECTED IN 1920, REACHING FROM NEW YORK TO OMAHA, MARKED THE HIGHWAY UNTIL THE ENTIRE STRETCH FROM NEW YORK TO SAN FRANCISCO WAS REMARKED BY THE CONCRETE MARKERS, ERECTED IN 1927

ONE OF THE THREE THOUSAND CONCRETE MONUMENTS ERECTED IN 1927 TO PERPETUATE THE HIGHWAY DEDICATED TO THE MEMORY OF ABRAHAM LINCOLN

He added that travel over one road increased 1,000 percent within two years after it had been marked.

Mr. Mitchell's organization was the only one in America that had done any extensive road-signing. Outside the territory covered by it the traveler was left to find his way with only the most primitive aid, as is instanced by the following incident related by Colonel Sidney D. Waldon:

"I was travelling out of Albuquerque," he said, "trying to get west on the southern route and I went to Colonel D. K. B. Sellers, a noted road enthusiast, for directions. Said he: 'Follow this mountain range 80 miles south to a stick in the fork of the road with a paper tied at the top. Take the ruts that lead off to the right.'"

At first, due to lack of money, the Association had to content itself with such marking as could be arranged through volunteers: but Secretary Pardington went to considerable trouble, as did Field Secretary Ostermann, to encourage and stimulate the work. Proper marking of the highway through his jurisdiction was made an important objective of each consul as soon as he was appointed.

The first markings were very simple, merely red, white and blue bands painted on a pole, rock or other convenient object. Later the Association designed its official insignia, consisting of red, white and blue rectangles with the letter L and the words Lincoln Highway in blue above and below the letter. The Association provided stencils of the official design and directions as to colors so that the work might be uniform; but the actual painting of the markers was done by good roads enthusiasts, automobile clubs, civic bodies and public-spirited individuals.

Communities along the route were quick to recognize the erection of Lincoln Highway markers as not only a worthy object for public-spirited endeavor but a powerful means of increasing their own revenue, because the markers stimulated traffic. The mayor of Bucyrus, Ohio, personally headed a party which marked the highway across Crawford County.

The city of Pittsburgh appropriated public money for marking the route through that municipality. Aurora, Illinois; Fort Wayne, Indiana, and some other cities had the insignia, worked out in art glass, made a part of their street electroliers on the route of the Lincoln Highway.

Several rural communities marked the highway with painted metal signs. Clinton County, Iowa, alone used 300 of them. Railroads voluntarily put Lincoln Highway markers on their bridges. Marking was done so enthusiastically, in fact, that Secretary Pardington said the road looked like "an elongated barber pole."

This first marking was not very effective. In some states, difficulties developed because the markers were not placed by the constituted road authorities. Telephone and telegraph companies objected to the placing of metal signs on their poles.

The painted signs wore out quickly, partly because they were placed by inexperienced painters and partly because unsuitable paints were used.

Pending official signing operations of its own, the Association in 1915 accepted an offer of the Sparks-Withington Company to place Lincoln Highway markers on the same posts with advertising signs which the company had already obtained state permission to erect along the route from Fort Wayne to San Francisco. Harry and Clifford Sparks, sons of the senior member of that firm, placed about 4,000 of these markers.

They were enamelled on steel and were distinct from the advertising signs. Had the Association been willing to accept any of several proposals to commercialize its markers, it could have had as elaborate a system as it desired, but all such offers were rejected.

Something official, uniform and controlled directly by the Association itself was needed, but the cost appeared too great to be undertaken until 1916. Then the organization obtained formal permission from the authorities in each state, as well as the various utilities companies whose poles were used, and undertook its first systematic marking. The actual work was done by a crew of painters who placed uniform, legible insignia wherever markers were needed.

The Association was helped very materially in this work by donations. The Willys-Overland Company supplied it with two Willys-Overland cars, specially arranged to carry supplies and equipment, and decorated in the Lincoln Highway colors. The Patton Sun-Proof Paint Company donated the paint. The Wooster Brush Company of Wooster, Ohio, donated the brushes. Cities, towns and villages along the road gave $5 to $75 each toward the work. The Association footed the remainder of the cost.

Starting from Jersey City in June, 1916, the painters worked west to the Nebraska-Wyoming line before weather conditions forced suspension for that year. They placed more than 8,000 markers, an average of five to each mile.

Meanwhile the California State Automobile Association, located in San Francisco, had marked the highway across that state; now negotiations were opened with a view to having the Automobile Club of Southern California mark the feeder road from Los Angeles to Ely, and the Lincoln Highway from Ely on east to Salt Lake City.

This part of the highway had already been marked by State Consul Hoag, as had the highway from Ely west to Eureka, Nevada, after a novel but effective method of his own. Mr. Hoag's practice was to obtain donations of worn-out boiler tubes from the smelter company at Ely, have them cut in four-foot lengths and pointed in the smelter's blacksmith shop, and then drive them into the ground beside the road. Painted in Lincoln Highway colors, they made a very acceptable marker.

Not least of their advantages was that they were permanent. Cattle, seeking something on which to scratch their necks, broke down the ordinary types of marker on high wooden posts, but never learned to get down on their knees to lean against Mr. Hoag's boiler tubes.

The negotiations with the automobile clubs failed to bear fruit for several years. Then, almost at the same time, the Automobile Club of Southern California agreed to do the marking from Los Angeles through to Ely and the California State Automobile Association undertook to extend its markings from the western Nevada border to Ely. Soon it was learned that the latter organization, too, wanted to sign the road on into Salt Lake City.

Both clubs' road signing crews were on the work at

the same time. When the southern club's men arrived in Ely they heard of the San Francisco organization's desire and, to retain the honor of the signing for their own club, hurried on that same night to place signs as far east as Schellbourne and completed the work into Salt Lake City within two days. Through arrangements subsequently completed between the southern club and the Lincoln Highway Association, the club marked the highway between Salt Lake City and Omaha, the Association bearing a part of the expense.

This gave the highway a complete system of permanent, enamelled steel signs from the Missouri River to San Francisco and also a completely signed connecting road into Los Angeles. The Association turned attention toward establishment of equally good markers from Omaha east.

There was no question about what should be done; the difficulty was the usual one—where could the money be found? John N. Willys helped solve it by permitting $15,000 to be withdrawn from the Willys-Overland trust fund and used for marking; the rest of the answer came from the towns and cities along the road between Trenton, New Jersey, and Omaha, which raised about $5,000, and from the Autocar Company of Ardmore, Pennsylvania, which donated two specially painted trucks for the use of the signing crews and paid their operating cost. This donation was arranged through the good offices of David S. Ludlum, a founder of the Association and president of the Autocar Company. Through the influence of W. C. Durant, the General Motors Corporation donated a Chevrolet car for the use of the crew foreman. With this assistance handsome enamelled steel markers bearing the official insignia were placed all along the road from Omaha east to Trenton. On the 60 mile stretch of the highway from Trenton to New York, state authorities set up special concrete posts and placed the signs at state expense.

The Association used eight foot redwood posts, donated by the California Redwood Association, for setting the markers in rural sections; in the business centers of cities the signs were placed on the poles of public utility companies, lighting standards and similar structures. Two signs were placed at each crossroad. Where there were no crossroads, signs were set beside the highways at least once in each mile. A total of 2,700 signs were erected in the 1,353 miles covered.

The work was completed in 1921 and the Association thought it had at last provided a marking which would remain serviceable for a long period. Yet at the end of 1924 Field Secretary Hoag reported:

"A check made in October showed 1,574 new poles and 2,157 signs needed to replace those destroyed or seriously damaged. Wooden poles rot, are handy for prying cars out of the ditch, and readily gravitate to the farmers' chicken yards. Enamelled steel signs are ideal targets; they react with a distinctive ping from either a bullet or a stone and are themselves badly scarred in the encounter. Once chipped, the metal rusts, destroying the remainder of the sign."

The mortality in signs, he said, was especially noticeable in sections where there was much hunting and in the vicinities of country schools. What was needed, he suggested, was concrete monuments bearing the Association's insignia in some non-fading, permanent material. However, even these would require a certain amount of maintenance, such as cutting of undergrowth to keep them visible at all times, replacement when damaged, and so forth. In any event, the Association had no money to erect them.

About this time an article which Mr. Hoag had written for the Lincoln Highway Forum began to bear fruit.

Driving through Noble County, Indiana, one day he had noticed that the mortality of signs was especially high and had evolved the idea that as this destruction was apparently the work of boys, maintenance of highway markers might well be made one of the objectives of the Boy Scouts. The article he wrote about the vandalism concluded with the words:

"What Noble County needs is more Boy Scouts."

This article, reprinted in the daily press, caught the attention of E. S. Martin, chief of the editorial board of the Boy Scout organization. Mr. Martin wrote to Mr. Hoag saying the scouts were anxious to participate in such public works and Mr. Hoag called on him to discuss the matter. Mr. Martin proposed that the Association finance a Boy Scout motor trip across the country to organize troops at country schools; in return the Boy Scouts would take over the setting and maintenance of permanent concrete monuments. They would, he said, dig the holes for the monuments, obtain volunteer local transportation to convey them to the point of erection and, to make the work spectacular and dramatic, set them all, from New York to San Francisco, in one day."

"Now you're talking, men!" said Mr. Hoag. "Now you've got a story!"

It seemed that at last a real solution had been found.

President Gunn of the highway Association thought so. Mr. Hoag thought so. Theodore Roosevelt, Jr., Barron Collier and other scout advisers and officials gave their approval.

Everything, in fact, seemed favorable except that to begin operations the Lincoln Highway Association must first design and manufacture and transport the monuments. They could find no method of financing this work and so the project languished, in spite of Secretary Hoag's recommendations, until the end of 1927. Then the Association, about to discontinue major activities, found $66,600 on hand, the unexpended portions of the Willys-Overland and General Motors trust funds. Roy D. Chapin suggested that this balance be drawn on to finance the permanent marking.

The directors approved, the donors of the money consented, and the Scout organization was enthusiastic.

Mr. Hoag helped the Scout chiefs obtain the donation of a truck from the Reo Motor Car Company to transport the boys and their equipment over the highway, and Mr. Chapin provided a Hudson car for the use of the scout officials in charge.

Designs for a monument were called for and over 200 submitted. None, however, was suitable. Eventually Secretary Hoag, Vice-President Bement and Colonel Waldon worked out the design which was used. This called for a concrete post, reinforced with four steel bars, bearing the Lincoln Highway insignia and a bronze medallion on the front and an arrow giving directional information on the side.

Means of casting the insignia in colored concrete were developed through cooperation with the Portland Cement Association, considerable research being done to discover pigments which would not be subject to quick fading. The colors finally used are as nearly permanent as could be found. The medallions carry a head of Lincoln in low relief, with the wording: "This Highway Dedicated to Abraham Lincoln."

A special form of arrow was designed by Colonel Waldon for easy visibility. The forms of these arrows and their location on the monuments are such that the motorist can recognize their indications without actually seeing the entire arrow. The monuments were seven feet in length, with an octagonal bottom section and square head, ending in a pyramid. They were manufactured in Detroit and shipped in carloads to strategic points for distribution.

As it was evident that monuments of this type could not be placed in large cities, arrangements were made to use in those locations the same sort of enamelled metal signs which had been put up in 1920, taking care, however, that they were affixed to metal instead of wooden standards. The chosen standards were all measured and the signs manufactured to fit.

While the monuments were being manufactured, arrangements for placing them were worked out in complete detail by Mr. Hoag and the Scout executives. As soon as it was announced that the Scouts were to undertake this activity, scores of letters and telegrams approving the project and promising cooperation flowed back to the Scout headquarters in New York. Even troops in towns miles off the highway volunteered to help.

Mr. Hoag went to New York and started a rapid drive across the country specifying locations at which the monuments should be placed and selecting the proper type for each location. With him went a Scout official, to make sure local Scout chiefs understood the plan.

Then Mr. Hoag prepared specific instructions covering each section of the highway, telling exactly where each monument was to be set, what type to set at that location, how far from the edge of the road to place it, how deep to dig the hole, and everything else needful to assure, accuracy in the work. Nothing was left to chance; nothing was omitted that would help all concerned to understand exactly what part each was to play. Even the shipments of monuments to each Scout organization were correctly assorted so that each group would have exactly those needed on its section.

To insure precision, the highly efficient organization of Lincoln Highway consuls was called into cooperation with the Scouts and also, in some places, American Legion posts participated.

Official state permission was obtained for setting the monuments and in many states the highway departments provided transportation for them from railroad depot to point of erection. Some also provided transportation for the Scouts who did the actual work.

The Scout caravan started across the country in midsummer and spent more than six weeks on the road. Numerous stops were made. Everything possible was done to arouse interest and insure that not only would the monuments be properly set but that they would be cared for after setting.

Shortly after the caravan had completed its trip, the Scouts dug the holes and, on September 1, 1928, on official word from their headquarters, placed the monuments.

Several of the troops set monuments on more than 100 miles of the highway on that one day. The troop at Fallon, Nevada, covered the greatest section of the route, from Austin almost to Sparks, a total of approximately 175 miles.

The only serious gap left was in Illinois, where a misunderstanding prevented the Association from obtaining immediate official permission. Later, special legislative authority was granted to the Association and the monuments were set by the Scouts.

Approximately 3,000 monuments were used. Two were placed at each important crossroad, one at each minor crossing, and others at sufficient intervals to assure the motorist that he was travelling the right road. They were set at the outer edge of the right of way to avoid interference with highway markers placed by the states.

Their permanence, and the value placed on them by the state highway departments, is evidenced by the fact that six years after they were set, less than 5 percent of them had been destroyed or removed. As a rule, when improvements were made, the highway department's maintenance men took up the monuments to keep them from being damaged by construction equipment, then replaced them in proper relation to the newly constructed road. In California, for example, all those from Auburn and Placerville east to the Nevada state line, a distance of nearly 100 miles, were taken up by the State Highway Department and stored while the roads were being reconstructed. The Highway Department promised to reset them when the new work was completed.

The setting of these monuments was a tremendous task and amazingly well done, especially as practically all of it was done in one day, by volunteer workers, and several thousands of persons participated in the work. That it succeeded at all, that it was nct absolutely swamped by endless confusion and misunderstanding, is a tribute to the organization work of Secreary Hoag and the Scout officials.

In this manner was fulfilled the Association's objective, the establishment of an appropriate and lasting memorial to Abraham Lincoln.

At different times, a number of feeder roads were marked by interests unconnected with the Association. The most important of these, of course, was the Ely-Los Angeles road. Others were the Chicago connections from Chicago Heights and Geneva.

The insignia designated by the Association for the marking of feeder roads was a rectangle of the same size and shape as the official highway marker, but the bands of red, white and red, instead of red, white and blue, and with the legend "To the Lincoln Highway" instead of the official "Lincoln Highway." However, this was not always used.

Away back in the early days, before women had received the suffrage and prior to the establishment of this special marker, the Chicago Heights connection was marked by the Political Equality League. The markers were of the saffron official suffrage color so there is at least a suspicion the leaguers were agitating as much for suffrage as for the Lincoln Highway.

The Chicago Heights feeder road is the only highway ever marked by name through the city of Chicago. The markers are especially noticeable in Lincoln Park, where they were the only markers of any kind until the erection of the U. S. highway numbers.

In addition to highway markers, many memorials have been placed along the Lincoln Highway, some by persons or organizations not connected with the Association.

John L. Hopley, late state consul for Ohio, and his brother Frank who succeeded him in the post, placed a number of very handsome brick monuments, each inset with an enamelled metal Lincoln Highway markers, at important points in Ohio. John Hopley, an attorney, fought through to the Supreme Court, and won, a case against a citizen who objected to establishment of one such marker in front of his property. Most of these markers are dedicated to men who gave special service to the cause of highway improvement, particularly the Lincoln Highway; among them Messrs. Joy, Bement, Seiberling and Ostermann.

John Hopley's own memory is perpetuated in a special roadside memorial in Bucyrus, his home city, erected by his friends.

Another noteworthy memorial was erected beside the road at Clinton, Iowa, by the citizens of that community, to the memory of W. F. Coan, Iowa's first state consul.

Outstanding among these monuments were those erected to the memory of Lincoln. J. E. Moss, of Scranton, Iowa, who though past 80 years of age was active as a Lincoln Highway consul, erected two handsome ones, bearing busts of the Emancipator, at either end of an important curve on the route. Mansfield, Ohio, erected a very notable one near the highway in Lincoln Park, the site where Lincoln first was mentioned for the presidency.

Mr. and Mrs. E. B. Wilson erected on the court house grounds in Jefferson, Iowa, the finest of them all, a standing figure of Lincoln in bronze, mounted on a granite pedestal with bronze tablet.

The Grand Army of the Republic and the Association cooperated in efforts to have bronze plaques, carrying Lincoln's Gettysburg address, erected at important points on the highway. The Association contemplated for a time erection of handsome granite markers at points where the highway crossed state boundary lines, each to carry one of these plaques and a similar one bearing the Lincoln Highway Proclamation. However, funds were not available and this project was abandoned. Instead of the granite monuments, artistic cast metal markers, mounted on special standards, were provided. These do not carry the proclamation but merely inform the traveller of the establishment of the boundary at that point. They were contributed, complete and ready for erection, by the Lebanon Machine Company of Lebanon, New Hampshire.

Motorists always placed great reliance upon the Lincoln Highway markers. They were ready to follow the red, white and blue signs unquestioningly, even when some other road was recommended as better. To assure control of its insignia, the Association copyrighted its official tricolored marker and its name, and also registered them in each state through which the highway passed. By establishing this legal foundation it was able to restrain persons seeking to make capital out of the highway's reputation. Once a whiskey merchant blandly labelled his product with the name and insignia of the Association until compelled to discontinue the practice.

On the other hand, the Association licensed several reputable firms to use the insignia on their products for a regular royalty. Among these were the Motometer Co., the Wayne Tank & Pump Co., the manufacturers of Crane's chocolates and a cigar maker.

Those who made unauthorized use of the insignia of the highway were not the only ones who sought to turn its prestige to their personal account. One gentleman planned to transport a large part of the Panama-Pacific Exposition over it, giving exhibitions in tents "similar, only bigger than Barnum & Bailey's."

Several women, and not a few men, sought Lincoln Highway support or sponsorship for organizations of various nature. Odd characters of all kinds addressed it on projects of amazing peculiarity. One of the few who actually did what he said he would do was "DeMers, the Hobo Magician," who walked the entire length of the highway, pushing a handcart.

Poor DeMers! When Secretary Bement declined to pay him to report on road conditions, he said he would do so anyway. And he did. His laboriously written long-hand reports are punctuated with tales of his handcart's breakdowns in the desert, his labors at remote ranches while awaiting spare parts, and his apprehensions regarding the "whiffenpoofs" and "rabicoyotes" which the fun-loving westerners told him roamed the country in ravenous search of just such tempting morsels as itinerant magicians encumbered with handcarts. Perhaps it is some consolation to him that the road today is vastly different from the one he travelled and that—who knows? —it may be that his reports played some part in its improvement.

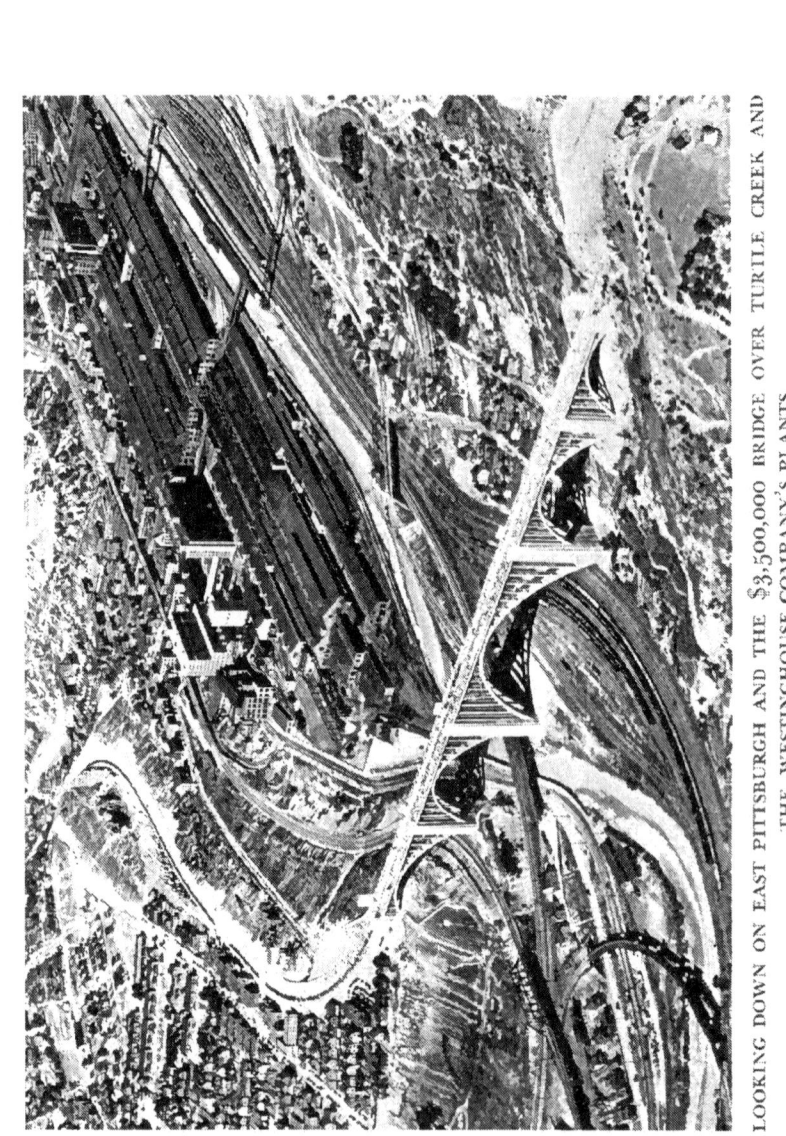

LOOKING DOWN ON EAST PITTSBURGH AND THE $3,500,000 BRIDGE OVER TURTLE CREEK AND THE WESTINGHOUSE COMPANY'S PLANTS

UNTIL THIS BRIDGE WAS CONSTRUCTED, TURTLE CREEK PRESENTED THE MOST CONGESTED BOTTLE NECK ON THE LINCOLN HIGHWAY. THE OLD HIGHWAY SKIRTED THE ENTIRE PLANT OF THE WESTINGHOUSE ELECTRIC AND MANUFACTURING COMPANY IN THE BOTTOM OF THE VALLEY. THE NEW ROUTE SAVES ITS USERS $1,500,000.00 A YEAR. THIS WORK IS DIRECTLY ATTRIBUTABLE TO JOHN S. FISHER, LINCOLN HIGHWAY STATE CONSUL AND GOVERNOR OF PENNSYLVANIA DURING THE PERIOD OF CONSTRUCTION

CHAPTER XVI

STRUGGLES FOR IMPROVEMENT

THE example set by the Lincoln Highway in its successive efforts to establish and maintain an adequate road-marking system stimulated wide-spread marking by other highway organizations, especially those engaged in promoting traffic along particular routes.

As the prime object of these promotional organizations was the building up of a profitable volume of tourist traffic rather than the construction of roads, they laid out routes mainly over existing highways, many of them frequently utilizing the same trunk road for long distances. One 1,500 mile stretch in the west was included in no less than fifteen of these named trails and highways, each sponsored by different promoters.

As the first thing these organizations did was to erect signs, it was not uncommon for a single pole to carry insignia of as many as a dozen routes, a condition highly confusing to the traveller.

Clarification of the situation was needed but difficult. Few states had adequate signing systems of their own and the markers placed by the highway bodies served a real need. Still, there were too many of them.

To remove the signs of some organizations and allow those of others to stand was not as unfair as it seems, because their relative values varied, but political considerations made this difficult. Removal of them all and substitution of some general system of marking which would merely identify the roads was the obvious solution. A system of numbers, instead of names, offered several advantages, chief of which was simplicity. Under it most roads would need but a single marker at each place where signs were required.

Naturally the highway bodies opposed removal of their markers, because any road-marking system which did not include the names of their routes would destroy the identity of the trails and highways and thereby bring the sponsoring organizations' careers to an end. However, no one had a better idea to offer and, in May of 1925, a joint meeting of state and federal highways officials in Washington approved the plan, voting for selection of a system of interstate roads to be designated as "U. S. Highways" and uniformly marked with numbers.

Some of the highway organizations battled vigorously against this idea; others, including the Lincoln Highway, sought to have their markers retained even though the numbers were placed as well. They gained support in many important quarters. The New York *Times* editorially said they were making "an effort to save the souls of the National Highways." It continued:

"The traveller may shed tears as he drives the Lincoln Highway or dream dreams as he speeds over the Jefferson Highway, but how can he get a 'kick' out of 46 or 55 or 33 or 21! The roads of America would still be on paper if the pleas that were made ten years or more ago had been made in behalf of a numerical code."

But the reasons for removal were too logical, and the difficulties of discriminating among the associations were too great. The numbers were set up and the names removed.

As the Lincoln Highway permanent monuments, however, were memorials to Lincoln and not road signs, the numbering system did not affect them. These monuments, coupled with the public interest aroused by fourteen years of uninterrupted educational work, are all that has enabled the Lincoln Highway to survive in the public mind. The monuments are not conspicuous and many a motorist passes over the road without realizing that he is actually travelling the great memorial to Abraham Lincoln.

"The government," wrote Mr. Joy to Secretary Hoag, "so far as has been within its power, has obliterated the Lincoln Highway from the memory of man, in spite of the fact that the press of the United States gave to the work very many hundreds of thousands of dollars worth of publicity to aid in putting this wonderful main arterial highway to the memory of Abraham Lincoln into actual service for the people of America.

"My thought is to send to the president, his cabinet and all members of Congress a copy of the Lincoln Highway Proclamation and along with it a printed slip saying:

" 'The Lincoln Highway, a memorial to the martyred Lincoln, now known by the grace of God and the authority of the Government of the United States as Federal Route 1, Federal Route 30, Federal Route 30N, Federal Route 30S, Federal Route 530, Federal Route 40 and Federal Route 50.' "

The thing that enabled the numbering system to gain a foothold was that it was applied at first under federal auspices and only to roads on which Federal Aid money had been expended, or which were eligible for such expenditure. All the U. S. Highways fell into this classification. Extension of the numbering system to state roads was a natural sequence.

Under the hit-or-miss Federal Aid provided by the early legislation, this condition could not have arisen, but the Association itself had labored long and earnestly for expenditure of Federal Aid money on a connected system of roads. Once this system was in a fair way of creation, establishment of U. S. Highways was a foregone conclusion. From that it was but a step to the plan of numbering them. To have named them, even for the country's greatest men, would have precipitated never-ending bickerings in behalf of favorite sons.

Thus, by its altruistic efforts in behalf of a sensible form of federal aid, the Lincoln Highway Association virtually destroyed the only basis on which it could arouse the public interest necessary to carry on its work. Fortunately, this did not come about until the two vital objectives for which it was formed had been assured— a connected system of national highways and permanent maintenance for them. That, in attaining these ends, the Lincoln Highway had practically lost its identity was regrettable but incidental. Federal Aid cost the country, in some part at least, a wonderful memorial to one of its greatest Presidents; in compensation it brought the first real system of roads the United States had ever known.

Federal highway construction, or grants of federal money to states for road-building purposes, is not a new thing in American history. When the Revolutionary War was over and the Congress began to consider means for developing the country, an improved highway to the west was one of the first plans adopted.

This highway, the old National Road or Cumberland Pike, was projected to Jefferson City, Missouri, by way of St. Louis, but its actual construction never proceeded beyond a point near Vandalia, Illinois.

The engineering of the Cumberland Pike was extremely good and bridges of very high quality for that day were built to carry it over the streams it crossed. The road construction itself, which was all of stone in the eastern part, was a remarkable enterprise for a people so limited in resources. Seven million dollars, an enormous sum for that time, had been spent on it over a period of 27 years before Congress, in 1833, abandoned it and turned attention from roadbuilding to canals.

With this as a precedent, legislators, alert to the growing sentiment for improved roads, several times sought federal appropriations for highway construction. In 1906 William Randolph Hearst, then a member of Congress, introduced a bill appropriating $50,000,000 to build roads.

What might be termed the parent of the federal aid bill eventually adopted was introduced by Representative D. W. Shackelford in 1911, and reintroduced in the same, or nearly the same form, by him or others, at every succeeding session of Congress until the Bankhead-Shackelford bill was enacted in 1916.

With this measure, the federal government returned to the policy abandoned eighty-three years before, when it suspended appropriations for the Old National Road, and again began to spend money to develop highway transportation.

The bill embodied one of two general theories of
government aid for highway building—it gave money to
the states for construction of roads. It was opposed by
many who feared construction done in such a manner
would lack continuity; that instead of creating a system
of roads, such legislation would merely permit the building of a large number of isolated pieces of road.

The other theory was that there should be a nation-
wide highway system constructed either wholly or partially at federal expense and without much regard to
service of isolated communities, the system being intended to connect main sections of the country. This
was the sort of federal aid the Lincoln Highway Association favored.

Representative W. P. Borland in a letter to the Association distinguished between the two plans as follows:

"The question is whether federal aid shall be used
as a means to secure a better system of roads; or shall
the federal money be frittered away in small payments
scattered into every congressional district and every road
district of the United States. The people are in favor
of the former and the politicians of the latter plan. The
latter plan is known as the pork barrel plan of federal
appropriation, by which everybody gets something and
nobody gets anything worth having."

The Association's interest in federal aid preceded its
formal organization. As early as March, 1913, Will Dobyns wrote to Mr. Borland about it, and in private correspondence only a little later Mr. Fisher said that if
the Ocean-to-Ocean Highway promoters could but raise
their projected $10,000,000 they would be able to obtain

at least $20,000,000 worth of aid from the government.

In 1914 Mr. Joy suggested that in the public land states the federal government should assume the burden of building the highway across such lands, thus promulgating a principle which was recognized in the Federal Highway Act of 1921.

The Association was not too well pleased with the 1916 bill; nevertheless, this measure made funds available for road construction. Secretary Bement promptly took action to assure expenditure of a portion of the new money on the Lincoln Highway. He sent letters to highway officials in states traversed by the Lincoln Highway and he wrote David F. Houston, Secretary of Agriculture, in whose department was vested the handling of the $75,000,000 aid appropriation, a very cogent and powerful letter, arguing for systematic rather than sporadic highway work. Secretary Houston gave considerable encouragement to this view, and Carl Fisher, to whom Mr. Bement forwarded the correspondence, commented:

"Thank God, Mr. Houston sees the light of day on a continuous backbone of good roads instead of the tapeworm variety."

Generally this view came to prevail and as precedent slowly grew regarding administration of federal aid funds, it came to be recognized that federal money should not be spent upon roads lacking connections with either centers of traffic or important travel routes.

In furtherance of this objective, Senator Charles H. Townsend of Michigan offered a bill to create a federal highway commission and to build through interstate roads with federal money. The Association supported it energetically but vainly. It failed chiefly because it invaded state rights. Had this bill been passed, the Association's objectives would have been assured. As it was, improvement of the Lincoln Highway across the eastern states appeared certain but a difficult situation prevailed in the west.

Western states had three main difficulties. They had long distances across which roads were urgently needed; they had little wealth and in each of them were tremendous areas of federally-owned public lands which were immune to taxation. They were barely able to build roads that would suffice for their own light local traffic. They were absolutely unable to finance through highways for the service of the thousands of automobiles crossing their borders from eastern, mid-western and southern states. For these reasons it seemed but fair that other states should help construct the western roads their citizens would use.

This, of course, meant federal assistance. Recalling the principle enunciated by President Joy in 1914, that roads across the federal domain should be financed with federal funds, Lincoln Highway officials initiated a campaign to gain this vital assistance for the west.

The fight was a strenuous one but the Lincoln Highway men were not alone in it. Logan Waller Page, chief of the Office of Public Roads; Thomas H. MacDonald, present chief of the Bureau of Public Roads; many western senators, western representatives, the officials of several western states, and numerous civic and automotive bodies gave support. So did a number of legislators from eastern communities who had grasped the larger idea of national highways as contrasted with state roads. The struggle continued more than two years but, late in 1921, senate and house conferees agreed upon a much-amended draft and, on November 9, President Harding made it a law by affixing his signature.

Under the old federal aid act, each state received one dollar of federal aid for each dollar of its own money it expended on a road project approved by the government. The new bill materially increased the amount of federal funds western states could obtain for each state dollar expended and made it possible for them to construct the highways so sorely needed by through traffic.

Important as this was, the measure contained another provision which the Association considered of even greater value. It required the states to limit to 7 percent of their total road mileage the routes on which federal funds should be expended.

Not in verbiage, but in results, it was exactly the federal highway legislation which the Association had always sought.

The earlier federal aid measures had been of tremendous value through stimulating highway construction in many different sections of all the states, thus educating the people to the worth of improved roads and creating sentiment favorable to highway betterment generally; this new act compelled concentration of all federal money and a great share of the state highway funds on important routes; and it compelled coordination of main routes into one cohesive interstate system. The two together were the real reason the founders of the Lincoln Highway Association could look back in 1927 and say "Our work is done."

The chief importance of federal aid was not the money

it made available, for soon the states were spending ten times as much, but the educational effects it exerted and the inducements it offered states to adopt sound highway measures. Chief of these measures was establishment of central highway authorities to have charge of state highways and to expend the federal moneys. The Lincoln Highway Association had long sought this centralization of authority.

Again, federal aid, either directly or by stimulation of highway appropriations, put money in the hands of competent state authorities so that highways could be relocated on better alignments, and through routes could be shortened by eliminating jogs and diversions.

It was chiefly by these means that the Lincoln Highway was shortened nearly 300 miles in only twenty years. True, there were some reroutings, one of which, in Utah, moved the highway some 50 miles from its former location; and another of which, in Ohio, moved it about 15 miles northward over a considerable section; also construction of bridges across the Sacramento and Missouri rivers permitted savings aggregating 60 miles; but most of this reduction of distance came from refinements, minor realignments, replacing of sharp corners with long, gentle curves, moving the road from arbitrary and right-angled section lines to the easy sweep of a railroad right of way, and reconstruction on better gradients in rough country.

The Lincoln Highway was rerouted all the way across New Jersey, reducing the distance nearly 10 percent and the driving time in even greater proportion, yet at no point is the present route as much as 3 miles from the old one.

Similar minor improvements are continuing. On the section between Sacramento and Oakland, California, where the distance was originally 126 miles and has now been reduced to 94.2 miles, realignments already scheduled will eventually reduce the distance by an additional 20 miles!

Lincoln Highway officials will be much surprised if, by the end of 1936, the removal of two "kinks" in Iowa, with a further shortening of 12 miles, has not been completed.

Moreover, it is the minor improvements which make greatest additions to motoring comfort and safety. The struggle for improvement began as soon as the Lincoln Highway had been proclaimed, for the association's leaders knew their road was far from perfect, just as surely as they knew it was the best available or possible at the time. As the Appeal to Patriots hinted in rather broad terms, politics had to be considered if there was to be any road at all; political pressure had to be given some sway in minor matters in order that the major end—a through, connected, transcontinental road—could become a reality. To obtain construction of any road whatever across some counties, the Lincoln Highway officials were compelled to accept construction on alignments which they knew, and which later experience has proved, were not the best.

Gradually, as road knowledge developed and as funds became available these have been eliminated until only one or two of the glaring instances remain. Soon, state highway officials say, even these will go.

The mileage involved in all the politically-compelled mis-alignments, however, was never very great. The major realignments have almost all been changes from the only roads which existed when the Association was formed to better roads constructed since, often at its inspiration and frequently with its active support.

In 1913 the Association had to accept whatever roads were available; later it could in a considerable measure procure construction of roads where needed.

One of the first sections where the Association's influence brought about a reduction of route mileage was in Wyoming, where highway officials were induced to change many miles of the route from the wavering alignment of the old wagon trail days to a more direct line, with better grades, largely on abandoned Union Pacific railroad rights of way.

Later, a great deal of even this improved alignment was abandoned in favor of a still better one which eliminated 12 of the State's 13 grade crossings on the Lincoln Highway: the sole remaining grade crossing is now in the town of Evanston, protected by gates and signals. The elimination of these dangerous crossings had been urged by the Association for years, but its arguments fell on deaf ears until L. E. Laird was appointed State Highway Superintendent. Mr. Laird had lost a son in a grade crossing accident and therefore appreciated the hazards such crossings offered.

In justice to other Wyoming officials, however, it must be remembered that funds for road improvement were very limited and that this third and present alignment for the Lincoln Highway could not be developed until federal aid had become available and also until the Association had donated $20,000.

The longest realignment ever brought about by the

Association was in Nebraska. In that state practically all roads followed section lines. As Nature had omitted to arrange the topography on any such orderly system, it followed that the traveller was constantly going around two sides of a triangle to get to his destination. Thus the Lincoln Highway motorist zigzagged his way for hundreds of miles across the state.

The answer was obvious—change the Lincoln Highway to follow the line laid down by the Union Pacific railroad, which Lincoln had encouraged to build the most direct possible route westward from the Missouri River back in the days when section lines were non-existent and Nebraska's most numerous inhabitants were Indians and buffaloes. Some Nebraska counties already had leaseholds from the railroad permitting them to run county roads along the unoccupied portions of the right of way and there seemed no sound reason why others should not make similar leases and rebuild their roads on improved routings. No reason, that is, except lack of money: when federal aid became a reality it appeared that even this difficulty had been removed.

However, federal officials would not consent to expenditure of government funds on such projects because the leaseholds all contained cancellation clauses. They held strictly to the principle that no federal funds should be expended on a road whose site was not certain to remain in state possession at least until the road was worn out.

The Lincoln Highway Association as an organization and several of its officials personally appealed to the authorities to have this ruling modified but without avail. As the Union Pacific had, and presumably still has, the idea of eventually building a four-track main line, it was reluctant to make long-term leases which could not be cancelled. The situation remained deadlocked until 1922, when Mr. Hoag, then field secretary, had a large and luminous idea.

Collecting figures from the railroad's own sources as to the numbers of accidents occurring at grade crossings on its lines, he went to Omaha. J. D. Whitmore, the enthusiastic Lincoln Highway consul at Valley, Nebraska, was the livestock agent for the Union Pacific and quite friendly with Carl R. Gray, its president. Together they called on President Gray. At that meeting the field secretary laid the Union Pacific's own figures before the railroad man. Said he in effect:

"Mr. Gray, if there were no grade crossings on your lines these would not happen, and the railroad would be saved a great deal of expense and trouble. The reason we have grade crossings is that we have such a wretched alignment here in Nebraska, with the roads following the section lines and zigzagging across the railroad. Now, if the Union Pacific will make the sort of lease that will give the counties, or the State, possession of a strip of your roadbed, which you do not use and are not getting anything out of anyway, for a term as long as a good highway will last, I think we can arrange so the Lincoln Highway will be laid out on that strip and these grade crossings eliminated."

Like most great ideas, this one could be compressed into few words. Mr. Gray saw the point at once. With his permission Mr. Hoag went into the land offices of the Union Pacific and picked out, section by section, the locations the leases should cover. He went farther than the Lincoln Highway Association had ever contemplated

THE OLD ROAD OVER THE SUMMIT OF THE SIERRA NEVADA MOUNTAINS FOLLOWED THE SOUTH WALL OF THE PASS. IT HAD GRADES RUNNING FROM 12 TO 18 PER CENT., FINALLY PASSING UNDER THE SOUTHERN PACIFIC SNOWSHEDS

THE ROAD COMPLETED IN 1933 SHOWS CHANGES IN LOCATION WHICH KEEP MORE TO THE NORTH WALL OF THE PASS AND HAS NO GRADE IN EXCESS OF $6\frac{1}{2}$ DEGREES

going and laid out virtually an ideal alignment from Omaha to the Wyoming line. Except for diversions to get through towns, this followed the Union Pacific all but a few miles of the way.

Mr. Gray was as good as his word. Through cooperation with State Engineer R. L. Cochran, arrangements were made for the counties to relinquish their short-term revocable grants and for the State to receive new non-cancellable 50-year leases instead. The Department of Agriculture accepted these long leases as guaranties of State possession of the roadbed for the necessary period, federal aid was forthcoming, and the excellent Lincoln Highway across Nebraska is the result.

This cooperation of the railroad in establishing a new alignment for the Lincoln Highway, the most heavily travelled through road in the state, reduced the number of its Nebraska grade crossings from 29 to 5. Four of these remaining ones were later eliminated by joint action of state and railroad in constructing viaducts; so that there is now, in the whole length of the Lincoln Highway in the Cornhusker state, but one grade crossing. This is at the main station in the city of North Platte, a division point, where all trains stop, and is protected by safety devices. What this improvement has meant to the motorist in reduction of mileage, higher speeds, freedom from annoyance and removal of accident hazard it is impossible to estimate.

A much longer struggle involving a much shorter section of the road, was that to realign the route between Pittsburgh, Pennsylvania, and East Liverpool, Ohio. It began soon after the Association was organized and did not end until 1929, although success had been assured several years earlier.

The old route west out of Pittsburgh followed the fogbound north bank of the Ohio River on a roundabout and winding alignment. From Pittsburgh nearly to the Ohio line it ran through a succession of boroughs so closely joined that no motorist could tell where one ended and the next began. Sometimes it ran over streets so narrow there was not room for both automobiles and streetcars. This was not the result of choice, but of necessity, for there was no other road.

As all these small communities had their own regulations for control of motor traffic and not a few of them looked to the transient motorist to reduce current deficiencies in the local treasury, the traveller was subjected to a succession of petty annoyances which no amount of protest from the Association could end.

There was a good route possible south of the river but it had never been improved. It involved crossing a corner of West Virginia and that state was ready enough to do its share but there was no sense in West Virginia's building an isolated and unconnected section unless Pennsylvania would do its part and build from Pittsburgh to the West Virginia line. And Pennsylvania wouldn't, though many Pittsburghers, the whole of East Liverpool and the Association all campaigned for the improvement.

Chiefly, the reason for refusal was that the piece of road the Lincoln Highway Association wanted built was not included in the state highway system. Secondarily, some of the boroughs north of the river did not want to lose the Lincoln Highway and the money its traffic brought. Midland, Pennsylvania, sought retention of the old alignment because it foresaw improvement of the Lincoln Highway and it wanted to be on a good road. The question became controversial, then acrimonious, then so bitter that it was difficult to keep desirable men in the post of Lincoln Highway consul in Pittsburgh. Boycotts were talked of here and there.

In 1923 Field Secretary Hoag induced E. K. Morse, an outstanding engineer, to accept the Pittsburgh consulate. Mr. Morse was enthusiastically in favor of the realignment, which some of his predecessors had not been. His prestige and the public confidence he enjoyed quickly put a different complexion on affairs. Through his influence, backed by the Association and the various local supporters of the change, the Pennsylvania legislature declared the road from Pittsburgh to the West Virginia line a state highway and it was designated for federal aid.

West Virginia was delighted to have even a small section of the route within its borders and its governor enthusiastically promised:

"We'll make this stretch the best on the Lincoln Highway."

Active construction was completed in 1928 in both states. The new alignment shortened the distance 13 miles, from 52.4 to 39.4. Though it added a toll bridge crossing of the Ohio River, which was against the Association's policy, the shortening justified it. Even greater improvement, however, was made in the reduction of driving time. An hour and fifteen minutes is ample for the new routing; three hours were frequently required for the old. Moreover, the new route was above the fogs and therefore much safer, while its scenic advantages and the freedom from petty police annoyances were much appreciated by the motorists.

Besides these and other efforts for major realignments, the Association always worked for routings which would keep the highway out of the business sections of cities or even take it outside municipalities altogether. Much of the improvement in route efficiency attained in New Jersey was the result of this avoidance of congested areas. This policy is now recognized as correct by all highway officials as well as most of the local interests which formerly opposed it.

However, in the earlier days, it was necessary to enter cities and towns and even to go down to and through their business centers, because the existing roads ran that way and there were no by-passes. Civic authorities —still less merchants avid for trade—did not then make the distinction between "passing traffic" and "buying traffic" which is now so generally recognized even in small communities. Everyone felt that the more people a community could induce to pass the doors of its shops and stores, the more money would be left with its business concerns. Nowadays, alert merchants know that the mere passerby is a positive detriment to business and they cooperate fully with the efforts of highway authorities to route through traffic away from the center of town, where it will not interfere with customers coming in to buy, and whom the downtown streets are chiefly intended to serve.

The Association at first sought improvement of the surface of the Lincoln Highway as a matter of keeping the highway passable under adverse weather conditions, which frequently paralyzed traffic over unsurfaced roads.

Later, as the economics of highways came to be more fully understood, it advocated hard surfacing as a matter of economy—economy in maintenance and economy in operation. This idea bore early fruit except in Iowa.

The Iowa difficulty developed first during the efforts to establish Seedling Miles; Secretary Pardington found that under Iowa laws the counties, which had full control of all road matters, were powerless to finance hard-surfaced highways even when the cement needed for the work was donated. The irony of this situation was that the Iowans were spending enough in maintenance to have amortized the cost of hard-surfaced construction in a few years. President Joy said they were practically rebuilding their dirt roads every summer and having them washed out by storms or torn up by struggling traffic every winter.

The Lincoln Highway leader, who had more than once spent 24 hours in an Iowa mudhole, or waited days in a country hotel for the roads to dry so he could continue a motor trip, raised a furore in 1916 by means of an article in *Collier's* which scathingly indicted Iowa road conditions. One paragraph said:

"Today, in the rich state of Iowa, not a wheel turns outside the paved streets of her cities during or for sometime after the frequent heavy rains. Every farm is isolated. Social intercourse ceases. School attendance is impossible. Transportation is at a standstill. Millions of dollars worth of wheeled vehicles become, for the time being, worthless."

Mark Sullivan, editor of *Collier's,* quoted this paragraph editorially and invited the people of Iowa to write

to him about it. Numbers of them did so, fervently and
often abusively, but the essential truth of the assertion
was conceded by many. Among these was no less an authority than E. T. Meredith, editor of Iowa's famous
agricultural paper *Successful Farming,* a man who later
became secretary of agriculture. Mr. Meredith wrote to
Mr. Sullivan:

"Your editorial regarding Iowa roads is more or less
merited and will do considerable good. If it raises a
storm of protest from the newspapers over the State,
that in itself will get Iowa to thinking about her roads
to an extent that no one has been able to get her to think
for some time."

Actually, the affair attained no immediate result, because Iowa legislatures, one after another, stubbornly
declined to amend the laws, even after federal aid had
been extended for highways. Not for many years did the
Tall Corn State decide to accept its full share of the
federal aid money and establish an administrative department having direct charge of highways instead of
merely ministerial duties. Iowa authorities consulted
the Lincoln Highway Association regarding the establishment of this department and the organization rendered considerable assistance in the framing of the new
highway statute.

Tradition has it that this change of heart on the part
of the Iowa legislators resulted from a rather odd cause.

The annual football classic of the State, always played
on Thanksgiving day, had aroused unusual interest.
Farmers by the thousands motored over the excellent dirt
roads to see the contest. During the game a heavy rain-

storm broke, turning the roads to mud, and hundreds of cars mired down and were abandoned by the wayside. Many of them could not be extricated for several days. Literally thousands of Thanksgiving dinners went uneaten because the diners were unable to get home.

The next spring the legislature reversed all previous stands and authorized the counties to issue bonds for road-building, the bonds to be retired from the proceeds of a state gasoline tax. Fred R. White, the state highway engineer and an ardent advocate of improved highways, had long foreseen what should be done. As soon as the counties made funds available, he had plans ready for work to commence. Before midsummer the counties had voted bond issues totalling high into the millions and the Marshalltown, Iowa, *Times-Republican* joyfully announced: "Iowa has gone hog-wild on paving."

While a good many years were required to get Iowa started, she more than made up for lost time and today has one of the best road systems in the west.

In addition to its campaigns for road improvement, the Association also carried on activities calculated to increase highway safety. One of these was based on an idea advanced by Mr. Hoag, which has since become very popular and is now the law in many states; namely, that pedestrians using the highways should walk on the left side of the road, so as to face the traffic. This movement was taken up by school authorities nationally and presumably will shortly become the rule throughout the nation.

Another was in behalf of the use of yellow as a standard color for tail-lights on automobiles, reserving red for stop-lights and danger signals generally. This was considered very seriously by the National Conference on Street and Highway Safety. This idea also was originated 'by Mr. Hoag. Both were the result of his experience in driving the highway, which he covered from ocean to ocean several times each year.

The current practice of painting white the trees, bridgeheads and similar danger-spots along the road for easy visibility was recommended by the Association as early as 1916.

The Association also initiated moves for elimination of grade crossings, as has been indicated, and cooperated in erecting warning signs at dangerous spots.

THIS BEARS A BRONZE PLAQUE READING "THE END OF THE LINCOLN HIGHWAY." IT IS SITUATED IN LINCOLN PARK, SAN FRANCISCO

CHAPTER XVII

THE VISION MADE REAL

ALTHOUGH the good roads movement in the United States was more than twenty years old when the Lincoln Highway was proclaimed, its progress had been slight ' and unimpressive. Fathered by far-sighted men who appreciated the need for improved roads, this movement was nursed through its earlier years by uninfluential local good roads clubs. Later the automobile clubs took over its direction. The aims of these organizations were many and diverse, their projects were all of minor nature; they could neither obtain wide support nor focus what they obtained on any single project.

The general movement languished, nor were various national road improvement organizations able to stimulate it because they fell into the easy error of propounding grandiose schemes, with bait for many sections of the country, instead of concentrating their efforts toward achievement of a single goal.

The Lincoln Highway Association provided this movement with direction by propounding a single, definite, concrete objective. This Association enlisted support from all quarters because its project was truly national in character, free from any taint of personal gain and carried the name of the Great Liberator.

"Here was a project," wrote President Joy a few years later, "big enough to stir the imagination and force the attention of a hitherto apathetic public. The name Lincoln Highway came to mind as most appropriate for this great national utility, which each year would be used and enjoyed by millions of people. The choice of the name gave a touch of sentiment and human appeal to a project hard as nails in its practical possibilities."

Having provided a definite national objective on which the country's growing enthusiasm for road-building could concentrate, the Lincoln Highway Association held that objective steadily before the public eye until sentiment for highway improvement throughout the country had reached an effective pitch.

This association was not the creator of the good roads movement; it was the factor that made the movement effective. While it had ever before it the goal of a national system of through connected highways, it believed the best way to attain this was to show the nation what good highways really meant by constructing one as an object lesson; therefore, it preached early and late on the text "Build a road across America first."

It believed results would be obtained most quickly by appealing directly to the people rather than to the custodians of governmental purses; its watchword was "Education" and its policy was tangible demonstration.

There is no phase of subsequent American highway progress which does not bear evidence of the success of this policy.

By offering to the nation, and particularly to those already interested in highway development, a specific project on which their energies and enthusiasms could be concentrated, it procured the establishment of a through, main, connected route on which there had been expended, up to the end of 1933, more than $150,000,-

ooo. This sum was once advocated by another organization as an adequate federal appropriation for building a national system of roads.

As this road, from the first, was so much better than other roads in the United States, it served as an object lesson to stimulate highway improvement all over the country, and even in foreign countries. The first evidence of this stimulation was in the establishment of feeder and connecting routes as a means of bringing profitable tourist traffic to particular communities. The second evidence was the establishment of other routes, some competing for traffic which otherwise would follow the Lincoln Highway and some seeking to develop new traffic.

The 1915 report of the Association says:

"Dozens of organizations have sprung into being in the past year with the avowed intention of working toward the construction of similar connecting improved roads, either parallelling or connecting with the Lincoln Highway. The organization of these many associations and their work has indicated that the original idea back of the Lincoln Highway, and one of the strongest which actuated its founders, viz., that the Lincoln Highway's establishment would be merely the first step in a nation-wide system of connecting improved roads, was a sound and wise one."

By 1919 there were 27 major and many minor highway promotion organizations, and this number increased very rapidly; even as late as 1925, after adoption of the numbering system had doomed them, there were 98 different highway organizations promoting 257 named routes!

A great many of these organizations patterned themselves upon the Lincoln Highway Association, which body also gave advice and information freely to all who sought it. Outstanding assistance was given the Dixie Highway, fathered, like the Lincoln Way, by Carl G. Fisher.

As each of these route and traffic promotion organizations was supported by its own special group of adherents, it was but natural that their local interests or local patriotism should engender rivalries. After all, there was only a certain amount of traffic available and each of them wanted more than its share. More than once the Lincoln Highway was attacked because it would not join in some other movement for highway development on a more general, and less effective, basis.

These rivalries not only failed to disturb the Association's leaders but were actually welcomed as evidences of growing interest in highway development.

The Lincoln Highway Association was organized not merely to build *a* road nor to establish the supremacy of one route over another; it was formed to educate the people of the country to the value of highways and to stimulate them to the building of *many* roads.

The second effect of the Association's policy was improvement not only of the Lincoln Highway, but of highways generally. And here began that amazing cycle which has brought about America's present highway system, in starting which the Lincoln Highway Association can truthfully be said to have played a major part. Each improvement stimulated traffic; motorists making up that traffic compared improved with unimproved sections of highway and demanded more improvements, which brought more traffic, and so on, down to the present and seemingly on to an indefinite date in the future. It is almost axiomatic with highway engineers that improvements stimulate traffic so rapidly they cannot build roads fast enough to keep abreast of its demands.

The Association sought and obtained improvements of many kinds, but the phase of this work most apparent to the motorist was hard surfacing.

The effects of each seedling mile of concrete road continued for many years after its construction, for it set aglow a new blaze of road spirit which was never satisfied with anything but high-type hard-surfaced road. Actually, the Seedling Miles created demand for improvement among classes which ordinary road propaganda simply left untouched.

Farmers saw their teams trotting with the traces slack when they drove over the Seedlings; they saw the same horses, hauling the same wagon, straining to move the same load at a walk over unimproved roads. Urban dwellers saw traffic proceeding over the concrete roadway regardless of wet weather, at the same time when they knew, a mile down the road, men and horses were floundering wearily through mud. The natural result was a desire for the better highway.

The amount of concrete road construction resulting from these Seedling Mile projects is beyond computation. In Indiana, within one year after construction of a Seedling Mile, sixty-seven additional miles of concrete road had been financed and some were under construction.

Seedling Miles spread the idea of concrete highways throughout the United States so that, when federal aid was made available the public mind was well prepared to expend the then large sums necessary for this economical type of construction.

Had the public not been prepared for such expenditures, had it not been educated, by Lincoln Highway example and Lincoln Highway publicity, to the value of concrete construction, it is quite possible that not even the federal influence for these highly improved roads would have been effective; and the whole national program of hard-surfaced construction which has been in progress since 1916 would have been delayed many years.

Indeed, had it not been for the educational effort of the Lincoln Highway Association and the object lesson effect of the Lincoln Highway itself, federal aid would have been only a vision, instead of a reality, at the end of 1916. The whole system of federal aid, including the state highway departments which the states were compelled to set up in order to benefit from federal appropriations, the 7 percent requirement which ended highway pork barrels, and even the present Bureau of Public Roads itself, are all natural sequences of Lincoln Highway influences.

It is the principle of concentration on main routes for which the Association labored so many years that today enables the motorist travelling anywhere in the United States to make all or nearly all of his journey over highly improved roads.

All this Association's activities had, and will continue to have, a very marked influence in stimulating traffic. This was, however, chiefly passenger car traffic until 1917, when railroad congestion thrust a tremendous truck movement onto the highways. Trucks manufactured in the Detroit area were loaded with munitions and driven to the Atlantic seaboard for shipment to France.

This government movement of trucks and munitions was feasible because there were roads available; it was economical because the Lincoln Highway afforded a reasonably direct improved road.

When the plan was first discussed, Roy D. Chapin, chairman of the highway transportation committee of the Council of National Defense, suggested to Secretary Bement that the Association might be of some assistance to the government. Mr. Bement went to Washington and he and Mr. Chapin offered the government the services of the Association without reservation. The offer was promptly accepted and Field Secretary Ostermann, who probably knew the roads of the east better than any other man, presently piloted engineers of the army and the Bureau of Public Roads over various routes from the truck production centers to the Atlantic Coast. Most of the way there was but once choice—the Lincoln Highway—but in Ohio a number of routes were driven in search of the best connection between Detroit and the Lincoln Way.

Meanwhile Mr. Bement broadcast to Lincoln Highway consuls and to state officials an appeal to put the highway into the best possible condition so truck movements could be stabilized and the railroads correspondingly relieved. This was in accord with a declaration of the Council of National Defense.

The states responded promptly. Soon the convoys were flowing, as one Pennsylvania newspaper put it, "like a stream" over the Lincoln Highway through the Pennsylvania mountains. When winter came and snow blocked the highway, the Pennsylvanians attacked it with motorized plows and cumbersome horse-drawn drags; when these failed to keep the roads clear, officials went back into the mountains, sometimes as much as 20 miles from the highway, and mobilized farm labor to work in the bitter cold that the never-ending flow of trucks and munitions might not be stemmed.

From December 16, 1917, to February 15, 1918, the men at work clearing the Pennsylvania highways for the trucks to pass numbered from 1,200 to 1,500; several times the high schools at Chambersburg and Beaver Falls were closed so the schoolboys, too, might be employed in this work.

Under the hammering of the heavy trucks the roads in several sections, constructed without thought that they would ever be used for such traffic, broke up and the Pennsylvania state council of defense set aside half a million dollars for repairs.

What tonnage of freight, what thousands of motor trucks, were moved in this way to aid in the winning of the war cannot now be stated. Certainly it was very large; enough, when the war ended, to have taught the country two lessons—that motor transportation of freight was feasible, and that highways, as then constructed, were utterly inadequate.

The reaction of the first lesson was an immediate and heavy increase in the use of trucks for ordinary commercial transport; that of the second was a move to keep trucks off roads constructed, as many persons believed, for the use of farm traffic and passenger automobiles. The answer of the Association to protests against this use of the highways was that traffic should not be adjusted to the capacity of the highways but highways be improved to meet the requirements of traffic. This principle is universally recognized today.

Thus the activities of the Association in laying out a through route, in procuring its improvement, and in promoting its use by the government truck trains, resulted in recognition of three principles of utmost value in American highway development.

Just as this intensive utilization of a portion of the Lincoln Highway was an object lesson in the use of motor trucks, so the constant improvements of the whole highway served as object lessons in their turn to bring about better alignments; to demonstrate the economies of grade separations; to stimulate hard surfacing, broadening, drainage, signing and other betterments on roads throughout the United States. In fact, the foundation of the American highway system as it exists today was laid by the Lincoln Highway. Let us examine the structure reared on this foundation and its effects on American life.

Because the Lincoln Highway Association worked long and hard for establishment of a national viewpoint on highways, as opposed to a local or political viewpoint, development has been concentrated on roads of greatest utility and untold millions of dollars saved the country. There are in the United States 3,009,066 miles of roads, of which some 325,000 are state highways. Only about 150,000 miles have a high-type surface, such as concrete, bituminous concrete or brick. These 150,000 miles carry so great a proportion of the traffic that the average motorist hardly realizes there are any other roads. He has become so accustomed to paved roads that he regards gravelled roads as difficult driving and unsurfaced roads, even in good weather, as approaching impassability.

If, instead of being concentrated on main roads, these 150,000 miles of paving had been divided equally among all geographic sub-divisions of the country, less than one-tenth of the traffic would be able to move over paved highways. If the money these paved roads cost had been spent for improving every mile of road in the United States, practically none of today's traffic would be able to move over paved roads. In fact, under such conditions, present traffic could never have developed.

That it has been possible, even after so many years of effort and careful expenditure of so many hundreds of millions of dollars, to improve so small a portion of the country's highways, is an outstanding vindication of the Lincoln Highway's policy of concentration. That such a relatively small mileage of paved roads serves so large a proportion of the people is a further vindication.

Development of improved highways has increased the value of rural property by tremendous amounts. In 1914, little more than a year after founding of the Lincoln Highway Association, Commissioner of Highways James R. Marker of Ohio estimated the increase in value of farms fronting on the highway in that state at from $10 to $50 per acre. The increase in value of properties near but not on the highway is more speculative but surely enormous. The aggregate increase in property values as a result of highway construction since that time reaches into the realm of imagination.

Construction of hotels, garages, filling stations, tourist camps and similar accommodations for those using the roads likewise reaches into enormous figures.

Tremendous savings in cost of transportation have been made possible by improved roads as opposed to unimproved roads, and by the use of the motor trucks which good roads made feasible instead of the horse-drawn transportation of mud-road days.

Studies made by several government bureaus indicate the cost of horse-drawn transportation over dirt roads is slightly more than 33 cents a ton mile and the cost of transportation by medium-sized motor truck, such as a farmer might own, over mixed concrete, gravel and dirt roads as 6.96 cents a ton mile. The saving in favor of motor truck transportation is 26.04 cents a ton mile, approximately 78 percent.

Taking the total American farm crop at 244,000,000 tons, and assuming that 15 percent of this never leaves the farm and further assuming the average haul from farm to market or common carrier is but seven miles, this saving amounts to more than $377,000,000 annually! The average haul from farm to market is speculative, and seven miles is admittedly a low estimate; $377,000,-000 is probably less than the actual saving. Let us apply known factors to a definite instance.

In 1931, trucks hauled 21,162,430 head of livestock into the 17 principal stock markets of the country. The total tonnage hauled was 3,000,000, divided into 1,750,-000 truckloads. The average haul was 65 miles and the ton mileage was approximately 195,000,000. Assuming, for purposes of comparison, that this tremendous movement could have been conducted by horse-drawn vehicles over unimproved roads, its cost would have been $64,-350,000. Trucks, whose operations were made possible by improvement of the highways, did the work for only

$13,650,000; a saving of more than $50,000,000!

Motor trucks are now hauling perishable' foodstuffs from farm and garden to centers of consumption as much as 700 miles distant. Profitable markets have been opened for producers who formerly were so far from centers of consumption that they could not compete. Trucking concerns picking up odd-lot shipments at points convenient to the farm have made it profitable to ship small quantities of commodities which otherwise would not have been marketed, as their value was less than cost of transportation by other means.

For certain classes of freight, such as garden truck and livestock, transport by motor truck is especially advantageous because it is more direct, more prompt, avoids loss by shrinkage, and delivers the commodity to the market in better condition. The swiftness and flexibility of motor transportation enables the producer to take advantage of favorable markets and actually acts as a stabilizer of prices. In the old days, when mud roads were the rule, every heavy rain stopped the flow of commodities from farmer to consumer; the resultant shortage sent the price up, and then, when the roads opened, there was a glut of produce to be sold and the price dropped. Good paved roads, not affected by weather conditions, permit orderly and regular marketing at all times. The saving in spoilage is also important.

The composite result of these factors is higher returns for the producer and lower costs to the consumer.

Nor are farmers the only producers to be benefited. Extension of roads has made profitable the opening of many mines and other sources of raw materials outside the railroad range.

Conversely, road improvement has lowered commodity costs to farms, rural communities and whole sections of the country which are isolated from other forms of transportation. The importance of this is greater than appears at first glance, because there are approximately 45,000 communities in the United States, involving 10 percent of the population, which are either without any rail connection whatever or have no freight station and so must depend mainly on the highways for transportation. Improved roads are directly responsible for a very considerable decentralization of urban population and the creation of literally hundreds of suburban and semi-urban communities which did not exist ten years ago. They have turned many a western ghost city into a prosperous community and given life to hundreds of cross-road villages.

The highways, in increasing the value of farm property, naturally increased taxable wealth and so indirectly repaid the sums expended on them. But they gave a greater return indirectly, through the automobile and its dependent oil, rubber, and other industries, which must pay taxes on property owned the same as any others. Owing to the wide ramifications of these industries, especially automobiles and oil, some part of this property appears on virtually every tax roll in the United States.

Development of new sources of raw material, already cited, also has increased taxable wealth. The business development of outlying rural property and the increase in value of suburban property created by highway improvement and motor transportation is staggering.

A still greater return is produced by the general and special taxes levied on the products of the motor industry, for not only are motor vehicles taxed as property but they are the only property whose owners are taxed for the privilege of operating them. In 1931 the taxes paid by motor vehicles, including that on gasoline, amounted to $1,025,735,112, or over one-tenth of the total of all taxes, local, state, and national, collected in the United States. In 1932, motor vehicles paid 12 percent of the total of all taxes.

Highway expenditures amount to $1,600,000,000 annually, 77 percent of which, according to the Bureau of Public Roads, eventually is paid to labor. Directly or indirectly, highway construction and maintenance, and motor vehicle manufacture, distribution, operation and maintenance, give employment to more than 4,000,000 persons, 9½ percent of those classed by the census as gainful workers.

Highway construction and maintenance affords direct employment for 325,000 persons; the motor industry gives employment to some 270,000 in motor vehicle factories; 175,000 more in parts and accessory factories; 350,-000 in sales work; over 400,000 in garage and repair activities. There are 380,000 chauffeurs and more than 1,500,000 truck-drivers.

The motor vehicle industry is the largest in the country, producing one-eighth of all manufactures. It turns out more than four-fifths of all the motor vehicles manufactured in the world. In 1929, the banner year, American retail purchasers paid $9,610,000,000 for automobiles, practically a fifth of all the money they spent for merchandise, and the industry exported almost 734,000 additional motor vehicles, worth $352,000,000.

While the automobile industry was already well established when the Lincoln Highway was proclaimed, it is to the development of roads that this industry owes its greatness. As early as 1918, leaders of the automotive world assumed and stated that the market for automobiles had become saturated, that all they could anticipate for the future was replacement business. And each year the development of highways opened new fields for automobile operation and surprised them with new markets, the end of which, perhaps, has not even yet been reached.

The highway and the motor vehicle really are a unit; neither is of value without the other and together they have wrought a revolution in American life. They made a nation of travellers out of the American people, broadening them intellectually and "tightening the Union" politically. Unquestionably, since millions of citizens began to travel back and forth over the highways, in daily business or pleasure trips, national solidarity and the unity of American thought has been vastly increased. Improved roads are a mortal enemy of sectionalism. With the creation of a system of improved highways, it was possible for the first time, for the average citizen to travel freely and enjoyably, seeing many sections of the country, developing acquaintance with the people of different regions, acquiring an appreciation of viewpoints other than those prevalent in his own community.

Travel in automobiles far exceeds travel by rail, partly because its economy, convenience, speed and flexibility have drawn much traffic from railroads, but even more so because the pleasure of motor travel has created an enormous volume of new traffic. Thousands upon thousands of families who formerly stayed at home now take vacation trips by automobile; other thousands take frequent short outings; often when one member of a family must travel for business, other members accompany him for the pleasure of the trip.

No longer is it necessary for these people to look in a geography to learn the principal products of a distant community; they have been there and seen for themselves. Who, having once driven through the mining regions of Pennsylvania, the tobacco fields of Connecticut, the cotton areas of the south, the citrus groves of California or Florida, the apple and pear producing regions of Michigan, can ever forget them? Travel by motor car brings the traveller close to the country, puts him in contact with its people and their activities in a way which no other form of transport can approach.

And travel by motor car is emancipated from the narrow restrictions of rails and rivers. Highways lead the motorist to a thousand, yes, to thousands, of scenic and recreation areas which no other form of transport reaches. Highways opened the national parks of the West, the mountain areas of the New England states, the lovely country of the Old South. Highways made possible the development of countless small local regions devoted to outdoor sports, from winter snowshoeing to summer picknicking. They have made the casual, unplanned outing a commonplace and inculcated a health-building love of the outdoors which conceivably is even now reflected in the increased life expectancy noted by actuaries. They have taken the city worker from the crowded flat in a congested community to a detached home of his own in the suburbs.

Highways ended the isolation of the farm. They made

the farmer's wife a person instead of a drudge. They gave farm boys and girls freedom and necessary social contacts. Whereas in former days the weekly trip to town for the mail was an event, now the rural carrier delivers mail at the front gate daily and farm dwellers think nothing of driving in for a motion picture after supper. Highways bring the butcher, the baker and the newspaper to the door every day.

Highways stimulate school attendance. Figures compiled in 1918 by E. T. Meredith, secretary of agriculture, showed that in states having a comparatively high proportion of improved roads, school attendance averaged 80 percent of those enrolled; whereas in states with a relatively small proportion of improved roads, school attendance averaged but 64 percent. Highways bring better education. The little red schoolhouse is almost a thing of the past. School busses, operating over improved highways, take the youngsters from the farms to modern consolidated schools in the morning and bring them safely home at night.

Similarly, when illness or accident necessitates medical attention, the farmer need not wait hours, or even days, until some heroic country doctor can plow through mud or flounder through snowdrifts to reach him. The doctor drives an automobile now, over roads that are passable in any weather. If a prescription is to be filled, the druggist sends it out almost before the hired man could have hitched up a team to go after it in the old days.

Something has already been said of the curious cycle in which highway improvement stimulates traffic and increased traffic stimulates improvement; two special aspects of this phenomenon remain to be examined. First, it was the growth of automobile traffic due to creation of the Lincoln Highway that led to abolition of the toll roads of Pennsylvania, the last of which was made free in 1918.

Second, erection of toll bridges and building of toll vehicular tunnels was stimulated by this same traffic, because states could not provide these expensive adjuncts of the highway as rapidly as traffic required them, and private enterprise had to be permitted to do so. As these structures will revert eventually to public ownership, the automotive operators, a special class of the population, will have paid for bridges and tunnels which are assets to the whole community.

The revenues to be obtained from automotive vehicle tolls are so large and so stable that they are now used even by States as a basis of revenue bonds for financing structures of this kind.

While all these effects were being brought about in the United States, Lincoln Highway policy was also exerting influence abroad. Since this road was virtually a laboratory for development of new methods in highway promotion, construction and improvement, the only one of its kind, engineers and others associated with highway work all over the world watched it very closely. In effect, the Association became a clearing house through which foreign engineers, highway improvement organizations and even governments obtained the latest information regarding highway progress in the United States. Its publications were even cited as authority by the United States Bureau of Public Roads.

Papers dealing with different aspects of the Lincoln

Highway were read before foreign engineering conferences so often they became a commonplace. Engineers and engineering publications in Australia, Japan, Chile, New Zealand, France, Holland and other countries asked and were readily granted inclusion in the Association's mailing lists. A Russian commission sent to the United States to study transportation motored over most of it. Civic organizations in several of the Latin-American countries sought advice from the Association on methods of promoting construction of needed roads.

Probably the greatest influence exerted was in Canada, where automobile and good roads leaders had long been aware of the rapid development of highways in this country and where a very real desire had grown up for a trans-Canadian road which would be to the Dominion what the Lincoln Highway was to the United States. Topographic obstacles were very great; difficult as it had been to pioneer an automobile route across the United States, it appeared that labor would be but child's play compared to a pioneering trip across Canada.

To stimulate such a trip, the Canadian Highway Association offered gold medals to those who should first drive from Halifax to Victoria and from Winnipeg to Victoria. Mr. Bement made the drive from Winnipeg west in the summer of 1924. With him went Edward S. Evans, a director of the Lincoln Highway Association. This trip was financed by the Packard Motor Car Company and sponsored by the Lincoln Highway Association as a friendly gesture toward the Canadian organization.

Messrs. Bement and Evans encountered their greatest difficulty in the canyon of the Fraser River, where the only passable way was that carved from the walls of the canyon by the Canadian National Railway. The two Americans fitted their automobile with railroad wheels and attempted to drive down the canyon on the rails, but the plan failed to work and they changed back to their regular tires and drove on the ties, one wheel between the tracks and other outside. On this section of their trip their car was dispatched and operated in the same manner as a regular train, and carried a regular railroad conductor who was responsible for its adherence to schedule.

Shortly afterward, the Canadian government selected this route as the line for trans-Canadian road improvement. All the winter of 1925 and far into the summer of 1926 workmen were busy cutting a way through the living rock so that other motorists might traverse the mighty gorge of the Fraser.

Now, what is to be the further result of all this?

President Henry B. Joy, in a paper read before a technical institute in 1917, said:

"The national interest in good roads will continue to increase until we have in this country a road system second to none, which will bind this country closer together, eliminate sectionalism, eliminate provincialism, make Americans cosmopolitans, and work wonders in the unification of American sentiment and in the forming of a cohesive empire of democracy, indissolubly linked together through just such a system of highways as was the foundation of Rome's greatness."

Everything he said has been proved by development, yet the prophecy is just as appropriate today as it was when he delivered it, for the effects of the Lincoln Highway's efforts are continuing and as far as can now be foreseen will continue indefinitely. This country, and perhaps some foreign nations as well, will owe an eternal debt to the men who, farsightedly and generously, founded the Lincoln Highway a score of years ago and so advanced, by at least a generation, the tremendous benefits which improved roads have conferred. The debt is not lessened by the fact that they worked hard, and paid liberally for the privilege of working, in this good cause, but always and forever its chief item must be that they provided the vision without which works are fruitless and vain.

The men who founded the Lincoln Highway Association and those who carried on its work have all had full and busy lives. The names of its leaders stand high in many fields of endeavor. There were among them no little men, no pettifoggers, no seekers after personal aggrandizement; they took broad views and they held high standards of accomplishment by which to judge.

They know well what is worthy and what is not. Mr. Joy, in 1933, spoke for them all when, looking back over a rich career, he said:

"I consider the Lincoln Highway the greatest thing I ever did in my life."

APPENDIX A

James A. Allison
Aluminum Co. of America
Autocar Company
Bibb Manufacturing Co.
Bijur Motor Lighting Co.
Henry E. Bodman
The S. F. Bowser Co.
Joseph Boyer
Briggs Manufacturing Co.
R. J. Caldwell Co.
Henry F. Campbell
C. G. Spring and Bumper Co.
Chandler Motor Car Co.
The Chrysler Corporation
Emory W. Clark
Dort Motor Car Co.
T. Coleman DuPont
E. S. Evans
Firestone Tire & Rubber Co.
Carl G. Fisher
The Fisk Rubber Co.
Edsel B. Ford
General Motors Corporation
Christian Girl

B. F. Goodrich Rubber Co.
Goodyear Tire & Rubber Co.
O. J. Gude Co.
Wm. Randolph Hearst
Hudson Motor Car Co.
Jenckes Spinning Co.
Henry B. Joy
Kelly-Springfield Tire Co.
J. H. Lane & Co.
Lehigh Portland Cement Co.
Lockwood, Greene & Co.
Miller Tire & Rubber Co.
A. C. Newby
Packard Motor Car Co.
Paige-Detroit Motor Car Co.
Peerless Motor Car Company
Perfection Spring Co.
E. E. Placek
Prest-O-Lite Co.
F. A. Seiberling
Sparks-Withington Co.
Stone & Webster, Inc.
Mary Clark Thompson
Timken-Detroit Axle Co.

J. Spencer Turner Co.

United States Rubber Co.

United States Tire Co.

Universal Portland Cement Co.

Willys-Overland Company

APPENDIX B

The following are the major contributions made to the Lincoln Highway Association:

Preliminary expenses contributed by Carl G. Fisher and James A. Allison, both of Indianapolis, Indiana.   Amount undisclosed.

Contribution to cover deficit:

Carl G. Fisher, Indianapolis, Indiana; Albert Y. Gowen, Cleveland, Ohio; Roy D. Chapin, Detroit; Henry B. Joy, Detroit; Frank A. Seiberling, Akron, Ohio; John N. Willys, Toledo, Ohio. $20,000

Underwriters' contributions:

W. C. Durant, Detroit; F. A. Seiberling, Akron, Ohio; Carl G. Fisher, Indianapolis, Indiana; A. Y. Gowen, Cleveland, Ohio. $66,000

Marquette Cement Manufacturing Co., Chicago; Chicago Portland Cement Co., Chicago; Northwestern States Portland Cement Co., Mason City, Iowa; German-American Portland Cement Co. $5,400

J. C. Dold, Buffalo, New York. $300

Cost of Printing "A Brief For the Lincoln Highway":

Henry B. Joy, Detroit, Michigan. $3,937

Preliminary expenses of Ideal Campsite

Edsel B. Ford, Detroit, Michigan. $4,500

Carl G. Fisher, Indianapolis, Indiana	$25,000
General Motors Corporation	100,000
Goodyear Tire & Rubber Co.*	75,000
Frank A. Seiberling, Akron, Ohio *	25,000
United States Rubber Co.	130,000
Willys-Overland Company	50,000
	$405,000

MATERIALS

33,000 barrels of cement.
Atlas Portland Cement Co., New York City; Chicago Portland Cement Co., Chicago; Crescent Portland Cement Co., Wampum, Pennsylvania; Marquette Cement Manufacturing Co., Chicago; Northwestern States Portland Cement Co., Mason City, Iowa; St. Louis Portland Cement Works, St. Louis, Missouri. $35,550

Steel Culverts.
    Nebraska Culvert Manufacturing Co. $1,000

3,000 Redwood posts.
    Redwood Association of California, San Francisco.

Lighting Equipment for Ideal Section.
    General Electric Co., Schenectady, New York $5,000

Drinking Fountains.
    Carl Parker, Los Angeles.

Twelve State Boundary Markers.
    Lebanon Machine Co., Lebanon, New Hampshire.

* Paid direct to officials of the State of Utah; not handled by Lincoln Highway Association.

Brushes.
 Wooster Brush Co., Wooster, Ohio $50
Paint.
 Patton Sun-Proof Paint Co., $1,000

EQUIPMENT

Packard Motor Car Company,—three touring
 cars.
Stutz Motor Car Co.,—automobile for Field Sec-
 retary for three years.
Studebaker Motor Car Co.,—two touring cars.
The Autocar Company,—two special trucks.
 The General Motors Corporation,—one tour-
 ing car.
 Willys-Overland Company,—two touring cars;
 two special trucks.
 Tires.
  Goodyear Tire & Rubber Co.
  United States Tire Co.
  Fisk Rubber Co.
 Tractor-Grader.
  Col. Sidney D. Waldon, Detroit, Michigan $1,085

DISPLAY ADVERTISING SPACE

Motor World
Motor Age
Motor Print
Automobile Topics
Hoosier Motorist
American Motorist
Canadian Automobile
Motor News (Washington)
Ken Motor Monthly

Motordom
Southern Motoring
Threshman's Review &
 Power Farming
Fechheimer Theater Pro-
 gram, Detroit
Miles Theater Program, De-
 troit
Gas Power

Lehigh Portland Cement Company
The Club Journal
Automobile Journal
Automobile Trade Journal
Motor
Motor Life
The Fra
Accessory & Garage Journal
American Cycle Car
Motor News (California)
The Spokesman
Motor Field
Implement & Vehicle Journal
Horseless Age
The Road Maker
Motor Truck
Packard Motor Car Co.
Pacific Motor
Garage Efficiency
The Automobile
Western Motor Car
Western Canadian Motorist
American Chauffeur
The Spectator
Automobile Dealer & Repairer
The Motorist
Detroit Motorist
Michigan Roads & Forests
Michigan Investor
The Light Car
S. F. Bowser Co.

$36,000

MISCELLANEOUS

Office Space
  Emory W. Clark, Detroit
  Edward Ford, Rossford, Ohio
2,000 Elm Trees
  Charles Gurier, De Kalb, Illinois
Photographic Services
  Ford Motor Company, Detroit
Sundry Office and Patent Attorneys' Services
  Packard Motor Car Co., Detroit
Publication of 65,000 booklets, Trego's "Hints to Motorists."
  Goodyear Tire & Rubber Co.

Services of band and transportation to accompany First
Army Transcontinental Motor Convoy.
Goodyear Tire & Rubber Co.
Auditing Services
Marwick-Mitchell-Peat & Co.

APPENDIX C

The original subscribers to the Coast-to-Coast Rock Highway; i. e., those who made subscriptions at the meeting held
in Indianapolis and called by Mr. Fisher in 1912, and the
estimated value of their subscriptions, were as follows:

American Motors Co., Indianapolis	$40,000
Archie Atkins Co., Indianapolis	2,200
Brown Commercial Car Co., Indianapolis	5,600
Cadillac Automobile Co., of Indiana, Indianapolis	8,000
Empire Automobile Tire Company, Indianapolis	3,500
Esterline Manufacturing Company, Indianapolis	10,000
Glover Equipment Company, Indianapolis	1,000
Gates Manufacturing Co., Indianapolis	500
Henderson Motor Car Co., Indianapolis	15,000
Gus Habich & Co., Indianapolis	1,000
Ideal Motor Car Co., Indianapolis	15,000
R. J. Irwin Manufacturing Co., Indianapolis	4,500
Marion Motor Car Company, Indianapolis	28,800
Mutual Printing & Lithographing Co., Indianapolis	2,000
The Motor Car Manufacturing Co., Indianapolis	10,000
Christian Off & Co., Indianapolis	1,000
Prest-O-Lite Company, Indianapolis	50,000
Premier Motor Car Co., Indianapolis	15,000
Pumpelly Battery Company, Indianapolis	500
Remy Magneto Company, Indianapolis	40,000

G. A. Schnull, Indianapolis	100
The Waverly Company, Indianapolis	15,000
Wheeler & Schebler, Indianapolis	45,000
G. H. Westing, Indianapolis	6,000
A Total of	$319,700

APPENDIX D

OFFICERS AND DIRECTORS

OF

THE LINCOLN HIGHWAY ASSOCIATION

A complete list of the Officers and Directors of the Lincoln Highway Association on December 31, 1927, when they adjourned sine die. All of these continue to hold their offices indefinitely.

F. A. Seiberling, President
Henry B. Joy, vice-President
Carl G. Fisher, vice-President
Roy D. Chapin, vice-President
Austin F. Bement, vice-President
Emory W. Clark, Treasurer
Gael S. Hoag, Secretary
B. F. Affleck
W. C. Durant
E. S. Evans
Edsel B. Ford
Alvan Macauley
C. S. Mott
W. O. Rutherford
Col. Sidney D. Waldon
John N. Willys

APPENDIX E

A ROSTER OF LINCOLN HIGHWAY CONSULS
BETWEEN NEW YORK AND SAN FRANCISCO

Arranged Alphabetically by Cities in Each State

NEW YORK

City	*Name*	*Title*
New York City	H. B. Lewis	State Consul

NEW JERSEY

Jersey City	Benjamin E. Farrier	Local Consul
Newark	R. C. Jenkinson	Eastern State District Consul
Newark	Wm J. Morgan	Local Consul
Newark	Jos. L. Reilly	State Consul
Trenton	S E. Kaufman	Local Consul
Weehawken	Alvin Hunsicker	County Consul

PENNSYLVANIA

Bedford	Lee F. Hoffman	County Consul
Bryn Mawr	H. Hoffman Dolan	Local Consul
Buckstown	Norman Boose	County Consul
Chambersburg	W. H. Fisher	Local Consul
Coatesville	T. L. Eyre	County Consul
Coatesville	Dr. S. H. Scott	Local Consul
Columbia	Alfred H. Meyers	Local Consul
Downingtown	Guyon Miller	Local Consul
East McKeesport	Jas. F. Woodward	County Consul
Everett	A. M. Karns	Local Consul
Gap	W. J. L. Walker	Local Consul
Gettysburg	H. C. Mitinger	Central State District Consul
Grafenburg	Robert C. Miller	Local Consul
Greensburg	Sam E. Patterson	Local Consul
Indiana	Hon. John S. Fisher	State Consul
Irwin	John L. Ridinger	Local Consul
Lancaster	J. G. Forney	Local Consul
Lancaster ·	Chas. M. Reiling	County Consul
Leaman Place	C. Morris Hershey	Local Consul
Ligonier	A. J. McColly	Local Consul
McConnellsburg	Leslie W. Seylar	Local Consul

City	Name	Title
Morrisville	Thomas B. Stockham	Local Consul
Mountville	M. E. Musser	Local Consul
New Oxford	Geo. S. Hummer	Local Consul
Philadelphia	B. D. Easling	Eastern State District Consul
Pittsburgh	Edwin K. Morse	Western State District Consul
Pittsburgh	Henry Tranter	Local Consul
Schellburg	Wm. Keyser	Local Consul
South Langhorne	Clarence J. Buckman	County Consul
South Langhorne	Jacob Good	Local Consul
Stoyestown	W. K. Walker	Local Consul
Wayne	Geo. L. Barnett	Local Consul
Wayne	Thos H. Garvin	County Consul
York	R. P. Anderson	Local Consul
York	F. H. Wogan	Local Consul

WEST VIRGINIA

Chester	Robert A. Douglas	State Consul
Chester	Geo. A. Arner	County Consul

OHIO

Ashland	J. L. Clark	County Consul
Beaverdam	Frank Huttinger	Local Consul
Bucyrus	Frank L. Hopley	State Consul
Bucyrus	E. G. Reid	Local Consul
Bucyrus	E. J. Songer	County Consul
Canton	Carl F. Duerr	Local Consul
Canton	J. A. Kress	County Consul
Crestline	J. F. McMahon	Local Consul
Dalton	T. C. Hunsicker	Local Consul
Delphos	A. B. King	Local Consul
East Liverpool	Robert E. Spencer	Local Consul
East Liverpool	Frank D. Swaney	Eastern State District Consul
Gomer	Dr. O. S. Robuck	Local Consul
Gomer	G. W. Williams	Local Consul
Kensington	Frank Cox	Local Consul
Lisbon	James M. Costello	County Consul
Mansfield	T. R. Barnes	County Consul
Massillon	Fred W. Justus	Local Consul
Upper Sandusky	Charles Artz	County Consul
Upper Sandusky	George G. Artz	Local Consul

City	Name	Title
Van Wert	W. J. Semple	Local Consul
Van Wert	T. C. Wilkinson	County Consul
West Cairo	Danial Harpster, Sr.	Local Consul
Williamstown	E. W. McKeon	Local Consul
Wooster	Emmett C. Dix	County Consul
Wooster	Donald Foss	Local Consul

INDIANA

Columbia City	Sam F. Trembly	County Consul
Columbia City	H. M. Miller	Local Consul
Dyer	Orin Fitch	Local Consul
Dyer	A. W. Stommel	County Consul
Fort Wayne	W. M. Griffin	State Consul
Fort Wayne	Martin H. Luecke	Deputy State Consul
Fort Wayne	Chas. R. Weatherhogg	Local Consul
Merrillville	Walter Bros.	Local Consul
Plymouth	Otto Fries	Local Consul
Plymouth	Frank Southworth	County Consul
Valparaiso	E. D. Hodges	Local Consul
Valparaiso	Chas. Wark	County Consul
Warsaw	G. D. Overmyer	County Consul

ILLINOIS

Ashton	Frank S. Hart	Local Consul
Aurora	James Lino	Local Consul
Aurora	Wm. H. McCullough	Eastern State District Consul
Batavia	Robt. Hollister	Local Consul
Chicago	W. G. Edens	Chicago Consul
Chicago Heights	B. H. Vannatta	Local Consul
DeKalb	Sam E. Bradt	State Consul
DeKalb	J. H. Jarboe	Central State District Consul
DeKalb	A. W. Marvin	Local Consul
Dixon	A. B. Whitcombe	Western State District Consul
Franklin Grove	I. J. Trostle	Local Consul
Fulton	M. W. Ingwersen	Local Consul
Geneva	Oscar Nelson	Local Consul
Joliet	T. R. Gerlach	County Consul
Joliet	Wm. Murphy	Local Consul
Malta	F. B. Willrett	Local Consul
Mooseheart	Rodney H. Brandon	Local Consul

City	Name	Title
Morrison	Ed. A. Smith	County Consul
Plainfield	U. S. G. Blakely	County Consul
Rochelle	W. P. Graham	County Consul
Rochelle	M. L. Pickle	Local Consul
Sterling	Roy R. Baer	Local Consul

IOWA

Ames	Parley Sheldon	County Consul
Belle Plaine	O. C. Burrows	County Consul
Belle Plaine	James Herring	Local Consul
Boone	J. B. McHose	County Consul
Boone	H. N. Streit	Local Consul
Carroll	N. M. Mackey	Local Consul
Cedar Rapids	W. G. Haskell	Eastern State District Consul
Cedar Rapids	Edward Killian	County Consul
Cedar Rapids	P. C. Rude	Local Consul
Chelsea	Roy R. Ryan	Local Consul
Chelsea	E. P. Willey	Local Consul
Clarence	T. R. Perkins	County Consul
Clinton	A. A. Daehler	Local Consul
Colo	Chas. R. Read	Local Consul
Denison	R. P. Conner	County Consul
Denison	H. B. Fishel	Local Consul
DeWitt	L. N. Williams	Local Consul
Dow City	W. E. Fishel	Local Consul
Grand Junction	T. R. Watts	Local Consul
Jefferson	P. L. Cockerill	Local Consul
Jefferson	E. B. Wilson	Western State District Consul
LaMoille	S. W. Myers	Local Consul
Lisbon	C. W. Carbee	Local Consul
Logan	Almor Stern	Local Consul
Marshalltown	C. H. E. Boardman	County Consul
Marshalltown	A. A. Moore	Central State District Consul
Marshalltown	H. A. Weisman	Local Consul
Missouri Valley	W. Allen Jones	County Consul
Missouri Valley	R. D. McEvoy	Local Consul
Montour	J. M. Buchanan	Local Consul
Mount Vernon	Dr. T. L. Wolfe	Local Consul
Nevada	F. M. Boardman	Local Consul
Ogden	Alvin Treloar	Local Consul
Scranton	James E. Moss	Local Consul

City	Name	Title
Stanwood	Homer Hart	Local Consul
State Center	Dr. I. D. Kauffman	Local Consul
State Center	E. C. Rohde	Local Consul
Tama	E. L. Beard	County Consul
Tama	D. E. Goodell	State Consul
Tama	F. S. Ingram	Local Consul
Wheatland	Henry Guenther	Local Consul
Woodbine	Lewis Haas	Local Consul

NEBRASKA

City	Name	Title
Alda	Frank Denman	Local Consul
Big Springs	Geo. E. Junge	Local Consul
Big Springs	A. L. Jensen	Local Consul
Blair	Reed O'Hanlon	County Consul
Brady	E. S. Springer	Local Consul
Brule	R A. Mills	Local Consul
Bushnell	F. O. Baker	Local Consul
Central City	Geo. J. Eoff	County Consul
Chappell	L. O. Pfeiffer	Local Consul
Chappell	J. R. Wertz	County Consul
Clarks	H. M. Moorse	Local Consul
Clarks	M. Shonsey	Local Consul
Columbus	A R. Miller	County Consul
Cozad	Dr. C. H. Sheets	Local Consul
Darr	Chas. S. Griffith	Local Consul
Dix	W. R. Ehlers	Local Consul
Duncan	John P. Sokol	Local Consul
Elm Creek	C. G. Bliss	Local Consul
Elm Creek	E. L. Sutton	Local Consul
Fremont	John Monnich	Local Consul
Fremont	John Sonin	Local Consul
Fremont	Geo. F. Wolz	State Consul
Gibbon	W. H. Buck	Local Consul
Gibbon	O. K. Campbell	Local Consul
Gothenburg	E. A. Calling	Local Consul
Grand Island	Thos. Bradstreet	County Consul
Grand Island	E. L. Brown	Local Consul
Grand Island	Ira T. Homan	Local Consul
Josselyn	J. D. Gwynn	Local Consul
Kearney	T. H. Bolte	Local Consul
Kearney	L. A. Denison	Local Consul
Kearney	C. F Tollefsen	County Consul
Kimball	John Filer	Local Consul
Lexington	G. E. Hammer	County Consul

City	Name	Title
Lexington	J. W. Morgan	Local Consul
Lexington	W. H. Wisda	Local Consul
Lodge Pole	A. B. Persinger	Local Consul
Maxwell	Chas. H. Kuhns	Local Consul
North Bend	R. C Brownell	Local Consul
North Bend	Roy Cusack	County Consul
North Platte	W. J. Hendy	Local Consul
North Platte	A. B. Hoagland	County Consul
North Platte	E. F. Seeburger	District Consul
Ogallala	J. S. Kroh	County Consul
Overton	H. H. Beltner	Local Consul
Paxton	H. L. Kildare	Local Consul
Potter	E. H. Biggs	Local Consul
Richland	G. A. Shonka	Local Consul
Schuyler	Anton Kopac	Local Consul
Schuyler	J. E. McNally	County Consul
Schuyler	Ed. Vrana	Local Consul
Shelton	W. E. Amos	Local Consul
Sidney	J. L. McIntosh	Western State District Consul
Sidney	Robert S. Oberfelder	County Consul
Silver Creek	John M. Vitamvas	Local Consul
Sutherland	John Palmer	Local Consul
Willow Island	Jerry Coston	Local Consul
Wood River	E. S. Leavenworth	Local Consul
Wood River	S. W. Wilson	Local Consul

WYOMING

Cheyenne	H. P. Hynds	Local Consul
Cheyenne	Gus Fleischli	Local Consul
Cheyenne	Warren Richardson	County Consul
Evanston	Payson W. Spaulding	State Consul
Fort Bridger	W. A. Carter	County Consul
Fort Bridger	W. C. Casto	Local Consul
Green River	Hugo Gaensslen	Local Consul
Laramie	Joe Lane	Local Consul
Lyman	M. E. Rollins	Local Consul
Medicine Bow	Fred Richards	Local Consul
Point of Rocks	Clarence Rader	Local Consul
Pine Bluffs	I. A. Peterson	Local Consul
Rock Springs	Dr. E. S. Lauzer	Local Consul
Rock Springs	John Hay	County Consul
Rawlins	N. R. Greenfield	Local Consul
Rawlins	Dr. Raymond Barber	County Consul
Wamsutter	A. P. Bugas	Local Consul

UTAH

City	Name	Title
Salt Lake City	Don. R. Lewis	Local Consul
Salt Lake City	E. M. Qualtrough	State Consul
Tooele	Harry G. Baker	County Consul
Wendover	Joseph Conley	Local Consul

NEVADA

Austin	N. S. Easton	Local Consul
Austin	C. F. Littrell	County Consul
Carson City	W. J. Maxwell	Local Consul
Carson City	Frank E. Meder	Local Consul
Dayton	M. J. King	County Consul
Ely	J. M. Lockhart	County Consul
Ely	B. L. Quayle	State Consul
Ely	Fred D. West	Local Consul
Eureka	Edgar Eather	Local Consul
Eureka	W. H. Russell	County Consul
Fallon	I. H. Kent	County Consul
Reno	John Blum	Local Consul
Reno	A. F. Frohlich	Local Consul

CALIFORNIA

Auburn	Verne M. Ford	Local Consul
Colfax	John M. Newman	Local Consul
Donner	W. B. Gelatt	Local Consul
Dutch Flat	K. W. Keasbey	Local Consul
El Dorado	Seymour Hill	Local Consul
Freshpond	J. B. Rupley	Local Consul
Gold Run	C. F. Collins	Local Consul
Kyburz	Ralph Kyburz	Local Consul
Meyers	B. C. Celio	Local Consul
Oakland	James A. Houlihan	State Consul
Pacific	Mrs. Estelle Poole	Local Consul
Penryn	H. E. Butler	Local Consul
Placerville	J. C. North	Local Consul
Placerville	T. G. Patton	Local Consul
Placerville	Guy E. Wentworth	County Consul
Riverton	Al Martin	Local Consul
Roseville	Dr. Bradford Woodbridge	Local Consul
Sacramento	Fred W. Kiesel	Eastern State District Consul
Sacramento	Geo. W. Peltier	County Consul

City	Name	Title
San Francisco	Earle C. Anthony	County Consul
Strawberry	J. T. Scherrer	Local Consul
Truckee	Charles B. White	Local Consul
Truckee	Dan D. Smith	Local Consul

APPENDIX F

CONTRACT
BETWEEN
THE LINCOLN HIGHWAY ASSOCIATION
AND
THE STATE OF UTAH

The following is a correct copy of a resolution passed by the State Road Commission of Utah at its meeting held March 21st, 1918.

Moved by Commissioner McGonagle,

Seconded by Commissioner Shields. Passed:

WHEREAS, the Lincoln Highway Association, a corporation organized under the laws of the State of Michigan, with its principal offices in Detroit, Michigan, has made certain offers to the State of Utah for the advancement of sums of money, aggregating $125,000.00 for the completion of two sections of road, one between Clover and Orr's Ranch, Utah, and one between the north end of Granite Point and Black Point, Tooele County, Utah; and

WHEREAS, It is agreed that in constructing these two necessary links in the route selected and thereby eliminating some 50 miles of the worst road conditions now existing on the Trans-Continental Highway, the Utah State Road Commission will accomplish a work of the greatest benefit, not only to the state of Utah but to the United States, in linking this great national strategic highway, with its resources and its people, to the states on the east and west and to the Atlantic and Pacific coasts, thereby complying with the recommendations of the National Council of Defense in bringing the Utah section of the Lincoln Highway into proper condition; and

WHEREAS, We see in this construction, now, more than ever before, the keystone of the Lincoln Highway arch, the most necessary step to be taken to provide a through route of an American highway transportation system; and

WHEREAS, Through our patriotic desire and support we believe that this construction will provide the only immediate opportunity for the Lincoln Highway Association and the State Road Commission of Utah to cooperate in achieving a result of vast national importance; and

WHEREAS, The State Road Commission of Utah is willing to accept the money tendered, in consideration of the fact that the said State Road Commission shall be allowed to make the construction requested and required, and in full compliance with the general road policy of the State of Utah.

Now, THEREFORE, BE IT RESOLVED, By the State Road Commission of the State of Utah, in regular meeting assembled, this 21st day of March, 1918, that the offer of $100,000.00 by the Goodyear Tire and Rubber Company and by Mr. F. A. Seiberling, its President, for the construction of that part of the Lincoln Highway hereinafter particularly described, to-wit:

Commencing at a point in Tooele County, Utah, known as the north end of Granite Point at Granite Mountain: thence in a westerly direction for a distance of approximately 17½ miles, to a point known as Black Point in Tooele County, Utah, which said points are the termini of the shortest

distance across what is known as the Great Salt
Lake Desert,

be accepted, and a roadway be constructed, not less than
eighteen feet in width and not less than one foot in elevation
of natural dirt soil, covered with a gravel surface of not
less than eight inches in depth at the center, nor less than
twelve feet in width, or of greater width if so determined by
the State Engineer of Utah upon further investigation;
also

BE IT RESOLVED, That the offer of $25,000.00 from Mr.
Carl G. Fisher for the construction of that portion of the
Lincoln Highway from Clover, Tooele County, Utah,
toward Orr's ranch, via what is known as Johnson Pass, be
accepted. Said $25,000.00 is to be used in constructing a
safe mountain highway with double track turnouts, with
suitable bridges to be erected where needed, the funds to be
applied where most necessary as indicated by said State Road
Commission after investigation and recommendation by the
State Engineer, said construction to cover a distance as
may be determined upon further investigation, but in no
case shall said funds be applied on a section or sections, the
total construction exceeding six miles in length.

The condition upon which said money is tendered to the
State of Utah, and accepted by it, to be that said road, for
the entire distance between Clover, Utah, and the Utah-
Nevada State line, via Overland Canyon, shall be designated
as a state highway by the State Road Commission on or
before the date that construction shall actually begin
thereon, the State of Utah first having secured proper right
of way where such construction is to be made.

FURTHER, That a road connecting the west terminus of the
Seiberling section and the present road through Overland
Canyon shall be opened up and made passable for motor

propelled vehicles by the State of Utah; and that a road from Johnson Pass, at the end of the Fisher construction, and west to Granite Mountain, be put in good passable condition for travel, in order to connect the Seiberling-Fisher memorial sections. Also that a connection be made by the State of Utah between the east terminus of the Fisher section and the town of Clover, Utah.

There shall be deposited with the State Treasurer of the State of Utah, as an evidence of good faith by said Seiberling and said Fisher, on or before the 1st day of May, 1918, or by the Lincoln Highway Association as their representative, fifty percent of the gross amount of money herein appropriated; and the remaining fifty percent shall be likewise deposited on or before the time when actual construction work shall have been commenced.

Said work shall be continued and completed not later than the first day of July, 1919.

The providers of the funds herein referred to and hereby accepted by the State of Utah shall be furnished with duplicate copies of the disbursement sheets kept in the office of the State Road Commission of Utah, showing the application of said money and the detailed items of expenditure as the work shall progress, which said statement shall be furnished monthly.

The desert section herein referred to shall be known and designated either as the Goodyear or Seiberling section as Mr. F. A. Seiberling shall hereafter determine; and Johnson Pass shall hereafter be known and designated as Fisher Pass, or by such other designation as Mr. Carl G. Fisher shall hereafter determine.

Said Seiberling and Fisher are hereby given authority to construct, at their own expense, at the termini of, or at such other places along such sections, suitable markers, monuments or arches for the designation of said respective sections in connection with the work herein referred to.

The Lincoln Highway's representatives are hereby given authority to inspect the work on said highway while the same shall be in progress of construction under the direction of the State Engineer and the State Road Engineer respectively.

FURTHER, Said Seiberling section, after completion, shall be kept closed to all travel until officially dedicated, jointly, by the officials of the State of Utah and of the said Lincoln Highway Association.

In consideration of the construction made by the State of Utah, whereby the Fisher and Seiberling sections are connected with and made a part of the State Highway system of Utah, it is agreed that Mr. F. A. Seiberling shall pay to the State of Utah for the proper upkeep of the Seiberling section such bills for maintenance as the State of Utah shall render, said amount at no time to be in excess of Five Thousand ($5,000) Dollars per year, nor for a longer period than five years, beginning with the year 1920.

IT IS AGREED that the State of Utah shall begin construction of the desert or Seiberling section not later than September 1, 1918, and failing so to commence work, all moneys deposited under this agreement, together with interest thereon at two percent per annum, shall be returned to the donors by the State of Utah on demand after October 1, 1918. It is understood that work having once been begun it shall be continued with reasonable diligence until the same shall have been completed.

IN WITNESS WHEREOF, We, the undersigned, have hereunto attached our signatures, this 21st day of March, 1918.

STATE ROAD COMMISSION OF UTAH
Harden Bennion, Vice Chairman
and Sec. of State
Dan B. Shields, Attorney General

Joseph Ririe, State Auditor
G. F. McGonagle, State Engineer
THE LINCOLN HIGHWAY ASSOCIATION,
by F. A. Seiberling, President.
THE GOODYEAR TIRE & RUBBER CO.,
F. A. Seiberling, President.
THE LINCOLN HIGHWAY ASSOCIATION,
Carl G. Fisher, Vice President
THE LINCOLN HIGHWAY ASSOCIATION,
A. F. Bement, Secretary
Carl G. Fisher
Attest: Ira R. Browning, State Road Engineer and Secretary.

APPENDIX G

Brief Biographical Sketches of Officers and Directors

SEIBERLING, FRANK A.: Manufacturer. Born in Western Star, Ohio, October 6, 1859. Student Heidelberg College, Tiffin, Ohio; President of the Goodyear Tire & Rubber Company, Akron, Ohio, 1898 to 1921; President of the Seiberling Rubber Company 1921 to date. Trustee of the Lincoln Memorial University, Heidelberg University, Western Reserve Academy, home Akron, Ohio. PRESIDENT OF THE LINCOLN HIGHWAY ASSOCIATION DURING TWO-THIRDS OF THE PERIOD OF ITS EXISTENCE.

JOY, HENRY BOURNE: Automobile manufacturer, now retired. Born Detroit, November 23, 1864. Son of James Frederick and Mary Bourne Joy. Educated Orchard Lake Military Academy, Pontiac, Michigan; Phillips' Academy, Andover, Massachusetts, 1883; Sheffield Scientific School, Yale University, 1886. Began as office boy Peninsular Car Company and became clerk, paymaster and assistant treasurer; in the mining business in Utah in 1887 to 1889; assistant treasurer, director, of the Fort Street Union Depot Company, Detroit, from 1889; married October 11, 1892, to Helen Hall Newberry, Detroit; President of the Detroit Union Depot Company, 1896 to 1907; receiver Chicago & Grand Trunk Railway Company, 1900 to 1903; Director of the Federal Reserve Bank of Chicago 1913, 1914; Chairman, President and Director of the Packard Motor Car Company 1903–1918; PRESIDENT OF THE LINCOLN HIGHWAY ASSOCIATION: Director of Chamber of Commerce of the United States of America; Vice-President and Director of Detroit Board of Commerce; American Protective League, American Fair Trade League; Vice-President of the Navy League of the United States; served in the United States Navy during the Spanish American War as Chief Boatswain's Mate of the U. S. S. *Yosemite;* served during World War as Captain and Lieut. Colonel, U. S. Army Signal Corps. Vice-President Lincoln Highway Association.

FISHER, CARL G.: Born in 1873, Greensberg, Ind. Received a common school education. Sold newspapers to get a start. He organized and built the Indianapolis Speedway, the world's greatest automobile testing ground, the instrument most forceful in developing the efficiency of modern automobile tires, ignition systems and auto construction generally. Next he entered the field of large scale real estate development, specializing on beach resorts. His first venture was on the Shores of Lake Michigan near St. Joseph, Michigan. Then he founded and developed Miami Beach, Florida. After the success of Miami Beach was assured he purchased a large acreage at the Eastern end of Long Island at Montauk Point and started a new development there which according to predictions by realty experts promises eventually to be one of the show places of the World. As Vice-President of the Lincoln Highway Association he conceived and promoted with a liberal expenditure of time and money the idea of a transcontinental highway —an ideal eventually realized in the completed Lincoln Highway.

For a number of years, Mr. Fisher was an underwriter

and large annual contributor toward the Association's promotion expense. And, in 1918, Mr. Fisher gave the State of
Utah $25,000.00 toward the construction of a road thru a
pass, which shortened the Lincoln Highway about 13 miles.
When Utah selected its Federally aided road system, a few
years later, it refused to include this section as well as another section toward the construction of which Mr. F. A.
Seiberling and the Goodyear Tire & Rubber Company had
donated $100,000.00, thus wasting both contributions.

CHAPIN, ROY D.: Manufacturer. Born, Lansing, Michigan, February 23, 1880. University of Michigan, 1899 to
1901. Identified with automobile business in Detroit since
1901; General sales manager of Olds Motor Works, 1904
to 1906; organizer, E. R. Thomas Detroit Company, 1906;
Treasurer and General Manager of the same, 1906 to 1908;
also Treasurer and General Manager of its successor, The
Chalmers Detroit Motor Company, 1908 to 1910; President
of the Hudson Motor Car Company, 1910 to 1923, Chairman
of the Board, 1923 to 1933, President since 1933; Secretary of
Commerce, under President Hoover, 1932 to 1933. Chairman of Highway Transport Committee, Council of National Defense, 1917 to 1918. Vice-President and Director
of Detroit Symphony Society; Director of Detroit Community Fund; Chairman of the Highway Transport Committee of International Chamber of Commerce; President
of the 6th International Road Congress at Washington
1930; Director Michigan State Good Roads Association;
Member of the Pan-American Confederation of Highway
Education (Executive committee); Highway Education
Board at Washington; President of National Automobile
Chamber of Commerce, 1927–1928, now a Director. Vice-
President, Director, and Member of Executive Committee
Lincoln Highway Association from its inception.

BEMENT, AUSTIN F.: Publicity Director. Born Toledo, Ohio, October 22, 1891. Educated in the Toledo Public Schools. 1909 Peninsular Engraving Company; 1910 advertising manager M. I. Wilcox Company, Toledo, Ohio, a jobbing house; 1912–1913 Advertising Manager, Electric Auto-Lite Company, Toledo, 1914 and for eleven years following successively; Publicity Director, Executive Secretary and Vice-President Lincoln Highway Association. Now Vice-President and General Manager Grace & Bement Inc., National Advertising Agency, Detroit, Michigan.

CLARK, EMORY W.: Retired Banker. Born in Detroit, Michigan, 1868. Became identified with banking business in 1904 as Vice-President of First National Bank Detroit, continuing in that capacity until 1911, when made President, relinquishing this office in 1925 to become Chairman of the Board, from which position he resigned in 1930. Nash Motors Company, Kenosha, Wisconsin; Michigan Bell Telephone Company; Detroit and Cleveland Navigation Company; Trustee-Mutual Life Insurance Company of New York. Member of Detroit Board of Commerce, Michigan Society, Colonial Wars. Treasurer, Lincoln Highway Association during its entire span of activity.

HOAG, GAEL S.: Born in Keeseville, New York, October 28, 1866. Educated in Northern New York State, Denver, Colorado and University of Michigan. Employed 13 years in the Business Department of the Rocky Mountain News, Denver. August 1897 to May 1902, Manager and Part Owner of the Cripple Creek Colorado Times Citizen. From 1906 to 1920 in mining promotion and fire insurance business in Ely, Nevada. Became interested in highway promotion in 1908. In 1909 organized the Nevada State Automobile Association, a branch of the American Automobile

Association. He was Nevada State Consul of the Lincoln Highway from 1913 to 1920 when he resigned to accept the employment of field secretary for the Lincoln Highway Association. He was made Executive Secretary to succeed Mr. A. F. Bement when he resigned December 1924.

AFFLECK, BENJAMIN FRANKLIN: Manufacturer. Born in Belleville, Illinois, March 1, 1869. Educated in the Public Schools. With Harrison Machine Works, 1885 to 1889. St. Louis, Alton and Terre Haute Railroads, now a part of Illinois Central, from 1890 to 1896. Illinois Steel Company, 1896 to 1906; Sales Manager at Chicago for Universal Atlas Cement Company, 1906 to 1915; President since 1915. Member of Portland Cement Association (President from 1916 to 1920). American Society Testing Materials, American Concrete Institute, American Iron and Steel Institute. Western Society of Engineers; Chicago Association of Commerce; Chamber of Commerce of the United States. Art Institute of Chicago; Field Museum of Natural History. Member Union League Club of Chicago (President 1928) Member Mid Day Club, Member Chicago Engineer's Club. Director Lincoln Highway Association.

DURANT, WILLIAM CRAPO: Manufacturer. Born in Boston, Massachusetts, December 8, 1861. Educated in Public Schools of Flint, Michigan. Founder of Durant-Dort Carriage Company, Flint, Michigan, 1886. Developed business reaching 150,000 carriages a year; organized Buick Motor Car Company, 1905 and General Motors Company, 1908; purchased Cadillac, Oakland, Oldsmobile and Northway Motor Companies in 1908 to 1909; secured controlling interest in General Motors Company in 1915 and in the same year organized Chevrolet Motor Company, an eighty-million dollar corporation with plants in 11 principal cities of the

United States; held controlling interest in General Motors Company and Chevrolet Motor Company until November 1920; organized Durant Motors Inc., January 1921; Chairman of the Board Liberty National Bank and Trust Company of New York; Director of Industrial Rayon Corporation, Loew Theatres Inc., Durant Motor Co. Inc.; Director of and generous financial contributor to Lincoln Highway Association.

EVANS, EDWARD STEPTOE: Manufacturer. Born in Thaxtons, Virginia, May 24, 1879. Law student at Columbian University (now George Washington University) Washington, D. C., 2½ years special course in Library Science. In the Library of Congress 1900–1904. Assistant State Librarian in Virginia 1904–1907; author of several historical works: Calendar of Virginia Transcripts, Encyclopaedic Guide to Richmond, Virginia and History of the Seals of Virginia. Organizer in 1915, and President and Treasurer, Evans Products Company of Detroit, Michigan. President and Treasurer of the Saven Corporation—Investments and Real Estate. President and Treasurer of E. S. Evans & Sons, Manufacturers; President and Treasurer, Evans Appliance Company, Manufacturers. Captain, Quarter Masters Corps., U. S. Army, 1918–1919–1920. Lieut. Colonel, Specialists Reserve, attached to U. S. Air Corps; 32° Mason, Knights Templar, Past Master, Palestine Lodge #357 F. & A. M., Detroit, Michigan; Fellow American Geographical Society; Member Detroit Club, Country Club of Detroit, Detroit Boat Club, Detroit Athletic Club. Holds record for circumnavigating the globe in the year 1926 in 28 days, 14 hours, 36 minutes. Was Manager Detroit Arctic Expeditions in 1925–1926. Director Lincoln Highway Association.

FORD, EDSEL BRYANT: Automobile Manufacturer. Born in Detroit, Michigan, November 6, 1893. Educated Detroit

University School; identified with his father who manufactures automobiles since beginning of active career. Now President and Treasurer of the Ford Motor Company. A member of the Arts Commission of the Detroit Institute of Arts. Director and generous financial supporter Lincoln Highway Association.

MACAULEY, ALVAN: Automobile manufacturer. Born in Wheeling, West Virginia, January 17, 1872. Lehigh University 1888 to 1890. George Washington University 1890 to 1892. Was admitted to the Bar in Ohio in 1897; practiced at Washington, D. C. three years; with the National Cash Register Company at Dayton, Ohio, 1895 to 1901; in 1901 became Assistant Manager of the American Arithmometer Company of St. Louis (original Burroughs Adding Machine Company). Was promoted same year. President since 1916. Member of the Detroit Board of Commerce; Automobile Manufacturer's Association (President); National Association of Manufacturers. Director and Member of the Executive Committee of Lincoln Highway Association from its inception.

MOTT, CHARLES STEWART: Vice-President of General Motors Corporation. Born in Newark, New Jersey, June 2, 1875. Graduated Stevens Institute of Technology 1897, Mechanical Engineer. Studied in Denmark in 1894 and in Germany in 1895. Secretary and Superintendent of the Weston Mott Company, 1900 to 1903; President 1903 to 1913; Director General Motors Corporation since 1913. Member of the executive committee 1915 to 1929. Vice-President since 1916. Member of Finance Committee since 1929. Served with the United States Navy in the Spanish American War; President of the Charles Stewart Mott Foundation; member of the American Society of Mechanical Engineers, Automotive Engineers, Detroit Aviation Society. Director Lincoln Highway Association.

RUTHERFORD, W. O.: Born October 31, 1874, in Fairview, Pennsylvania. Died July 18, 1935. Was Vice-President of B. F. Goodrich Tire & Rubber Company; President of the Pennsylvania Rubber Company, President of the Rubber Manufacturers' Association of America. President, Motor and Accessories Association: member Pan-American Association for Highway Education. He belonged to the Lotus Club, New York, the Portage Country Club, Akron, Ohio, the Detroit Athletic Club, Detroit, Michigan, and the Greensburg Country Club in Greensburg, Pennsylvania. Knights Templar, 32° Mason, Tadmor Temple, Akron. Was Director and active cooperator in the work of the Lincoln Highway Association.

WALDON, COL. SIDNEY D.: Born London, England, January 29th, 1873. Attended London day school and South Kensington Science & Arts night school. Apprenticed with Hobbs-Hart & Company, lock and safe manufacturers. At age of 19 came to United States with his family and settled at Mt. Vernon, Ohio; was employed by John Cooper Engine Company and Mt. Vernon Bridge Company. Left parents to work for Ball Engine Company at Erie, Pennsylvania, and in 1900 became superintendent of factory making steam automobiles in Rochester, New York. In 1901 took part in the New York to Buffalo automobile endurance contest. In 1902 joined James W. Packard, Warren, Ohio, moving with the factory to Detroit in 1903, and remained with that company until 1915. Became director of engineering of the Cadillac Motor Car Company, and enlisted in the Aviation Section of the Signal Corps U.S.A. December 1916. Organized Equipment Division of the Signal Corps, and in September 1917 went to France with Major-General Fulois to establish and equip aviation assembly plants, depots, etc. Served Detroit on Street Railway and Rapid Transit Commissions, developed Detroit's Master Plan of Superhighways, and has always promoted improved facilities in all departments of transportation. Was director and member of the executive committee of the Lincoln Highway Association from the beginning.

WILLYS, JOHN N.: Manufacturer, Foreign Diplomat. Born Canandaigua, New York, October 25, 1873. Began in the bicycle business in Canandaigua in 1890; removed to Elmira, New York, and organized the Elmira Arms Company, also engaged in selling automobiles on an extensive scale. Purchased the Indianapolis plant of the Overland Automobile Company in 1907 and two years later purchased the Pope Toledo Plant at Toledo; later Chairman of the Board and co-receiver of the Willys Overland Company of Toledo, also of Willy Morrow Company, Elmira, New York; Ambassador to Poland 1930–1932. Director Lincoln Highway Association. Died July 1935.

GUNN, JAMES NEWTON: Born Springfield, Ohio, September 3, 1867. Graduate of Public and High School, Private Tutors—Chemistry, Mathematics and Engineering, Certified Public Accountant—State of Connecticut, Fellow American Institute of Accounting and Engineering Factory Organization and Administration. 1901 Founder and President of Gunn, Richards and Company, Consulting Engineers. 1911 —Called in Advisory capacity, as General Manager of Studebaker Corporation (December 1911 to September 1913), October 21, 1915—United States Rubber Company— Vice-President and Director, also November 10, 1915—Acting President United States Tire Company, April 6, 1916,

President, United States Tire Company. Also Director of numerous subsidiary companies of U. S. Rubber Company. Resigned from U. S. Rubber Company and subsidiary companies June 7, 1923. Following this retirement he soon entered the engineering field again as a consultant. He served as receiver for the Hodgman Rubber Company and on the engineering staff of Lockwood, Greene and Company, at the same time acting in an advisory capacity for several other corporations. During the World War, Mr. Gunn was a member of the War Industries Board as a representative of the Rubber Association. He was President of the Lincoln Highway Association and did much to bring that enterprise to its completion.

OSTERMANN, HENRY C.: Born, Tell City, Indiana, 1876. At the age of 6 years he was a newsboy in New York City, living in a newsboys' home; at nine he became a bellboy in a hotel and in turn thereafter a cash boy and cigar clerk. At seventeen he was discharged from the Navy following three years of service. He drifted through California, picked oranges and worked on the west coast steamers. From 1895 to 1897 he traveled with Buffalo Bill's Wild West Show, ranched in Montana and North Dakota, became a flagman on the Illinois Central Railroad. He was promoted first to brakeman, and then conductor. In 1906 he invented and developed a grain door for freight cars. To promote this he organized a car building concern, Ostermann Manufacturing Company. In 1913 he expanded still further when he started an automotive business in Deadwood, South Dakota, there he distinguished himself in public service; the Chamber of Commerce of Deadwood adopted formal resolutions of appreciation for certain of his efforts. Just as his future appeared to be established, investment in a smelting concern proved disastrous and he was left with practically

nothing. His service with the Lincoln Highway Association
started from Detroit and his travels carried him many times
across the country. His duty was to make contacts with
wealthy citizens and induce them to subscribe and to
travel along the highway stirring up local interest and disposing of certificates. It was not realized at that time that
the retention of Mr. Ostermann was to provide one of the
main driving forces of the organization in the days to come.
His work proved incomparable and while he lived his service to the Association brought untold admiration and respect not only from his associates in the work but from all
whom he encountered. His accidental death in 1920 was
mourned sincerely by thousands of friends. He was a member Detroit Athletic Club, F. & A. M. and Medina Temple.

PARDINGTON, ARTHUR R.: Born in Lexington, Michigan,
July 30, 1862. He attended grade schools in Detroit and
graduated from the High School at Tecumseh, Michigan.
Later he entered New York University for a course in medi-
cine and pharmacy. This led to the position of Superintendent of the Methodist Hospital (then Seney Hospital) in
Brooklyn, N. Y. Following this connection he went with
the New York Telephone Company and became a district
manager with that company in Brooklyn. After promoting
several smaller projects he became associated with the Long
Island Motor Parkway Association, which was a Vanderbilt-
Whitney enterprise for building a motor road through
Long Island to Montauk Point to compete by automobile
with the Long Island or Pennsylvania Railroad for the in-
coming ocean mail delivery. The Parkway was finished as far
as Lake Ronkonkoma. At about this time, Mr. Pardington
became actively interested in Mr. Carl Fisher's Coast-to-Coast
Highway. With Mr. Fisher, the preliminary work of the
proposed transcontinental road being completed, the idea

was introduced into automobile circles in Detroit and the Lincoln Highway Association was formed in 1913. Mr. Pardington became Vice-President and General Manager and held this office until his death.

He was a Spanish War veteran, having served in the Naval Militia for many years. At the time of his death he was Lieut. Commander, 2nd Bat. N. Y., with quarters aboard the old Granite State at the foot of 96th Street, New York. He was also one of the early members of the A.A.A. in New York and a member of the Crescent Athletic Club of Brooklyn.

In Detroit he was a member of the Detroit Athletic Club and the Yacht Club.

In his connection with the A.A.A., Mr. Pardington was for many years official Referee at the Indianapolis track and for the various Vanderbilt Cup races.

INDEX

Alger, Russell A., Co-indorser of note, 75; Executive functions, 22, 26, 43, 44, 149; Resignation of, 151

Allison, James A., Contributions, 72, 82, 173; Director, 150; Founder, 81; Partner of Carl G. Fisher, 81

American Automobile Association, Batchelder, A. G., Secretary, 12, 14

American Institute of Architects, Architectural treatment of bridges, 131

American Road Congress, Resolutions, 12, 14

Ammons, E. M., Governor of Colorado, 55, 60; Protest on Denver loop, 158

Annual Reports, as publicity medium, 104

Apperson Automobile Factory, Edenburn, W. D., advertising manager, 28

Ashton, Fred W., Nebraska "Seedling Mile," 130-131

Atlas Portland Cement Company, Cement donation, 127

Autocar Company of Ardmore, Contribution, 215

Automobile Club of Southern California, Competition for route, 157; Highway marking, 214-215

Baker, Fred L, Consul for southern California, 141

Baker, Newton D, Secretary of War, 110

Bamberger, Simon, Governor of Utah, 180; Suspension of Utah road construction, 180-183

Bankhead–Shackelford Bill for Federal Aid, Provisions of, 231-232

Bailey, Willard F., County consul at Kearney, 132

Batchelder, A. G., Secretary of the American Automobile Association, 12, 14, 16

Bement, Austin F., Activities of, 67, 85, 109, 134, 177, 179, 187-188, 199-202, 209, 218, 219; Dedication of monument to, 223; Director, 150; Financial reports of, 84-86; Publicity work of, 92, 100-102, 107, 148, 198-199; Secretary, 82-83, 149, 152, 172-175; Traffic estimate, 118-119; Vice-president, 151

Benefits of Good Roads, 249-269

Bennett, George W, Vice-president of Willys-Overland, 13-14

Beveridge, Senator Albert J., First board of directors, 14, 43, 149; Praise of consuls, 145-146; Publicity work, 99, 103

Bit and Spur Magazine, Publicity in, 100

Bodman, Henry E., Joy's attorney, 26-27; Resignation of, 43-44

Bond Issues For Highway Construction, Facilitated by military expedition, 113

Booklets, Publicity in, 104

Bookwalter, Charles A., Ex-mayor of Indianapolis, 26-27; Speechmaker, 35

303

CPSIA information can be obtained
at www.ICGtesting.com
Printed in the USA
BVHW041833240122
627047BV00010B/417